HOW TO BE A SUCCESSFUL COMPUTER CONSULTANT

Alan R. Simon

Fourth Edition

McGraw-Hill

New York San Francisco Washington, D.C. Auckland Bogotá
Caracas Lisbon London Madrid Mexico City Milan
Montreal New Delhi San Juan Singapore
Sydney Tokyo Toronto

Library of Congress Cataloging-in-Publication Data

Simon, Alan R.
    How to be a successful computer consultant / Alan R. Simon.—4th
    ed.
        p.   cm.
    Includes bibliographical references and index.
    ISBN 0-07-058034-0 (hardcover).—ISBN 0-07-058029-4 (pbk.)
    1. Business consultants.   2. Electronic data processing
consultants.   I. Title.
    HD69.C6S58   1998
    658.4'06—dc21   97-46907
                                                                    CIP

McGraw-Hill

A Division of The **McGraw·Hill** Companies

1 2 3 4 5 6 7 8 9 0   DOC/DOC   9 0 3 2 1 0 9 8

ISBN 0-07-058034-0 (HC)

ISBN 0-07-058029-4 (PB)

*The sponsoring editor for this book was Scott Grillo, the editing supervisor was
Stephen M. Smith, and the production supervisor was Tina Cameron. It was
set in Fairfield by Dina E. John of McGraw-Hill's Professional Book Group
composition unit.*

Printed and bound by R. R. Donnelley & Sons Company.

CONTENTS

**CHAPTER THREE. PLANNING AND ORGANIZING
YOUR CONSULTING BUSINESS**   **51**

**CHAPTER FOUR. MARKETING YOUR
CONSULTING BUSINESS**   **67**

CHAPTER FIVE. FINANCIAL CONSIDERATIONS OF CONSULTING   91

CHAPTER SIX. PUTTING IT ALL TOGETHER: THE BUSINESS PLAN   109

PART TWO. YOUR PRODUCTS AND SERVICES

CHAPTER SEVEN. DEVELOPING INFORMATION SYSTEMS   135

CHAPTER TWELVE. HOW TO STAY CURRENT— YOUR LIVELIHOOD DEPENDS ON IT   253

CHAPTER THIRTEEN. THE NEXT STEPS IN YOUR CONSULTING CAREER   271

CHAPTER FOURTEEN. DETERMINING YOUR ROLE AS A CONSULTANT ON *THIS* ENGAGEMENT   279

PREFACE TO
FOURTH EDITION

How times change. Back in 1992, when I began work on the Third Edition of this book, much of the computer industry was just beginning a slow, tenuous recovery from the recession of the early 1990s. Certain parts of the United States had been affected much worse than others; many computer consultants who worked in New England, the mid-Atlantic states, or out in California probably felt as if the Great Depression had returned.

I remember giving an after-dinner presentation at the New York City chapter of the Independent Computer Consultants Association (ICCA) in the Wall Street area in the autumn of 1992, and one of the questions posed to me was, "How can I possibly hope to make a living as a computer consultant when clients only want to pay $25 per hour for my services?" I launched into my standard spiel about upgrading one's skills, the need to be persistent in marketing, how external factors such as the regional economy factor into the supply-demand picture, etc.—all solid advice, make no mistake about it, but all tinged with a "how to survive in tough times" philosophy.

So here we are in early 1998. What has happened to displaced COBOL programmers, the most unloved, unwanted information technology (IT) professionals (consultants or employees) of the early 1990s? Can you say "Year 2000 consultant"? Can you say "extremely high demand"? Can you say "high billing rates that are going even higher"? Sure—I knew you could!

Make no mistake about it, prospects for computer consultants have been booming for the past few years. Even those parts of the United States—indeed, the world—where economic fortunes were most adversely affected in the early 1990s have come roaring back. New England? Hiring bonuses all around! New York and Philadelphia? Tremendous consulting opportunities, in all industries; come on, don't be left out!

But wait—can this last forever? Remember the early and mid-1980s and the birth of the PC, and what this meant in terms of computer consulting opportunities. That time period came before the ugly days of the late 1980s and early 1990s, right?

No one knows what the future will bring. Year 2000 consultants have tremendously bright prospects right now, but what will happen in a few short years when that activity dramatically drops off? How about Webmaster consultants—will they be in as much demand three or four years from now? No one knows for certain.

That's where the basic skills, techniques, and strategies of *How to Be a Successful Computer Consultant* can help. I only have to look at my own career and the long and winding road (apologies to Paul McCartney) it's taken. I started in the early 1980s as both a dBASE III "expert consultant and software developer" (or so I thought I was) and, at the same time, a developer of communications and systems software for Sperry Univac mainframe–based, real-time military applications. In the mid-1980s I did a stint working with office information systems and LAN technology, followed by a late 1980s divergence into the vendor community with Digital Equipment's Database Systems Group, which laid the groundwork for my 1990s emphasis on data warehousing and business intelligence.

At one time, such "flexibility" in specialties would probably have been viewed as a lack of stability, the inability to choose a particular area of emphasis and grow within that domain to become an "expert." Nowadays, as we all know, any computer consultant who doesn't quickly and aggressively reinvent himself or herself as necessary is destined to be left behind as new waves of technology drive major changes among our client base.

I've tried to achieve a balancing act in this Fourth Edition of *How to Be a Successful Computer Consultant*. There is material that is virtually untouched from the First Edition, which was written in 1983–1984 and published in the summer of 1985. I have decided to retain this material because many readers of this Fourth Edition are new to computer consulting, either as a result of a shift in their career orientation (i.e., moving from corporate IT positions into consulting) or because they are relatively new IT professionals (recent college graduates, for example). For these readers, I have removed material that has been superseded and left what I hope are nuggets of advice they can use. Although this book still retains its orientation toward independent consultants, there is good information for the growing legions of consultants who are part of some type of consulting company.

Recognizing that there will (hopefully) be many readers who are already experienced consultants (including some who may have read one or more editions of this book), I have augmented this edition with advice (I don't dare call it "wisdom"!) based on my own experiences in the consulting arena. I've consulted to and developed software for small independent businesses, mid-sized companies, and some of the largest companies in the United States. I've been engaged by business users under the guidelines of, "Here's my business problem; I don't care what you do, but produce something that will meet my needs." Then there's the flip side: assignments in an IT department with an extensive list of standards, opinionated managers, consultants from other companies on whom I've been dependent for meeting the client's needs, etc. One thing I've learned is that while every consulting assignment has one thing in common—producing something of value in return for financial benefit— there are far more differences than similarities among assignments, and it is essential that you develop a "sixth sense" as to what to do and what not to do on each of them.

Being a successful computer consultant means more than building up a toolbox of technical aptitude and experience. It means being able to sense changes in technology and market direction and, one way or another, reinvent yourself to take advantage of those opportunities and avoid being left behind. It means having a keen sense of how to market and sell your abilities, regardless of whether you're an independent or working with a larger consulting firm. And it means learning how to be successful—today and tomorrow.

With this in mind, I've added to this book entirely new chapters that are part workbook and part "hints and tips" from my own experiences. In many ways, the material in these chapters reads like "Machiavelli on consulting", given the discussion of hidden agendas, identifying your enemies, etc. But as the more experienced consultants among you will agree, there are engagements that turn into situations with plots not unlike those of novels or television series, and, as I continually point out, it's in your interests to identify the consulting landscape as accurately as possible before you find yourself in a very nasty, no-win situation.

I hope that all readers, those new to this title and those who have read one or more of the previous editions, will be able to directly use this new material.

Alan R. Simon

PREFACE TO FIRST EDITION

In November 1982, after reading several magazine articles extolling the potential rewards of computer consulting, I began investigating that profession as a supplement to my U.S. Air Force programming job. Chief among my reasons were (1) staying abreast of the microcomputer explosion, (2) supplementing my Air Force income, and (3) allowing for more flexible future employment options.

Over the next year I acquired a collection of books (as well as numerous periodicals), dealing with small businesses, consulting, and microcomputers, that supplemented my already bulging library. The lack of one comprehensive, concise reference source necessitated my massive search.

During the planning and growth stage of my business, Computer Education and Consulting, I often wished that just such a comprehensive guide existed for the computer consulting profession to aid the research process. This book is an outgrowth of that desire. I have attempted to combine in one volume all of the major topics that I found were critical in building a computer consulting practice.

Since, as I mentioned, information was gleaned from many sources (most of which are complete books themselves), it is impossible to cover every topic in exhaustive detail. Some subjects, such as the legal aspects of software writing, are merely summarized, with references to places where more detailed information can be obtained. If every topic had been covered to the degree they were in their original form, this book would probably have been titled *The Encyclopedia of Computer Consulting* and comprised several volumes!

Nevertheless, the subjects were covered in sufficient detail for this book to be both a tutorial and a comprehensive reference source for anyone considering a career in computer consulting. Since two chapters are devoted to contract and commercial software development, respectively, this book will also be useful to someone who doesn't wish to become a consultant but rather a software developer. Using the business and organizational material which is critical to building and managing a business, the reader can choose exactly what he or she wishes to provide to the public and pursue that avenue.

Much of the material is supplemented (either stated or implicitly) by personal knowledge learned through trial and error, especially the advantages and disadvantages of pursuing a consulting career on a part-time basis (and writing a book on top of that!).

Much time and effort has been devoted to making this book reflect the promise of its title. I sincerely believe that a computer professional, or anyone who possesses the skill and devotion and is willing to put forth the effort required to build a successful consulting practice, can do so by following the guidelines presented in the following chapters. Again, when I feel additional information is required for a more complete understanding of a topic, I have cited comprehensive references.

The book is divided into three major portions. Part 1 discusses the planning stages and early life of your consulting practice. Part 2 presents a detailed look at the major products and services your consulting firm will likely offer. Finally, Part 3 concludes with subjects of continuing concern after your practice is established, including management of your business operations and planning for the future.

No author's preface would be complete without the appropriate expressions of gratitude. Therefore, I would like to thank the following people: Sandy Davis, without whose typing and editing assistance you would not be reading these words now; my business partners, Ted Davis and Michael LaFollette, for reviewing portions of the manuscript and putting up with my preoccupation with this book; my brother, Jordan, for loaning his flexible name to my fictional consultant in the book; and finally, my parents, Bernie and Sandra (whose names have also been used in the text), for instilling in me the drive for success that was so critical in conceiving and finishing this book.

Alan R. Simon

ACKNOWLEDGMENTS

I'm indebted to many people for their assistance with *How to Be a Successful Computer Consultant*—this Fourth Edition as well as the previous three.

First, I'd like to thank all of the McGraw-Hill editors with whom I've worked on the various editions of this book: Tyler Hicks, who first showed faith in this project back in 1983 and was responsible for launching my writing career; Steve Guty; Theron Shreve; Kay Magome; Jeanne Glasser; John Wyzalek; and Scott Grillo. I'd also like to thank the production staff at McGraw-Hill, most notably Stephen Smith, who has supervised the editing of all my McGraw-Hill books to date.

Next, I'm grateful to the people I interviewed during preparation of previous editions, especially Chris Date and Donald Jacobs, the highly successful consultants who were so willing to share their time and expertise with me and with this book's readers.

I'm also grateful to those people over the years who have helped me in my own consulting and writing career, including my original business partners, Ted Davis and Mike LaFollette, with whom I first explored the field of computer consulting by trial and error. Ann Mergo has assisted me throughout the years, as have innumerable consultants (and clients!) with their insights into both technology and the consulting profession.

Finally, I'd like to thank my brother Jordan, and my parents, Bernie and Sandra, all of whom provided an atmosphere for learning and success over the years.

ABOUT THE AUTHOR

Alan R. Simon is the author of many different books about information technology and career development. The previous editions of *How to Be a Successful Computer Consultant* have guided over 100,000 readers through their consulting careers. He is currently the director of data warehousing with an international consulting firm.

PART ONE

THE BEGINNINGS OF YOUR CONSULTING CAREER

AN OVERVIEW OF THE CONSULTING PROFESSION

If you've been in the computer profession for even a few years—say, since 1990—you've seen a flurry of changes that not too long ago would have taken several decades to occur. We've seen:

- The emergence and widespread acceptance of Microsoft Windows, beginning with Version 3 and continuing to Windows 95, spawning an entire paradigm shift toward making graphical user interfaces (GUIs) the standard mechanism for interacting with "real business applications"—not just personal productivity applications
- The pheonomenal growth of the Internet and the frenzied shift of applications and packages toward "Web enablement"
- The coining of the term *data warehousing* and the development of an entire subindustry built around the concept
- Growing acceptance of three-tier client/server models, middleware, distributed objects, and other distributed computing models and components

We've also seen a brief but vicious economic downturn that affected the northeastern United States and California (both among the strongest economic areas in the United States during the 1980s) and the ensuing recovery and renewed growth in these areas. We've seen "downsizings" (mass layoffs) of tens of thousands of employees at some of the largest companies in the United States and around the world, followed by complaints on the part of many of these same companies of "shortages of skilled workers."

We've seen the pace of globalization increase, and we've seen it extend to former Eastern Bloc countries and emerging nations. We're also seeing growing concern—some would say panic—related to the coming of the Year 2000 and its impact on much of the world's computing infrastructure (discussed in Chap. 2).

So what's the relevance? Simply this: As a result of the items listed above and related factors, the computer consulting profession is experiencing *unprecedented* growth—leading to unprecedented opportunities for computer consultants.

Computer consulting, whether done on an independent basis (i.e., working for yourself) or as an employee or affiliate of a larger consulting organization, offers the information technology (IT) professional the opportunity to take charge of his or her career. The often near-chaotic pace of change in business landscapes, economic fortunes, and emerging technologies represents *opportunity* for the computer consultant— and that's what this book is about.

WHY BE A CONSULTANT?

In the previous section we discussed becoming a computer consultant from a defensive point of view, of career survival in the face of industry and economic turbulence beyond your control. There are, however, some additional reasons you are likely to consider consulting as a profession; let's discuss them.

As a consultant, you will find yourself facing challenges and opportunities that often are unavailable to a person working in a large corporation or similar organizational setting, at least for a long while. Your income, growth, and reputation depend on a combination of *your* business skills, technical expertise in your specialties, and your dedication. By business skills I mean not only the mechanics of starting and managing a small business (such as filing the appropriate forms, keeping accurate accounting records, and similar routine tasks), but functions such as determining the market for your consulting services, finding clients, and winning business.

As a self-employed computer consultant, you are your own boss; no one but you will determine the projects and contracts on which you'll work. Unlike many computer professionals who find themselves locked into a finite set of job functions, working on hardware and software that rapidly is losing favor in the industry because technology is marching by, you can decide to focus your skills on the hot, highly marketable technologies at any given time; these include (in today's environment) open systems, client/server computing, and many of the other areas we'll discuss throughout this book.

To a large degree, the same is also true for those who choose to pursue computer consulting not as an independent but rather working with (or through) a larger organization. Flexibility and encouragement—even the necessity—to learn new technologies and architectures are hallmarks of any successful computer consultant's career, regardless of the environment in which he or she works.

In other words, the computer consulting business offers you myriad opportunities that you probably wouldn't face until much later in a traditional computer career, even without the overriding issues we discussed earlier in this chapter. You can function as the operator of a business, the marketing staff, designer and developer, and financial manager—all at once and all within the context of your own firm. Again, however, it's important not to underestimate the greatly increased responsibility over that with which you may be familiar. In most cases, no one else will find your clients for you, no one else will do proposals for the projects you intend to develop, or, on the flip side, no one else will complete the projects that you propose, win, and put under contract; in short, you need to have a much broader tool kit of skills than someone who works within the narrow confines of a typical corporate job description.

WHY CLIENTS USE COMPUTER CONSULTANTS (SEE FIG. 1-1)

The importance of processing information in all areas of business, government, and even the home has become increasingly evident in recent years, particularly since the personal computer revolution that began in the late 1970s and gained steam in the early 1980s. Despite tremendous strides in the placement of computers in homes and schools to train the next generations of this work force, it will be many years before the general population of the United States and around the world is familiar and competent with computers. In fact, an increasing paradox has developed where many "older" people (OK, the over-thirty generation to which many of us belong) are less comfortable with computers in their business and homes than younger people. These "computerphobic" people may have bad memories from that mandatory FORTRAN programming class in college from which they barely squeaked by with a C, or they just aren't willing to give a user-friendly personal computer with a GUI—or even a Web browser—and easy-to-use application software a chance in their business operations, preferring to do things manually.

Despite this resistance to computerization, which seems to be diminishing in the Internet age but still hangs on stubbornly in some corners, business and government increasingly rely on information processing. Until recently, this growth in infor-

---

1. Need for computer-literate general developers/advisers.
2. Need for specialized HW or SW skills unavailable internally.
3. Corporate downsizing eliminated the workers, and work still needs to be done.
4. Temporary project without adding headcount.
5. Advisory services.

FIGURE 1-1   Reasons clients hire computer consultants.

mation needs was accompanied by a shortage of qualified programmers, analysts, and other computer professionals to meet those requirements, and a large application and system development backlog developed. Today, as we discussed earlier in this chapter, the computer professional shortage *in terms of raw numbers* is greatly diminished or has even evaporated.

However, the growth of certain types of technologies that we also discussed earlier in this chapter has created something of a mismatch between the skill levels of the typical computer professional and those needed by businesses and other organizations with computerization and automation needs. "The mainframe is disappearing," many industry observers cry. That may be a bit overstated—particularly given IBM's astounding recovery and strong showing in recent years—but it is inarguable that the centralized corporate mainframe (generically speaking, not singling out IBM or any other vendor) no longer is the default development platform environment, and that alternatives such as departmental midrange systems and local area network (LAN) environments are viable alternative candidates for development, often with substantial cost savings over a mainframe system.

Because of this rapid downsizing shift, which gained momentum as the 1980s became the 1990s, the skill set of the typical computer professional did not evolve quickly enough to meet the requirements of distributed smaller-scale computing, which is oriented around systems integration and interoperability. This resulting imbalance has created a shortage, at least at present, in professionals who are skilled in relational databases, object-oriented technologies, LANs and MANs (metropolitan area networks), client/server computing, and other individual technologies. And so, this imbalance has created additional opportunities for computer consultants experienced in new, emerging technologies.

And what of those people with a skill base that is now "obsolete"? How about the classical "endangered species," the mainframe COBOL programmer for standard business systems development? There are even consulting opportunities for these people.

As an example of how rapidly—and dramatically—events can change for computer consultants, consider what I wrote in 1993 in the Third Edition of this book:

Think about many of the layoffs and personnel cuts with which you are familiar, perhaps at your current or former company or that of someone you know. In many cases, the victims of "The Turk" (for those of you who aren't football fans, The Turk is the assistant coach who tells someone about to be cut, "coach wants to see you—and bring your playbook") are the real workers within an organization, those who are unfortunate enough to find themselves without the appropriate political clout and connections to survive the massive layoff. As companies routinely lay off 10,000, 20,000, even 50,000 or more employees, it's hard to reach that number exclusively from "the fat" of the organization without touching a single individual who actually is performing mission-critical work. (A side note—are you detecting an anti-corporate bias yet on my part?)

Anyway, enough social commentary; the point is that when a company eliminates, say, an entire computer operations department or a group of "obsolete mainframe COBOL programmers" often there is work left that needs to be done, at least for a while. There may be existing code that must be maintained and possibly enhanced while a new system is developed and deployed. Perhaps an employee resigned from some Company A to start his or her own consulting business, and Company A has a hiring freeze in effect for the next two years. If that employee had been performing tasks such as mainframe programming or other functions that aren't exactly on the list of hot technologies, that role may need to be filled by outside help, typically by a consultant. In this case, having a skill base that at first glance appears to be diminishing in career opportunities may turn out to be a door opener for a consultant.

So now it's 1998—and what was envisioned as opportunities for "simple maintenance" a few years ago has turned into the Year 2000 fix-it-up frenzy that we'll discuss in Chap. 2. The lesson? "Obsolete" is relative. Consider *every* skill you ever learned as having the potential to bring you consulting opportunities at some point in the future.

Another reason a client may want to use a computer consultant (or more than one) is for a short-term development or implementation project. A given client may want to develop a small business management application or upgrade a LAN. The smaller the client is in terms of business size (such as a small music and video store as compared with a *Fortune* 500 company), the greater the chance is that at project start time there is inadequate in-house support. Rather than hire an individual or a team for which there is expected to be no work after the project's completion, often it makes good business sense to bring a consultant aboard for the duration of that project.

Finally, there may be cases where a client simply wants advice from an expert about a specific computer-related matter, which may range from something simple about what types of PC and LAN are appropriate, to more complicated items, such as assistance with long-range strategic information systems planning for a multinational corporation; or highly specialized technical matters such as choosing a set of standards against which all future corporate development will occur. In cases such as these, retaining an outside consulting service to provide the expertise for the matter at hand often is desirable.

TYPES OF COMPUTER CONSULTANTS

The point above, that of providing advice, gives rise to a question you may be asking yourself: What exactly is a "computer consultant"? Notice that the advice mentioned above ranged from advice on fairly routine matters (for computer professionals, anyway) such as basic hardware and software selection to advice on high-level business or technical matters.

In the original edition of *How to Be a Successful Computer Consultant*, I focused discussions and examples primarily on what might be considered low-level consulting activities, such as developing and selecting standalone or small LAN systems for small and medium-sized businesses. To many beginning consultants at the time (the mid-1980s), this was an extremely fruitful market due to the initial widespread automation of small business operations with PC-based systems.

Upon reviewing that first edition while preparing this book, however, I realized that my focus on that area neglected other types and levels of computer consulting. Therefore, it will be beneficial if we take the time to develop a taxonomy of computer consulting against which we can frame our subsequent discussions and which you can use in your own start-up and subsequent business planning.

You might look at computer consulting as consisting of three levels (Fig. 1-2). The lowest level, in terms of technical expertise and *breadth* of skills, is oriented around software development and basic advisory services. A consultant in this group might focus his or her efforts exclusively on, say, C or Ada development of a certain type of business or commercial application, or might specialize exclusively in Microsoft Windows environments for small businesses.

Someone who enters the computer consulting field with a fairly narrow range of skills—one or two programming languages, and familiarity with a given hardware platform, and who has spent his or her entire career working on a particular family of applications, may have an easier time trying to tran-

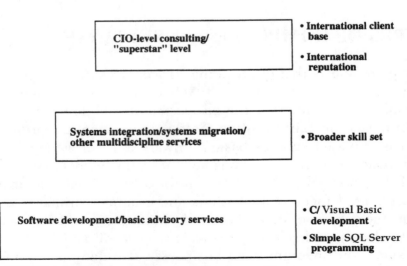

FIGURE 1-2   The three levels of computer consulting.

sition into the consulting profession at this lower level than at a higher level. This ease, or lack thereof, of entering the profession has to do primarily with the pool of potential clients and types of projects available at these different levels. At this first level, projects typically will revolve around system selection and basic application software development (as we mentioned earlier) rather than a top-level type of assignment such as strategic IS planning or other tasks that require a broader range of skills.

At the second level, we find consultants with broader skills than at the first level. For example, an individual may be familiar with a number of different development environments from several different programming languages (including fourth-generation languages, or 4GLs) to computer-aided software engineering (CASE) technology for requirements collection, design, and code development or generation. "Extended" skills such as systems integration and system migration are part of this person's repertoire, permitting him or her to not only develop new information systems but integrate new components with old ones and plan for an orderly transition from old technology to new environments. A consultant at this level may be familiar with a variety of development environments, ranging from desktop computers to midrange systems to mainframes.

Finally, our top level consultants—the true "superstars" in the field—are those who have an international client base and are recognized as being among the world's experts in one or more areas. Those areas may be of a technological nature (examples: database management systems, object-oriented technology, or open systems) or of a business or procedural type (example: world class experts in transitioning to open systems or strategic MIS and technology planning).

Note that at this level a consultant may or may not have a broad range of skills, depending on the type of specialties he or she has. For example, someone recognized as a world expert in multilevel database security may not be very familiar with developing and maintaining small business accounting applications or with graphical user interfaces; however, he or she is not being retained for a broad range of skills, but rather for a specific area of expertise. By contrast, someone specializing in advising multinational corporations on which of the many national and international standards efforts to use for their long-range multi-billion-dollar commitments should have extensive expertise in databases, networks and communications, repositories, operating systems, security, and the many other areas applicable to standards efforts.

As stated earlier, you should take a long, *honest* look at these various levels during your initial consulting business planning. Most of us would like to see ourselves as superstars, chairing international conferences and billing clients at rates which would make even a lawyer proud, but in truth there is only so much room at the top. If, however, you're entering the consulting field after a long career oriented primarily around a narrow range of specialties, initially you should focus your efforts nearer to the low end of the hierarchy. True, it's more competitive there and billing rates (and potential earnings) will be less than at the higher levels, but in all honesty, you will have a better chance for success with projects within the bounds of your skills.

This isn't to say that you can't, or shouldn't, aim to move up the ladder, since growth in this manner is not only desirable but is also critical to your business success. A decade and a half ago, in the early 1980s, you could comfortably make a living developing standalone, menu-driven applications using database platforms on microcomputers for a client base consisting exclusively of small local businesses. As these skills, not to mention rapid development techniques like code generators and GUI toolkits, put this expertise into the hands of more and more computer professionals and even end-users, that market becomes quickly saturated. Even small businesses who hadn't automated and computerized during the first round of the PC revolution will likely want their initial systems to be LAN-based, possibly with communications links to remote services or support for electronic document interchange (EDI), automated faxing of orders, and other capabilities that wouldn't have been cost-effective not too long ago. Therefore, it is imperative that you broaden your skill base as you progress in your consulting life.

This doesn't mean, however, that every consultant should start at the bottom and progress from development-intensive work to a goal of high-end consulting, many years down the road. A "new" consultant who may have been a chief information-tion officer (CIO) or a company president or chairman in his or her previous corporate life may be highly qualified—and much more at home—with high-end consulting, focusing on the types of projects and tasks we mentioned earlier. It is up to each individual to determine the types of services, the potential client base, and other factors at which he or she has the greatest chance of success, and to pursue those targets.

WHAT CLIENTS LOOK FOR IN A COMPUTER CONSULTANT

When a client hires a computer consultant, he or she is looking for more than just technical expertise. If an individual or business representative is to commit funds to you in exchange for your services, you should possess the traits that make the client feel comfortable about your expertise. These traits are common to computer consultants, whether their client base consists of small businesses outside the computer field, or computer vendors to which they provide a specific type of expertise. These traits include:

1. *Understands the general principles of a client's business.*   In order to propose a solution to a business's problem or opportunity, you need to understand the intricacies of a client's business. If you are hired to design a realtor's property management computer system, you must understand the unique principles of property management: what types of information are stored, how often this information is updated, what reports are important to a property manager, what alarms should be included, and so on. If your client is a computer software vendor and your expertise is in integration of CASE

tools, then you should understand the client's current product line, the client's major competitors, and the general trends in CASE integration technology.

This is not to say that prior to your first meeting with your client you must know his or her business intimately; many businesses conduct their operations in a nonstandard manner or consider certain information more important than similar businesses might. You should, though, know generally what a "standard" business in that industry does and be able to discuss that business intelligently. Only when you understand these nuances can you successfully fill your eventual consulting role.

2. *Speaks the language of the business.*   If your client base consists of individuals and organizations outside of the computer industry, you should have an understanding of that business's terminology. Your client will likely question your capabilities if you require a translation of every industry-specific acronym or term used. You probably won't know every such term, but you should be able to discuss business operations without saying "What does that mean?" every five minutes.

3. *Doesn't overuse technical computer jargon.*   Again, if your client base consists of those who aren't necessarily computer literate, your client shouldn't have to ask *you* for a translation every time you describe a computer topic related to his or her business. This doesn't mean, however, that you should appear to be condescending, or talking down to your client if he or she happens to have some computer expertise. I had one client who wrote dBASE IV programs himself on the side, and he was in the construction business. I could discuss technical matters with him with relative ease.

You should gauge your terminology not only by your client's familiarity and expertise but also in a manner appropriate to the situation. If you are discussing a record store management system with a business owner, you should purge your vocabulary of terms such as "reentrant," "call by reference," "instruction set," and similar phrases that have little to do with the matter of developing a small business computer system. Alternatively, if your client is a computer vendor or perhaps an MIS director at a large corporation and your task is to discuss the implementation of security standards, then discussions of authentication, nonrepudiation, and traffic padding are highly appropriate to the situation.

If you must explain computer concepts to a client who isn't computer literate, describe what you are talking about in English (or whatever your native language is, for those of you outside of the United States) without delivering a 45-minute lecture about the history of virtual memory or the miracles of fiber optics. Don't elaborate just to impress your clients with your technical knowledge; they are impressed by results, not jargon. Explain those subjects in terms of the benefits they provide for the client's particular business. (Example: "By standardizing on an electronic mail system that is compliant with the X.400 standard, you should be able to implement electronic document interchange by the end of the next fiscal year.")

If I seem to be saying that you should make the effort to learn your client's business language *and* translate your computer jargon into a middle ground, you're right. Remember your client is paying you to perform several functions, one of which may be to make computers and information technology more understandable and less threatening.

4. *Proposes sensible, cost-effective solutions.*   The term *right-sizing* applies here—the right technology for the job. Not too long ago, it was realtively easy to determine the technology to apply to a given business problem: mainframe solutions for large corporate problems, mid-range or minicomputer solutions for departmental systems, and simple PC-LAN environments for smaller businesses. Today, a consultant who specializes in LAN-based applications needs to understand all of the issues and complications surrounding, for example, the difference between a 20-seat departmental environment and a 2000-seat enterprise solution with multiple synchronized servers. Again, you need the right technology for the job at hand, taking a fresh look at technology, architecture, and cost for *every* consulting engagement.

5. *Appears to be a business person.*   In the First Edition of this book, I wrote that "no matter how adept you may be in computer design and programming, blue jeans and a T-shirt will not draw the professional clientele that a successful consultant desires." I've mitigated my view on the dress code somewhat in the intervening years, having spent some time working at a computer vendor where *I* was considered odd for wearing a suit and tie to important meetings. Besides, as I'm typing these very words I'm wearing jeans myself (but not meeting with a client, of course). You might say that I'm doing consulting-related work, just not at a client site.

You should, however, *strongly* consider dressing appropriately (suit, or sportcoat and tie for men, business wear for women), at least at initial meetings with clients or during other public appearances such as speeches and presentations. You may find that your client's dress code is extremely informal, or nonexistent. If, say, you're developing a small business system for a garage or a record and video store, and everyone, including the owner, dresses informally, then subsequent meetings and on-site work may in fact be accomplished when "dressed like the natives." The important thing is to use common sense and dress appropriately, depending on the particular situation.

CHARACTERISTICS AND BACKGROUND OF A SUCCESSFUL COMPUTER CONSULTANT

As stated earlier, a successful computer consultant needs an appropriate mix of technology and business skills to build and manage a consulting firm. Additionally, certain personality traits and general skills tend to be characteristic of a successful consultant. A study done by the Association of Management Consultants (AMC) lists essential attributes of successful consultants, including:[1]

- The ability to deal with people
- Integrity
- Objectivity
- Problem-solving skills
- Written and verbal communications skills
- Professional etiquette
- Self-confidence
- Creativity
- Ambition

A consultant, particularly in a self-employed capacity, must be able to operate successfully in an environment of uncertainty. Even though we've discussed how independence from corporate uncertainty and turbulence can be a major factor in choosing a consulting career as an alternative, you still must be able to sleep at night knowing that your current project ends next week but a subsequent project has not yet been put under contract.

Another important attribute is learning to adapt to a new style of working and a different culture. Much of the traditional organizational culture politics and gamesmanship, including the ever-popular covering your…well, tail, no longer applies when you're a consultant. Since your business is your own, and for the most part you are the person responsible for the success or failure of a client's project, finger-pointing and blame-shifting can't be used as frequently—or at all—as in larger companies.

Still another characteristic is the ability to learn from your mistakes. In the golden days of corporate life, it was politically expedient—and it made good business sense—to be involved in mentoring relationships, where a senior manager would take an underling under his or her wing and help guide career and business decisions. Particularly for self-employed consultants, being able to launch pilot programs and judge potential marketability, or learning valuable lessons from disastrous projects, is important for long-term success.

TECHNICAL SKILLS

A computer consultant's primary assets are his or her information systems knowledge, of course. You are being hired as an expert in your field to analyze problems and opportunities for your client, whether that client is an end-user or someone within the computer industry seeking your particular expertise. Unless you can propose commonsense solutions to solve those problems or exploit those opportunities, you may quickly find yourself with a failing practice. The essential information systems skills you should possess are:

1. *Demonstrated ability.*   You must have the ability to analyze a client's business operations, technological strategy, or other "raw material" and successfully implement a solution to problems or opportunities. You need more than classroom theory in systems analysis and design. For example; you should have initiated, developed, and completed a project with similar characteristics to the one you now face.

2. *In-depth knowledge.*   You should possess in-depth knowledge of your particular areas of specialization, as well as a fairly complete understanding of the information systems industry as a whole. You may, for example, specialize in developing small departmental LAN-based systems using desktop PCs and servers, but you should also have some working familiarity with Unix-based workstations, open systems trends, and similar other items to provide a frame of reference for new products and services.

3. *Knowledge of where to find the answers.*   Keep these words and phrases in the front of your mind: Internet, search engine, CD-ROM—you get the idea. Whereas not too long ago knowing where to find the answers was only half of the solution—the tedious job of digging out the data was much more difficult—the Internet age has done wonders for quick, at-your-fingertips access to unprecedented amounts of information. While some may worry about "information overload" or other social concerns, to the computer consultant, the knowledge that can be gained from the Internet is *essential* to success.

The key is not to try to know everything—it would drive you absolutely crazy to even attempt that—but to know where to find the answers quickly. Chapter 12 discusses a *methodology* for keeping current with computer, communications, and business matters. As long as you know in what direction to begin an information search, you are halfway to solving problems facing you.

4. *Familiarity with hardware requirements.*   You must have some level of familiarity with different classes of hardware: personal computers, desktop workstations, mid-range and minicomputer systems, and mainframes. You may specialize in special-purpose computers or supercomputers, leading to additional requirements for your knowledge base. As you propose solutions to client's end-user systems, you need to have some idea of capacity, relative performance, compatibility, and other issues of members of these various classes, as we discussed earlier, in order to propose sensible and cost-effective solutions.

5. *Familiarity with software.*   You need to have knowledge of:

- Operating systems
- Graphical user interfaces
- Database management systems
- Interoperability software
- Repositories
- Applications software
- Other types of software

You should know what applications software is commercially available (or what is being developed) both for the general computer user in your industry segments or areas of speciality (example: new versions of an operating system, or new DBMS products), as well as for any industry in which you are specializing (real estate, medical, legal, etc.).

You should be able to analyze existing software for ease of use, freedom from bugs, reliability, expandability, and execution speed. It is also helpful to have an understanding of the relative tradeoffs among the computer languages and technologies used to develop software (3GLs such as C and COBOL; 4GLs; CASE-based code generators; and so on) to help analyze existing systems or contract for developing new applications.

6. *Programming.*   Not every consultant needs to be a programmer, though a repertoire of development skills—not only coding, but also analysis and design techniques, testing, quality assurance, and so on—is helpful for understanding the philosophy behind the software and systems you evaluate. More importantly, you won't be forced to either refuse or subcontract projects that require new programming or maintenance of existing software, at least not because of a lack of skills.

BUSINESS SKILLS

As has been stressed, your business knowledge and skills are critical for the growth and survival of your business. Unlike a large corporation, a single-member consulting firm doesn't have a marketing director, chief financial officer, accounting staff, personnel director, and legal officer.

Obviously, you may find yourself contracting for outside assistance in certain areas: Your accountant probably will prepare your tax return and provide advice with tax planning matters; your attorney may handle incorporation or other complicated tasks. However, you don't want to have to run to your outside advisers every time a business decision needs to be made. They are professionals just as you are, and command compensation that may be forbidding for a beginning business on a regular basis. Therefore, your business skills should include:

1. *Marketing.*   This is probably the most crucial. Without the ability to determine and analyze a target market, develop products and services to meet the market's known and projected needs, choose a competitive and profitable price, and make your market aware of the availability of these services, the best computer analysis skills, business background, and personality traits won't make you successful in your consulting venture. You must find the most appropriate and cost-effective means of advertising and distribution, and, as we'll discuss in Chap. 4, your marketing encompasses far more than just advertising, but rather a comprehensive overall strategy of publicity and business building.

2. *Finance and accounting.* You should have a basic understanding of different types of costs, budgeting and forecasting, and projecting capital requirements, and should be able to manage at least a simplified set of income and expense books. As your business grows, you should know the relative tradeoffs of financing sources such as banks and venture or seed capital firms, and the tradeoffs between "bootstrapping" your business or seeking outside investment. And, of course, you must determine an appropriate fee structure for your services.

3. *Business law.* As a consultant you will be party to many types of contracts. You should know how to protect both yourself and your products (software, books, etc.) from liability and infringement, as well as how to develop contracts that are fair to your clients.

4. *Personnel.* When your practice expands you may find yourself hiring other consultants to meet the increasing workload, or administrative help to manage office functions. You need to know how to manage and motivate people to achieve maximum performance, balancing those goals against avoiding worker exploitation. Issues such as compensation (salaries, bonuses, and other incentive pay) and federal and state laws relating to your employees (unemployment insurance, worker vs. contractor status, family leave and health care requirements, and so on, many of which we will discuss in Chap. 11) must be within your grasp.

5. *General management.* The above-mentioned functions don't operate in isolated environments; they all interact very closely with one another and form (hopefully) a cohesive management strategy free of ambiguity and contradiction. For example, as you prepare your business plan (Chap. 6), your financial projections must be supported by your marketing analysis and your available resources.

CAUTIONS AND RED LIGHTS FOR POTENTIAL CONSULTANTS

So far, we've concentrated our discussion around the benefits of consulting, focusing on the high points and advantages with respect to your own career growth. You should now examine your own attributes to see whether you should consider a consulting career. Everyone's situation is different, of course, and as we discussed earlier in this chapter, consulting does not necessarily imply self-employment; there are other consulting avenues within other frameworks. The guidelines throughout this chapter are not set in concrete; you should, however, not only examine your own personal characteristics and experience against those items, but consider the list below. Those of you considering self-employed consulting may want to consider issues such as whether you have any of the following shortcomings:

1. *Inadequate or inappropriate experience.*   Until recent years, a minimum skill set—analysis and design techniques, coding, testing, and other related abilities—was required to develop even standalone PC-based systems. Today, the growth of code generators, development toolkits, and similar productivity enhancers has brought *basic* application development skills within the realm of more people, even those who aren't necessarily computer professionals.

The real world is full of considerations that are covered lightly, or not at all, in an educational environment: disaster management and recovery (What happens if a fire destroys the environment? Where should backup data be stored? How often should data be backed up?), security, and so on. Even small business clients must address most of these concerns. Therefore, if you are a "whiz bang" C programmer but have little experience in the overall development life cycle, or with corollary issues such as those mentioned above, you may want to consider limiting your initial contract-based work to simple coding projects while you gain experience in these other matters. For example, you may try to handle a couple of contract systems on a part-time basis for friends' businesses; this may give you a clue as to how competent you would be consulting on a regular basis in a "full functioned" capacity, that is, more than just programming.

2. *Insufficient business knowledge or aptitude.*   Many graduates of computer science departments that are either associated with engineering colleges or independent programs may have had their university curricula filled with electives and core courses from engineering, liberal arts, or other general-studies programs, but few or no business courses. A person who graduated from a business-oriented information systems program, however, probably attended courses in marketing, finance, accounting, business law, and similar subjects. While the computer science major arguably may be more technically adept at the intricacies of hardware, operating systems, compiler optimization techniques, and similar subjects, the business IS graduate may have a stronger combination of the business and computer skills required of a successful consultant.

In many cases, this imbalance evens off after additional education (such as a graduate degree) or real-life work experience. In fact, one of the subjects in my book *The Computer Professional's Survival Guide*[2] is the complementary nature of undergraduate and graduate education programs, depending on one's career objectives [example: combining an undergraduate computer science degree with a master of business administration (MBA)]. Early in one's career, however, the business skills necessary to run and manage a small business may be lacking; this could impede your operating a consulting firm successfully.

Additionally, some people just don't have the aptitude or desire to manage a business, including a consulting firm. Those individuals may want to consider focusing their consulting efforts on working within an existing firm's or organization's framework.

3. *You feel uncomfortable with a lack of job security.*   When I wrote the original version of this topic in the First Edition of this book, there was a general feeling that, for the most part, corporate and government careers equaled job security. Even computer professionals who found themselves unemployed as a result of downsizings in the early and mid-1980s often found new corporate-based work immediately. Obviously, job searches take much longer today, and corporations (and government organizations, too) with long-standing policies of lifelong employment have changed their tune.

It's important to note, though, that in most cases there still is an increased degree of security within a larger organization than for a consultant "living on the streets," seeking contracts from a variety of clients. Many people just can't handle this level of uncertainty; others may have the appropriate attitude but not necessarily the financial resources through which they can survive between projects (or before that first client is acquired). We'll talk about various financial issues throughout this book, but just as important is the mental attitude with respect to the lack of the security of a "regular" job.

4. *You take setbacks as personal defeats.*   Consulting can be a lot like dating in high school: a long series of false starts, and many commitments cancelled at the last minute—basically, a lot of rejection. I've seen many "certain" contracts suddenly cancelled, often at the last minute. Someone with whom you are trying to build a consulting relationship—say, a person from a consulting search firm (discussed in excruciating detail in Chap. 4)—may tell you in person or over the phone that you are "the perfect person for a client's project," and then you never hear another word about that business opportunity.

You must be able to shrug off each setback and look ahead, and learn from any mistakes you have made. Don't view each bad turn of events as a personal loss, but rather as part of the business.

5. *You aren't a self-starter.*   A great deal of your work, perhaps most of it, won't be performed on a 9-to-5 basis within an office environment, with your immediate supervisor giving you a well-defined set of tasks and finite deadlines. The hours in the consulting profession are irregular and typically long, usu-ally far more than the traditional 8-hour workday and 5-day workweek. While this is also true for many corporate jobs, you must be an exceptional person, highly self-motivated, to continually kick yourself in the tail and do your necessary work—not only client and customer activities but overhead and administrative tasks as well.

It's often tempting, when working in your home office, to watch the daily sequence of reruns on the TV in your den. Some people can work well with background distractions (such as TV or radio), while others can't. Just as you made a personal decision as to the type of study environment best suited to your own particular needs when you were in high school and college, you need to do the same for your home-based consulting work. If you can't work effectively and efficiently with distractions in the background, you must be able to avoid the temptation of the soaps, the reruns, or the talk shows.

SUMMARY

This chapter has presented an overview of the information systems consulting business. While it is a profession with virtually unlimited opportunities and rewards for the person willing to extend the effort and make the sacrifices, many additional responsibilities that the typical computer professional doesn't face now may become major concerns later. The attributes and backgrounds of successful consultants were discussed, along with an overview of client-customer relations. After reading this chapter, you should have a clear understanding of the computer consulting profession and of whether or not you should seriously consider entering the business. Succeeding chapters will discuss many of these topics in further detail.

Let's now meet someone who will travel through the subsequent chapters with us. Bernie Jordan is a senior software engineer for a major computer vendor. He began his current job after receiving his master's degree in information systems from the State University College of Business.

During his first five years employed by this vendor, he was involved in a number of projects, primarily as a software and systems developer for the company's customers. Typically, Bernie would be assigned to a customer project for a period of three to nine months, and, as part of an on-site team, would analyze customer requirements, develop software using C or 4GLs, and sometimes perform training and maintenance functions.

In the past year, though, the business of this particular company has fallen off markedly. The firm's hardware and operating system profile is aging, and market share has been diminishing. For at least half of the past year, Bernie hasn't been "billable"—that is, assigned to a revenue-earning project.

The rumor mill in the company whispers of as many as 5000 layoffs during the next fiscal year, including software engineering not only from the product development area but also those specializing in client application development. The salary freeze that was implemented eighteen months ago is still in place, and promotions among the general population of developers are virtually nonexistent. Bernie has quietly been sending his resumé to many different companies, both in response to position advertisements and unsolicited, but has not even had an interview, let alone a job offer. The local corporate recruiters—the headhunters—basically have told him that there are few openings in which they could place him, and that they "will keep his resume on file."

Three articles in recent business magazines caught Bernie's attention. The first dealt with the growing trend of information systems users to migrate away from proprietary environments to "open systems," those built around standards-based hardware and software with more or less interchangeable components. Even though open systems are perceived as being inherently good, there is still a major issue of maintaining current systems and business functions while a transition occurs, not to mention choosing from among the many off-the-shelf commercial hardware and software options.

The second article mentioned the growing role of computer consultants in keeping businesses informed about the rapidly exploding technology advancements. Many MIS directors are having a tough time dealing with the many issues of their current environments, and have neither the time nor the resources (in terms of additional staff) to explore the wide array of new technologies.

Finally, the third article dealt with an anticipated growth of open computing environments in the legal profession, primarily due to the rapid growth of on-line legal databases and the need for easy access to the volumes of information stored in those databases.

Thinking about his own experience, Bernie is contemplating switching his career focus to computer consulting. His corporate experience has been oriented on a project-by-project basis, switching among multiple clients (and occasionally working for two or more clients simultaneously). Additionally, Bernie has a strong background from his graduate school business courses, which ranged from accounting to marketing to financial management—and business law. Since his corporate career path to management appears blocked—possibly gone forever—these business skills are in danger of never being utilized.

Bernie has always been very self-motivated, having held several part-time jobs while in college despite a heavy course load. He also has always enjoyed challenges, and the thought of starting a consulting business is exhilarating to him.

Stay tuned...

END NOTES

1. Robert E. Kelley, *Consulting: The Complete Guide to a Profitable Career,* Scribner's, New York, 1981, pp. 15–16.
2. Alan R. Simon, *The Computer Professional's Survival Guide,* McGraw-Hill, New York, 1992.

C H A P T E R

T W O

CHOOSING YOUR SERVICES AND SPECIALTIES

As a computer consultant, you can specialize in, well, just about anything. Even back when I began consulting, when there were relatively clearly defined demarcations among technologies (mainframe, minicomputer, and the then-emerging PC world), there was a tremendous range of possibilities for a consultant building a professional career.

Today, the opportunities are even greater, which makes it that much more important that you:

1. Carefully choose one, or perhaps two or three, areas of emphasis

2. Continually monitor the marketplace for erosion in your specialties, so that you can take preventative action

3. Continually assess new opportunities (such as the Internet and related services) that didn't exist when you last staked a claim to a particular specialization

In this chapter, we'll look at a very broad range of areas in which you can build a consulting business (or, if you're not an independent, areas of emphasis for your consulting career in general). Keep in mind that this is the fourth time I've compiled such a list—in *The Computer Professional's Survival Guide* (1992), in the Third Edition of *How to Be a Successful Computer Consultant* (1994), and in *Downsized But Not Out*

(1995). And as you might expect, the list has changed dramatically over the past six years. For example, the Year 2000 problem certainly was around in 1991, but few consulting opportunities existed in an era when COBOL programmers were being dumped out on the streets en masse and the downsizing frenzy was reaching full steam. Could you have imagined that COBOL skills and knowledge could command a premium in the consulting marketplace? Neither could I.

At the same time, consider CASE. While it is still a viable specialty (no, CASE is not dead!), it is far from the hot specialization area that it once was. Given a choice between specializing in CASE-based application design and specializing in Year 2000 consulting over the next few years, many consultants would, in effect, say, "Show me the money!" and brush off those once-sneered-at COBOL skills. Can you say "PROCEDURE DIVISION"? (That's a COBOL sort-of-joke, for you newbies not skilled in the black arts of the language!)

YEAR 2000 CONSULTANT—GENERALIST

Description.   The vaunted "Year 2000 problem" has been with us for years, but in that wonderful tradition of procrastination, it has been only recently that the business and information systems community has raised its collective eyebrows and said, "Uh-oh!" Simply stated, the long-accepted practice of not using century indicators (the "19" in 1976 or 1985, for example) when storing and manipulating dates—in the interest of storage efficiency, "better" utilization of available space on users' terminal screens, and other related considerations—is going to cause a *major* problem when dates with a "20" century indicator appear with more frequency in calculations; the resulting decisions made within the body of program code are likely not only to be incorrect, but to force incorrect business processes to occur (incorrect amounts for billing, erroneously determining that a product has expired because "00" is less than "98," and so on).

A Year 2000 consultant can be a generalist—someone who is engaged almost exclusively to hunt down code and data that are Year 2000–susceptible and fix them. For this consultant (as contrasted with those with other Year 2000 consulting specialties, discussed next), the primary skills are (1) analytical (being able to track the logic of complicated, often antiquated code) and (2) technical (being able to make the appropriate fixes).

Outlook.   Well, until the Year 2000, it's going to be a seller's market for these types of skills. Every company has a Year 2000 problem even if it doesn't have a Year 2000 problem. Doubletalk? Not at all. The burden of proof is on every company and organization to *certify* that it isn't susceptible to Year 2000–related problems if it is among the lucky ones that do not have massive time bombs waiting for them in their information systems—and if it's like most companies, it does have time bombs that need to be defused. Enter the Year 2000 consultant, "fixer of problems under the pressure of time." Rates are at a premium for skills once considered passé, and they aren't likely to drop anytime soon.

YEAR 2000 CONSULTANT—QUALITY ASSURANCE

Description.   Most consultants—like most computer professionals in general—despise quality assurance (QA) work. The drudgery, the testing-instead-of-development orientation, the after-the-fact nature of the work—many qualified professionals shy away from this type of work.

In the Year 2000 world, though, quality assurance is a necessity! An army of Year 2000 generalists can spend tens of millions of dollars of a client's money fixing code, but until that code is *proved* to be immune to Year 2000 problems, there is still cause for concern.

Enter the Year 2000 QA specialist. Sure, developing and executing test plans and documenting the results may be tedious, but going rates for this type of work far exceed "typical" QA-related compensation.

Outlook. The discussion for the Year 2000 generalist consultant also holds true here. Hint: One area of opportunity for independent Year 2000 QA consultants is to provide validation that the plans and deliverables from large consulting firms specializing in this area will meet clients' business needs.

YEAR 2000 CONSULTANT—STRATEGIST

Description. To fix or to replace—that is the question.

No, that's not Shakespeare; that's the quandary faced by every company with respect to its Year 2000 liability. One camp holds that the Year 2000 problem is so enormous that attempting any type of migration away from these applications (a replacement strategy) adds far too much risk, and that the correct approach is to first fix the applications and then, at some later date, replace them.

The other camp argues that expending so much effort on once again patching hard-to-understand code that probably doesn't even meet today's business functionality is a pretty darn stupid idea, and that despite the high migration project failure rate in the late 1980s and early 1990s during "the great client/server hype" (i.e., the hysteria that demanded that all the mainframes in the world be replaced by networks of workstations and PCs), the smart thing to do is to leave your problems behind and quickly develop new applications using the latest in high-productivity visual development tools and corresponding client/server technology.

So what is a company to do? Enter the Year 2000 consultant who specializes in the strategic side of the question. By analyzing (1) the company's exposure to Year 2000 problems, (2) the company's tolerance and capability for change, and (3) the technology landscape available, appropriate strategies can be put in place.

Outlook. Well, 1998 is getting pretty late in the game to put a Year 2000 strategy in place, but consider:

1. There are still laggards that are just getting started with their Year 2000 programs.
2. There are opportunities for consultants to come in and try to redirect some companies' efforts after several years' worth of poor results from existing Year 2000 service providers.

YEAR 2000 CONSULTANT—PROJECT MANAGER

Description.   Leading a Year 2000 effort *demands* top-notch project management skills, for the simple reason that there is *no* room for error. Unlike a "typical" development project, where, in the worst case, money is wasted and people are unhappy, but the project can be started again, learning (hopefully) from past mistakes, there is a fixed deadline for most Year 2000 efforts. I say *most* because some applications are already exposed to Year 2000 problems, particularly those that either store future dates (e.g., expiration dates) or add some period of time to a date and then do calculations within the body of the code. These situations are even more challenging for a project manager because development and deployment activities are being complicated by real-world business problem management.

In any case, the Year 2000 problem demands top-notch project management skills. You could look at the Year 2000 problem as the "final exam" for any project manager. Corporate politics need to be brushed aside; teamwork is essential; adherence to schedules is mandatory; quality assurance can't be overlooked; and so on.

Outlook.   It's one thing for a client to plan to solve its Year 2000 problem; it's another for that client to make a *commitment* to doing so. Those that are committed to doing what is necessary to prevent upcoming problems that could potentially be disruptive to business—and even threaten the survival of the company—are willing to pay a premium for project and program leadership that will increase the chances of their Year 2000 effort being successful. Therefore, the outlook for project managers looking to spend a few years in this arena is good, and it will no doubt get better as January 1, 2000, approaches.

DATA WAREHOUSING CONSULTANT— GENERALIST

Description.   Depending on what survey you read and when it was taken, somewhere between 90 and 98 percent of all large organizations have at least one data warehousing initiative under way. Translation: *lots* of opportunities for consultants.

A generalist data warehousing consultant is capable of:

- Developing an architecture that takes into consideration the data that should be in the warehouse, the sources from which the data will be obtained, and how the data will be used
- Developing project plans and leading a data warehousing implementation project
- Doing the hands-on "dirty work" of modeling the contents of the warehouse and mapping elements from data sources to the target warehouse

The consultant also performs related tasks and functions.

Outlook.   Excellent, for the foreseeable future. Though many would argue that first-generation data warehousing technology is somewhat constrained in providing the full range of analytical and information delivery capabilities needed, a new generation of data warehousing technology is on the horizon, and a consultant could specialize exclusively in helping his or her clients assimilate these new technologies into new data warehousing efforts. No matter what way you look at it, data warehousing is here to stay—and so are opportunities for data warehousing consultants.

DATA WAREHOUSING CONSULTANT—BUSINESS INTELLIGENCE SPECIALIST

Description. "Business intelligence"—the umbrella that incorporates on-line analytical processing (OLAP), executive information systems (EIS), general querying and reporting, and the relatively new area of data mining—can be a subspecialty for a data warehousing consultant. Basically, this consultant would work with users to determine that if, indeed, a data warehouse is built, what are the purpose(s) for engaging in this development—in other words, what work models will be supported when the data warehouse is available?

Outlook. This is an underrecognized specialty at the time of writing this (1998), but as more and more data warehouses are deployed—to the displeasure of those who "just can't get the right information out of them"—the need for these types of services will become more apparent to the client base as they struggle to avoid wasting money the second or third time around the data warehousing block.

CLIENT/SERVER APPLICATION DEVELOPMENT CONSULTANT

Description. This is the "bread-and-butter" application development consultant. Working alone or as part of a project team, the charter here is to analyze, develop, and deploy applications for your clients using distributed computing technology (e.g., client/server models and architectures).

Outlook. Though a wide range of computing professionals have basic development skills, and more and more are coming out of universities and other training programs every year, the mid-1990s has seen a tremendous imbalance between open positions and available resources. As a result, demand for developers who understand the basics of client/server computing, particularly when it comes to multitier environments (discussed under "Middleware Development and Architecture

Consultant"), have been commanding premiums in the marketplace and are in high demand at present. The marketplace tends to run hot and cold regarding various skills and the rates paid, but the basics—teamwork, an understanding of architectural and design principles, and the ability to learn new technologies and products quickly—will help any consultant stay in demand.

DATABASE APPLICATION DEVELOPMENT CONSULTANT

Description.   Many client/server developers concentrate on the "front end" of applications, i.e., that which is deployed using visual development tools and which runs on client-side PCs and workstations. A database application development consultant would (1) model and design the database environment, (2) create the databases (often with the assistance of a client's database administrator), and (3) develop stored procedures that are part of the overall application logic.

Outlook.   Not to sound like a broken record, prospects here are also very good. As an increasing number of applications using distributed computing logic are deployed, it is imperative that clients obtain qualified assistance in all of the roles that would be part of this individual's job description. As a result, the demand for inclusion of "database-qualified developers" on the ever-increasing number of consultant-led projects will continue to lead to premium pay and a wealth of opportunities for these individuals.

MIDDLEWARE DEVELOPMENT AND ARCHITECTURE CONSULTANT

Description.   For several years, there has been talk about the first generation of client/server computing ("two-tier models") being supplanted by multitier, more complex alternatives.

Increasingly, large scalable environments—particularly those using Internet technologies—feature some degree of middleware, or distributed computing services, as part of the overall environment.

Outlook.   In many ways, middleware is where the worlds of "real computing" and client/server converge—the ability to deploy mission-critical applications and systems across distributed platforms composed of PC clients, workstations, and servers. While "traditionalists" have often sneered at the suitability (or lack thereof) of distributed computing to handle "real applications," there have been tremendous advances in the past few years in base services and technologies that make new platforms a reality for applications that at one time would have been automatically deployed on the corporate mainframe. To ensure that these applications are architecturally sound, though, requires a great deal of thought and understanding concerning interoperability models, distributed transactions, and other capabilities that fall under the umbrella of "middleware." Even mainframe environments are increasingly being enhanced with messaging capabilities delivered through middleware such as IBM's MQSeries. The outlook: Lots of blue skies ahead for middleware consultants!

DISTRIBUTED COMPUTING SECURITY CONSULTANT—GENERAL

Description.   Security has long been a concern of corporate IT, and as the open systems era has developed since the late 1980s, the need for consultants who understand the security impacts of distributed computing—not only the network portion (e.g., encryption), but also security services such as authentication (i.e., proving that a user or application is who he/she/it says he/she/it is) has increased. A great deal of the wariness of distributed computing on the part of traditional IS organizations has been because of the relative immaturity of security capabilities in these environments. A consultant specializing in distributed systems security—architecture, implementation, etc.—can help plug the holes.

Outlook.   Strong, and getting stronger. As distributed computing becomes mainstream, security consulting and engineering is increasingly recognized as an imperative. Because of the seriousness of what can happen when security breaches occur—and the potential losses—consulting services in these areas command a premium.

SECURITY CONSULTANT—INTERNET

Description.   Take everything just stated regarding distributed systems security and make it far more complicated because of the extra-enterprise focus, and you have Internet security consulting opportunities. At the time this is being written, the major Web browser products had been identified as having security issues—in one case which a "malicious Web site" could access the contents of the hard disk of *client PCs* accessing that site. Sure, the holes are being plugged quickly, but as electronic commerce (discussed later) becomes an increasingly important part of any forward-thinking company's growth and distribution strategies, consulting services specializing in Internet security issues and solutions will increasingly become a necessity.

Outlook.   Very good—the stakes are high, and companies have to be sure that if they expose their computing environments to the outside world in general, they have adequate protection.

INTRANET APPLICATION DEVELOPMENT CONSULTANT

Description.   Marry the world of the Internet with client/server development, mix in a little Java, and you have a consulting subspecialty of developing applications using intranet capabilities within a client's computing environment.

Outlook. Just about everyone is at least experimenting with intranet applications, and a consultant who can not only whip together a browser front end for "play applications" but also do *serious* architecture and development—using new database-browser interfaces, for example—should be in high demand for some time to come.

INTERNET WEB SITE CONSULTANT

Description. Just about every company and organization has a presence on the Internet. Since the early days of the World Wide Web, when there were, quite honestly, some fairly bland Web sites (and some highly elegant ones with horrendous download times because of all the graphical content), companies have turned their external images over to "Webmasters" who have not only a sense of the content but also the design, layout, and technical underpinnings to develop high-quality Web sites.

Outlook. While many companies have their own internal Webmasters, the general demand for home-page and site development will continue to create demand for consulting services in these areas. The rates may start to stagnate as services in this area become more of a commodity and tools become easier to use, but it's fun work!

INTERNET ARCHITECTURE CONSULTANT

Description. Taking all of the Internet and intranet material we've discussed so far into consideration, it is apparent that any company that is serious about the Internet needs to have a firm architectural foundation for its external *and* internal sites. Internet architecture isn't only about developing correct site maps (the flow of pages within a site), but also about the underlying technology—and choices that have to be made.

Outlook.   The technology in this realm is flowing faster and faster. If the convergence of computing and other media (e.g., television) happens as expected, then an entire new world will be opened up—one that will require architectural services that will typically be provided by knowledgeable consultants.

ELECTRONIC COMMERCE CONSULTANT

Description.   The Internet is more than just advertising through an on-line medium. Increasingly, it will be an integral part of how a company conducts business with its partners, suppliers, and customers. This area, commonly known as electronic commerce, is expected to grow exponentially over the next few years.

Outlook.   This means near-endless opportunities for consultants who not only are literate in Internet technology and architecture, but also can architect and deliver commerce models for on-line banking, automated order entry and delivery, etc.

WORKGROUP COMPUTING CONSULTANT

Description.   Though acceptance of groupware and workflow technology has been somewhat spotty (with the noticeable exception of Lotus Notes), it is expected that a new generation of products, coupled with Internet technologies, will give a lift to these areas.

Outlook.   Rates and prospects for those who specialize in this area may not reach those in loftier, higher-profile areas such as Internet security, but companies that have already seen productivity gains from early and mid-1990s initiatives will increasingly want to take the next step and add collaborative capabilities to their systems. A consultant who is skilled not only in these technologies but also in the "softer" areas of workgroup computing—for example, the often overlooked cultural issues—will have a steady supply of business.

"UPSIZING" CONSULTANT

Description.   Suppose that your consulting specialties for the first few years of your practice have centered on smaller-scale systems—a mix of standalone, PC-based applications and small-scale LANs. Increasingly, organizations find themselves outgrowing their first-generation implementations as their businesses grow, their sophistication about what can be done through computing increases, etc. One niche specialty you could consider is to help organizations such as these in their "upsizing" programs—taking the next step toward more complex computing environments.

Outlook.   This is a niche area. The prospects are unknown, but in general, there is a market for consultants who can not only implement these next-step environments but also assuage clients' nervousness and fears.

OUTSOURCING ADVISORY SERVICE

Description.   A trend that will continue—with slower growth than in the recent past, but growth nonetheless—is for corporations to "outsource" entire blocks of their information systems operations to a consulting firm. An area of specialization for an independent consultant might be to act as an advisor to a company that is thinking about doing this: what areas should be outsourced, how qualified are the competing firms for *that client's* particular needs, and so on.

Outlook.   While this is partially within the realm of management consulting (discussed later), it is a specialization within that overall area. There probably isn't room for a whole lot of players in this market, but for those with some experience in outsourcing, it may be worth trying to capitalize on that knowledge.

DESKTOP PUBLISHING

Description.   A common victim of early 1990s downsizing was the corporate department that produced brochures and other graphical material—much to the glee of independent consultants, who, powered by the latest in PC-based desktop publishing, built successful businesses that catered not only to corporate America but also to smaller-sized firms.

Outlook.   The market is getting crowded and the pressure is sometimes relentless because of "I need it yesterday" demands from clients, but there is steady work in this area for those who don't necessarily want to do "computing work" but would rather use their computers as a tool to provide aesthetically pleasing, creative, content-oriented solutions to their clients. *Hint*: An interesting combination of services might be desktop publishing and Web site development.

CLIENT/SERVER MISSION-CRITICAL CONSULTANT

Description.   Traditionally, the world of mission-critical applications—those that are "must haves" for a client—has been mainframe-based (with some scattered minicomputer-based deployments). The challenges (high availability, high throughput, etc.) could be met only by mature technologies. Now, as client/server computing matures and capabilities steadily improve, companies are increasingly turning to this model of computing for deployment of new mission-critical applications or migration of existing ones.

Outlook.   To put it bluntly, typical client/server consultants—those who have been developing departmental-type solutions for a while—have little background in the nuts and bolts (or even the requirements) of mission-critical applications. There is a high demand (and one that will continue to grow) for consultants who can marry the latest in technology with the requirements of the mission-critical world and, as a result, can architect, design, and develop the next generation of these types of applications.

NETWORK ADMINISTRATION CONSULTANT

Description.   As network complexity continues to grow, so does the need to gain control over the vast array of routers, hubs, bridges, switches—the list goes on and on. Most corporate networking support staffs are stretched thin—very thin—these days and have their hands full trying to maintain uptime and provide operational support for a company's networking environment.

Outlook.   So enter the networking administration consultant—someone who can look at a client's particular environment and help develop a "command center" capability for supporting this environment. The promises of network administration have been slow to appear, but as increased capabilities come about, companies will start getting more serious about engaging consultants in these areas. Watch for prospects to grow.

SYSTEMS ADMINISTRATION CONSULTANT

Description.   The discussion concerning network administration also applies to system administration—disks, PCs, servers, etc. In fact, the convergence of network and system administration is a growing area.

Outlook.   This isn't the most exciting work a consultant can do, but it is nonetheless important. For example, a consultant who specializes in electronic distribution of software to large-scale enterprises is in high demand from—well, just about any company with a large base of PC users. The era of the "common desktop" has occurred, and consultants who understand the client and server sides of administration and how all the pieces fit together can make a client's life a whole lot easier.

SUPPORT SERVICES CONSULTANT

Description.   Supplementing internal staff at the traditional "help desk"—or performing this function in its entirety—has long been a mainstay for consultants.

Outlook.   Very often this is entry-level work, but it's a good way for a beginning consultant to not only learn technology and products but also see firsthand what some of the most commonly occurring user problems are. This will help him or her in future consulting endeavors (e.g., helping to develop more user-friendly interfaces).

IT MANAGEMENT CONSULTANT

Description.   A spinoff of the traditional management consultant, an IT management consultant is someone who specializes in areas such as managing application portfolios, assisting with IT budgets, helping business organizations sell their computing plans to their senior management, and so on.

Outlook.   The rates are often very good, but you have to know what you're doing. Credibility is key; it might be tempting to fake experience, but at some point your inexperience will be noticed. A consultant specializing in this area should treat his or her deliverables as seriously as if they were code or a design; if they are thought of as simply "business-speak" and half-considered action plans, there will be a whole lot of dissatisfied clients in someone's future.

SYSTEMS MIGRATION AND TRANSITION CONSULTANT

Description.   The great client/server boom of the late 1980s and early 1990s was notable for a number of things, including (1) the overselling of the capabilities of the distributed technology of that era, and (2) abnormally high project failure rates as companies attempted to migrate existing systems to new platforms. True, the technology wasn't there, but in many cases, the projects failed because of horribly mismanaged migration efforts. Now, as a new migration boom occurs—due in part to the Year 2000 problem, in part to the Internet, and in part to a general understanding that the new technologies make sense—there is a desperate need for consultants who not only can develop "new things" but also can move data and functionality *in an orderly manner* from old environments to new ones.

Outlook. Very good—but this is very stressful work. Rates are high, but the hours are typically long and the projects are, by nature, more complex than "from-the-beginning" development.

INDUSTRY-SPECIFIC CONSULTANT

Description. Take any of the areas we've discussed so far and add in expert-level knowledge about a specific industry, and you have an industry-specific consultant.

Outlook. Unclear. On the one hand, many clients insist that their data warehousing consultant or their electronic commerce consultant be intimately familiar with the business models and peculiarities of a given industry. Typically, though, they balk at paying a premium for this knowledge. Other clients take the approach that a consultant who is *not* an industry expert is actually a better fit for their needs, particularly analytical ones, because the questions asked during facilitated work sessions and interviews typically raise out-of-the-box thinking about different ways to accomplish business goals (i.e., process improvement).

VENDOR-ORIENTED CONSULTANT

Description. Some consultants who are technology experts concentrate their efforts on product vendors. For example, someone who is a data warehousing expert may work with vendors in that area to help them design transformation tools, develop OLAP products, and so on.

Outlook.   This is kind of a small market, but for those in whom a vendor places trust, there will probably be steady work ahead. Be careful, though, about the exclusivity of your services as a tradeoff for "inside knowledge" of what's coming up in vendors' product releases.

DEVELOPMENT CONSULTANT WITH OBJECT-ORIENTED EMPHASIS

Description.   Objects have been coming for over a decade. Though object-oriented programming languages (e.g., C++) have been around for a while, it is only recently that "end-to-end object models" [those based on the Common Object Request Broker Architecture (CORBA) or Microsoft's Distributed Common Object Model (DCOM)] are being commonly used to deploy application environments.

Outlook.   Though conceptually simple, object technology is, in reality, difficult to master for many IT professionals grounded in procedural programming and other traditional roots—meaning a wealth of opportunities for consultants who specialize in object-oriented architecture and/or development.

TRAINING AND EDUCATION CONSULTANT

Description.   The old saying, "Those who can, do; those who can't, teach" is definitely *not* true when it comes to technology education and training. Although many implementers have little interest in communicating their knowledge to others through training or teaching, there are tremendous opportunities for those who are interested in this area.

Outlook.   Chapter 8 discusses training and seminars as part of a consultant's service offerings. Interestingly, the early

1990s featured a remarkable slowdown in the technology training and seminar business as a result of economic pressures (corporate downsizings and budget cuts, the 1990 recession, and so on), but when recovery came, it brought with it a phenomenal boom in technology training, much of it due to pent-up demand, but also fueled by the Internet, data warehousing, next-generation client/server computing, etc. There will probably be downturns in this sector in the future, but if history is any teacher, each will be followed by a frenzied demand for consultants who can communicate and educate.

RECRUITER

Description. Tired of all types of consulting? One option is to shift your emphasis to the recruiting area, working within a larger firm, or possibly on an independent basis. A consulting recruiter does more than just scan resumes and schedule interviews; a good recruiter also spends time learning about technology trends—what's popular and what the demands are likely to be for certain sets of skills—and then tries to filter through resume jargon to determine what a candidate's *true* capabilities are.

Outlook. Currently, the growth in consulting services has put pressure on the recruiting channels at most firms, so the opportunities are certainly there for a consultant who wants to try a slightly different path in his or her career. What is likely to happen, though, is that when the next downturn hits, there will be pressures in the recruiting side of consulting; anyone who takes this path should have a contingency plan in place (e.g., going back into the world of implementing, at least for a while).

STAFFING SPECIALIST

Description. This specialty is related to recruiting. A consulting staffing specialist typically is responsible for (1) managing a pool of consulting resources, particularly their assignments and their availability for various projects, and having a knowledge of their respective skills, and (2) making recommendations as to assignments that should occur on upcoming engagements.

Outlook.   Basically, the same as for recruiting—high demand now; uncertain demand during the next economic downturn.

ACCOUNT MANAGER

Description.   A consulting account manager sells (1) projects (actually, business solutions), (2) staffing support, or (3) both. An account manager has to be more than just an "order taker"—he or she not only has to have basic sales skills, but also must be able to produce proposals, deliver presentations about company capabilities, and, in general, make sure that services are sold.

Outlook.   Again, the good times in the consulting business have led to an increase in the number of opportunities for account managers. Unlike recruiters and staffing specialists, though, an account manager has some control over his or her fortunes; someone who is a "natural seller" can probably survive even tough times.

CONSULTING FIRM ADMINISTRATION AND MANAGEMENT

Description.   Another path for consultants is to "advance" into management. From corporate management to running the marketing or sales organization at a consulting firm, to managing a practice (e.g., data warehousing) at a consulting organization, there are many opportunities for those who want to take a break—at least for a while—from the hands-on aspects of consulting.

Outlook.   Fairly good, as a result of the growth of so many firms.

INDUSTRY ANALYST

Description. A spin on consulting is to become an industry analyst, that is, someone who doesn't necessarily deliver solutions to clients, but rather synthesizes a broad range of inputs and helps to forecast trends, future directions of technology, etc. Many consultants are familiar with The Gartner Group, Meta Group, and other firms that specialize in providing these types of services.

Outlook. This is a very tight market, but the major players and some up-and-comers are usually seeking to add staff with specialties in emerging technology areas. It's very high-profile work; you have to really know what you're talking about.

"CONSULTANT TO CONSULTANTS"

Description. Finally, we have someone who gives advice to other consultants—as I do, with this book and all of its previous incarnations, as well as my other technology and career-oriented books.

Outlook. Interestingly, when the First Edition of this book was published in 1985, it was almost the only book on the market on the subject of computer consulting. Since that time, many other authors have created works that in many cases are complementary to this book in that they covering different material, or similar material but with a different approach. There is always room for a consultant to share his or her experiences with others.

PLANNING AND ORGANIZING YOUR CONSULTING BUSINESS

Now that your firm's products and services have been determined, your next step is building a business organization around them. As you will see, unless you have a strong business organization to support these services, success in the consulting arena becomes difficult or unlikely. This chapter will cover the preliminary organizational requirements such as choosing a business name, planning your first expenditures (and keeping your costs to a minimum), building a computer system for your own use, making the "full-time versus part-time" decision, and finding a business location.

CHOOSING A BUSINESS NAME

By what name should your consulting firm be known? The first decision is whether or not your own name should appear as part of the business name (this doesn't mean Al's Consulting and Garage). Many consultants operate under their own name, such as Mary Jones Consulting Service or simply Mary Jones, Consultant. This follows the practice of the majority of accountants, lawyers, and physicians: no gimmicky names, just a statement of the person or people involved and possibly the service offered. Other consultants prefer a simple name such as Computerized Medical Consultants.

When should you use your name and when should you choose a fictitious name? If you have strong name recognition in your geographic consulting area (local, state, or national, whichever you choose to market your services in), your own name serves as a marketing and advertising tool as much as or more than any descriptive title. Of course, a combination name, such as Mary Jones Computerized Accounting Consultants, provides a description of services provided for those currently unfamiliar with your name.

My own choice when I began consulting was Computer Education and Consulting because of a lack of name recognition in the Colorado Springs area. The name was a simple statement of the services provided by my firm: general computer consulting and educational (computer literacy and training) services. In retrospect, however, the name may be descriptive in print but is a mouthful to say when answering phone calls or otherwise speaking the name because of the number of syllables.

Another consideration when selecting a descriptive name is *not* to inadvertently limit your potential business by your chosen name. Computerized Accounting Consultants may have a hard time convincing a client legal firm that they do indeed know the legal-applications area as well as accounting ones and aren't just moonlighting to gain additional business. If the firm evolves into specialties different from the original target markets, as was mentioned in Chap. 2, a name change may be necessary to realign the business specialties. Business Microcomputer Consultants still defines a target market (small business computers, as opposed to home systems or mainframes) but allows for a wide evolution of service lines within the range implied by the firm's name. Your advertising could then be targeted toward the specific applications areas for which you are aiming.

Once you choose your name, how do you keep someone else from using it? Similarly, how do you make sure that you are not treading on someone else's territorial rights? This

```
STATE OF ARIZONA
COUNTY OF MARICOPA

Bernard Jordan_____ of the County of Maricopa_____
in the State of Arizona, being first duly sworn upon oath deposes and says that
Jordan Business Computer Systems_____
is the name under which a business or trade is being carried on at _____
7300 N. 27th Ave. Phoenix, AZ 85021
in the County of Maricopa, State of Arizona.
That the full name and address of all the persons who are represented by the
said name of Jordan Business Computer Systems is as follows,
to wit:Bernard Jordan 7300 N.27th Ave.Phoenix, AZ 85021

                        Bernard Jordan

  NOTARY    Subscribed and sworn before me this 30th day of November,
  PUBLIC    1984. My commission expires January 31, 1985.

                   Jon Anderson
```

FIGURE 3-1   County name registration form.

depends on your form of business organization (discussed later in the chapter). The business name of a sole proprietorship or partnership is usually registered at the local, county, or state level by the appropriate recorder (see Fig. 3-1). The name must be registered for each geographical area in which you will be operating (multiple cities or counties). If your business is incorporated, you can choose a name that will be registered with your state's corporation commission at incorporation time. If you plan to be incorporated in more than one state, you must register that name in each state.

Once you decide on a name, your next trip should be to the local or county recorder or corporation commission. They have a list of all registered business names that are in effect in the covered area. Occasionally you may need to do a little searching, since they might have an alphabetized computer printout effective through the beginning of the month, for example, and a handwritten, unalphabetized, temporary log for all registrations since the printout and prior to the next update. Others may have an online system that is continually updated. Normally a small fee is required for registration and notarization; $5 is typical. Incorporation, of course, is more expensive.

If you are using your own name you are less likely to find a conflict. You may if you have chosen John Smith Consultants, but you are highly unlikely to find too many Stanislaw Fontanez Consulting Groups. If you do find a business name conflict, don't go to your lawyer and change your own name; change the business name slightly—for example, John Smith Consulting Group.

If you should find subsequently that another group is using the same name that you have registered, contact the individuals involved and inform them that you have registered that business name; they may simply be unaware of the registration rights. If they don't cease operating under your name, legal action may be necessary.

MINIMUM BUSINESS NEEDS

When viewing a lucrative contract prior to officially beginning practice, new consultants may be tempted to purchase full-page advertisements in the *Yellow Pages,* buy 2000 business cards and 10,000 letterhead-envelope sets, and run weekly display ads in the Sunday newspaper's business section. Before they know it, the profits from the first contract have been converted into fixed overhead costs and the next contract is nowhere in sight. The rule to remember is to provide for your minimum business needs without spending your life savings or mortgaging the next 3 years' profits. The absolute minimum you should consider includes:

1. *Business cards.*   While they may be cheaper in lots of 2000, 500 business cards will go a long way. Remember that every time your business location, phone number, or anything else changes the cards become outdated and it's reordering time. Old business cards may be great for writing phone messages on, but scrap paper is cheaper: Don't be stuck with a lot of unused cards.

Shop around, also, as prices and quality vary widely among printers. Find high-quality cards that reflect favorably on your business and professionalism and are reasonably priced. You may or may not choose to include a business logo on your cards, but *don't* spend several hundred dollars at the beginning to have a logo designed. If you insist on one, do it yourself or let the printer design it or find a starving art student to do it for you.

2. *Letterhead and envelopes.*   The above rules also apply to your business stationery. Shop around, don't buy extraordinary amounts, and get good-quality paper (20-pound bond, for example).

3. *Advertising.*   You should be listed in the *Yellow Pages* under Computer Systems Designers and Consultants or a similar title; when people "let their fingers do the walking," you don't want them to walk right by you. You should not, however, spend $75 per month for a display ad when you have little or no business; a bold-faced entry with a surrounding box could serve the same purpose for less money. A sample box listing is illustrated in Fig. 3-2.

Be cautioned if you choose to work out of your home and don't have separate phones for business and personal use: you may have to convert your residential phone to a business one and pay the higher business rate in order to be listed in the *Yellow Pages*. You can keep your personal listing in the white pages for a monthly "additional listing" charge. The advertising as well as the difference between a business and residential listing is tax-deductible as a business expense, of course.

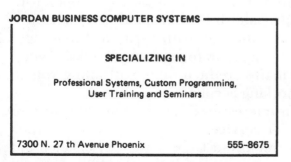

FIGURE 3-2   Yellow Pages box advertisement.

Check with your local phone company for their business and residential policies.

Additionally, there is no way to ignore the Internet when it comes to advertising. Even independent consultants can benefit from a professional Web site that not only promotes whatever your services and specialities happen to be, but also can be updated at a moment's notice to take advantage of new opportunities, strategies, and markets.

4. *Office supplies.*   You will need file folders, paper, pens, paper clips, and other office material. You should wait to purchase expensive material such as file cabinets, bookshelves, and others until you have enough revenue to cover the expenses.

5. *Post office box.*   If you base your consulting business in your home, you may want to rent a post office box for business mail. This is especially useful if you have several partners in the business, all working from their own residences. Rather than designate one location as the principle business location you may choose a post office box. This is helpful when one or more partners are out of town for long periods of time; all mail will still be accessible to the remaining partners. It could also prevent reprinting business cards and stationery when addresses change or a partner leaves the firm (if his or her address had been the one used). Small post office boxes cost around $15 for 6 months.

6. *Checking account.*   Even if you are starting your consulting business on a part-time basis you should still establish a separate checking account for business expenses and revenue deposits. This will prevent the mixing of business funds with personal ones and help establish in your mind that your business is a separate financial entity with separate funds flow, regardless of whether it is a separate legal one. Banks, savings and loans, and even many credit unions will allow you to establish a business checking account.

Shop around for an interest-bearing account with little or no minimum balance or service charge. Business accounts that pay no interest or require a large minimum balance but offer interstate network access are of little use unless you will be conducting business over a wide geographical area and plan to either travel a lot or establish business locations in many of these areas.

7. *Invoice forms.* Since you are not in an industry with large daily volume, simple letterhead with a typed statement of services performed and associated fees is usually sufficient; there is no need to purchase several hundred preprinted invoice forms. This will also save on overhead expenses.

8. *IRS registration.* If your business is operated as a sole proprietorship, no Internal Revenue Service registration is required; your business tax identification number is just your social security number, which appears on the rest of your tax forms. A partnership, however, needs to register a separate tax identification number to be used with any tax information returns (since more than one person is involved in a partnership, one partner's social security number would be insufficient).

9. *Answering machine, voice mail, or answering service.* A beginning consultant probably doesn't need an expensive answering service. The widely accessible nature of voice mail within the past few years can, for slightly more than a cost of an answering machine, give even a home-based office a professional touch to clients and prospective clients calling you. Regardless of what option you choose, there should be some means of receiving messages left for you.

10. *Computer system.* It probably would not seem appropriate to your clients if their computer consultant didn't have a computer system of his or her own. Additionally, you will probably need a computer for evaluating software and possibly developing your own, for internal use or commercial sale.

A minimum system that you could use for your own business operations should have (*a*) word processing software, for typing business letters and reports, (*b*) a spreadsheet program, for conducting financial analysis of your own and your clients' operations, and (*c*) a database or file manager, for maintaining mailing lists, organizing your reference material, and other data management needs. As your practice expands an accounting program will help save you valuable time in organizing your receivables and payables and present an accurate picture of how business operations are doing.

Something to keep in mind, though, is that if you are going to be specializing in, or at least involved in, LAN-based applications evaluation and/or development, then your own computer system should be capable of supporting those activities. That is, you may want to install an inexpensive 2- or 3-PC LAN to permit testing and evaluation of applications. Given how inexpensive LAN components and computers themselves are today, you most likely will recover your costs rather quickly. For your purposes, you most likely won't need a high-capacity, high-powered "tower" server; you probably can get by using "below production grade" components for your development environment.

FULL-TIME OR PART-TIME CONSULTING?

One of the most crucial decisions you must make is determining whether you should enter the consulting profession on a full-time or part-time basis. There are many tradeoffs that you must consider. While it may be tempting to quit your present job, make a relatively small investment for overhead expenses, and then watch the money roll in (or so the scenario goes), you need to consider your present and projected situation, financially and otherwise.

Bureau of Labor statistics show that approximately four million people work at two jobs, with half of them being managers, executives, professionals, and technicians.[1] Why would you want to begin your consulting career on a part-time basis? There are several reasons.

1. *Security.* If you maintain your present employment until your consulting business is *very* well established, you gain a chance to test the waters—to see if your market analysis, business projections, and computer skills meet the requirements

of the consulting marketplace. Rather than forfeit the security and steady income of your current job, you can begin your business organization and early contracts as supplementary income.

2. *Infeasibility of quitting your present job.*   Sometimes it is difficult or impossible to terminate your present employment prior to embarking on your consulting career. If, for example, you have another three years until you are vested in your company's retirement plan, it may not be desirable to leave their employment at this time. You may not want to postpone beginning your consulting career, though, because of extremely promising market niches that you wish to exploit. Part-time consulting may be the answer, at least on an interim basis.

The same principle applies to someone who cannot leave his or her present job because of contractual agreements; a military officer with two years left until separation from the service can't walk into the commander's office and say, "Sorry, sir, I'm resigning to become a consultant." Because I was an Air Force officer when I founded Computer Education and Consulting, I am especially familiar with this situation.

3. *Growth.*   Until you gain more experience and confidence in all of the business and computer topics we've discussed, you can use part-time consulting as a learning forum.

4. *Burnout.*   A consultant is likely to be dealing with many new situations and responsibilities not previously faced. Many hours will be spent mastering the "consulting learning curve." At periodic intervals you may feel burned out. A part-time consultant can take a break from consulting responsibilities and still have regular income from a full-time job.

Of course, there are disadvantages to coupling your consulting tasks with another job. The major one is time. Your consulting activities are likely to cut deeply into your leisure time. This problem is compounded if you have a spouse and family. There are many times that a part-time consultant may spend eight to ten hours working at a regular job during the day and then have to spend five more hours in the evening working on a design project or software task. It's because of these situations that burnout can result. You must determine if you're willing to make the extra sacrifice required for this type of lifestyle.

Another potential problem is conflicts of interest with your present job. As a military officer you cannot maintain any off-duty employment with a company (your own or otherwise) that conducts business with the defense department; therefore, an Air Force computer officer is forbidden by law from providing third-party contract software to another Air Force agency.

You need to check with your present employer to determine what restrictions, if any, exist for outside consulting activities. Many employers consider legal action if you leave a firm and clients follow you to your new employment; you must be aware of any contracts that are binding upon you.

Inconveniences can result if you are currently employed in an 8-to-5, Monday-through-Friday job. Not only will you be doing almost all of your consulting work in the evenings and during weekends and holidays, but many of the management functions you need to do, such as visiting your accountant, going to the bank, and arranging for printing must be accomplished during lunch hours. Many of your potential clients may not desire to meet with you during weekends and evenings, and this can cost you business opportunities. If your current job is one with flexible hours, this problem can be alleviated, of course.

Another problem may occur when you are suddenly flooded with many opportunities that you can't possibly handle yourself during the limited time you have available. You might then find yourself forced to refuse certain contracts (though we will see later that subcontracting these opportunities provides an opportunity to alleviate this predicament).

Some clients may view a part-time consultant as less professional than a full-time one; they may feel that if you were worth the fees that you charge you would be consulting full-time. Others may not see you this way, especially if you are consulting part-time because of contractual agreements. I've had clients take both stands; most seem to understand that as an Air Force officer I had to consult part-time. Even they, however, sometimes have doubts about the time, though not the capabilities, I would have to complete a contract.

Finally, a full-time job that requires substantial or unpredictable travel can be a great hindrance to one's part-time consulting practice, particularly in the area of client support. I've been able to overcome that problem over the years through partners and subcontractors who were capable and available to fill in for me when I've been unavailable because of travel.

If you decide that the time involved and other deficiencies of starting part-time are too great and therefore wish to take the plunge into full-time consulting, you should ensure the following:

1. You have at least one *guaranteed contract* that will provide enough income for living expenses, early business growth, etc. While this contract is underway you can begin or continue marketing efforts for subsequent business.

2. In case the first contract falls through or additional business doesn't follow as quickly as you had planned, you should have *sufficient savings* to provide you with living and business expenses. How much is sufficient depends on how long you are willing to stick it out and what your actual living and business expenses are.

If you have an office with a $1500 per month lease, your business expenses are obviously greater than if you are working in your home. Living expenses will be greater in a city like San Francisco than a small city like Tucson or Colorado Springs.

3. You *limit your initial expenses* just in case things don't work out as planned. That's why a limited purchase of business cards and letterhead is a wise decision until you see what directions your business takes you.

WORK AT HOME OR LEASE AN OFFICE?

Thought you were done with the difficult decisions, didn't you? It is highly recommended that a beginning computer consultant base operations out of his or her home. The added expense of a monthly office lease could absorb business capital and revenue at a quick enough pace to force you to give up consulting. Many of your meetings will take place at your clients' business locations; an office is basically an expensive prestige item.

There are several things that you should be aware of regarding working out of your home, however. You must separate your "work time" from your "home time." Just because you don't get into your car and drive to a business location every morning doesn't mean that you aren't working; you must avoid household distractions (including your spouse and children).

Also be sure to check your local zoning laws. If you are just basing your operations in your home rather than having clients constantly trooping through, you shouldn't face any problems. Some neighborhoods, though, may have covenants providing some restrictions; be sure of what you sign and know your own zoning laws.

When meeting clients at your home, you must present a businesslike appearance. Your office or den should reflect the professional nature of your consulting profession. Interruptions and distractions are a wonderful way to lose a client.

You must also check with your local or county zoning commission to learn exactly what zoning laws are in effect for your neighborhood. Some neighborhoods have covenants that prohibit a business from being operated in a residence; usually this refers to a retail operation. Others restrict the number of clients you can meet with at one time. If this is the case, you may not be able to hold a large seminar at your residence.

If you are operating your practice from your home, you are most likely eligible for tax deductions of a percentage of your home mortgage or rent for business use of the home. This will be discussed further in Chap. 11.

If you *must* rent an office because of the infeasibility of working at home, investigate leasing a small one-person office or desk space within an office suite. Your costs will be much less and often copying, telephone answering, and secretarial services are included with your rental fee.

FORM OF BUSINESS ORGANIZATION

You will probably begin your consulting business in the simplest of the three legal business forms, the *sole proprietorship*, meaning you are running your business as a solo effort. You and your business are the same legal entity; this is business talk for "You are personally responsible for your firm's financial and business obligations." If your sole proprietorship tallies up $100,000 in business debts or is successfully sued, your personal assets are open game to meet these obligations.

The second major form of business organization is the *partnership*. As you might suspect, you need at least one partner to be considered a partnership. You are still considered responsible for the financial and legal obligations of your firm, but not by yourself.

Finally, there is the *corporation*. The primary benefit a corporation offers you is the legal separation of your business from you (and your partners, if applicable). Bankruptcy or legal liability by the business will only affect you to the extent of your stated investment in the business; only those assets are subject to loss.

Which business form should your practice have? If you will be designing and marketing much software, either for a limited number of users or for the commercial market, incorporation may provide protection from potential lawsuits by competitors, software publishers, or customers. Remember, ours is a litigious society, and successful businesses are often targets of lawsuits.

Bear in mind that incorporating just for prestige is probably not worth the incorporation and legal fees; you should have a legitimate need for the protection. If your primary services are seminars, training, and writing, your lawsuit potential is less than if you actually provide operational software, either by recommending its purchase or actually developing it.

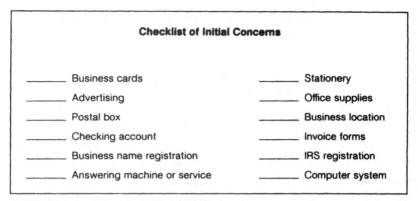

FIGURE 3-3   Checklist of initial concerns.

ADDITIONAL CONSIDERATIONS

When you register your business (usually when you apply for your business name), check with your local, county, and state business governing agencies for any regional regulations that may apply to you. You shouldn't have to worry about collecting and remitting sales tax, since you most likely won't be selling any taxable goods, but rather services.

Be sure to review Chaps. 4, 5, and 11 for additional operational concerns such as bookkeeping, tax filing, and advertising. A checklist of preliminary business considerations is provided for your use in Fig. 3-3.

SUMMARY

Well, what is Bernie Jordan up to? He is more convinced than ever that he can enjoy a successful career as a computer consultant. He begins planning for business operations, first choosing the name Jordan Business Computer Systems to provide both name recognition for himself and define his area of expertise. Though he will begin by emphasizing legal systems, he does plan to expand his applications base as business grows and doesn't wish to change the firm's name as new specialty areas develop.

Bernie contracts with a local printer for 250 business cards and 500 letterhead-envelope sets. He also begins a business checking account at his current bank. Bernie already owns a personal computer that he uses for investment management; he feels it is sufficient to use for his consulting practice. He currently has word processing, spreadsheet, and database software. He has decided against spending $1000 for an accounting system because early business volume is expected to be light enough to manage accounting data manually, assisted by his spreadsheet and database programs. After business volume increases he can then write or purchase an accounting system.

Even though the layoff rumor mill is still churning at Bernie's company, he is a bit reticent about jumping ship just now. There are several reasons for this. First, one of the other rumors is that there may be a round of voluntary severance incentives to leave the company, which could give Bernie some excellent seed money for his consulting business if he hangs around long enough to collect it.

Second, even though he has been lining up potential small business clients, the local business climate is still a bit shaky, and until he reaches his business financial goals (discussed and illustrated in Chap. 5) he is not sure he wants to take the plunge full-time.

Therefore, Bernie decides to pursue the consulting activities on a moonlighting, part-time basis for now, always keeping his plans for full-time activities updated in case he needs to, or finds the opportunity to take that route on short notice.

END NOTE

1. William C. Banks, "You're Not Alone in the Moonlight," *Money*, April 1984, p. 219.

MARKETING YOUR CONSULTING BUSINESS

INTRODUCTION

Networking and communications, networking and communications...no, I'm not talking about LANs, WANs, and protocols, though those subjects obviously are very important to computer consultants in these days of distributed computing. Rather, I'm talking about the keys to marketing your consulting business. In this chapter we'll discuss the many steps that lead to successful marketing. These range from defining your target market, to forming strategic relationships, to the always tricky (but potentially lucrative) area of selling your consulting services back to your former employer.

You might as well learn the following equation right now, so we can keep our discussion in focus:

$$Marketing \neq Advertising$$

That's right; advertising, while an important part of reaching your intended market for your services, is *not* the same as marketing, but rather is only one piece of the overall marketing strategy. In fact, many successful computer consultants build their practice through marketing means other than advertising, especially using channels which are either no-cost, low-cost, or possibly more cost-effective than most advertising.

So far in this book we've discussed one of the so-called "4 Ps" that comprise an overall marketing strategy. These are:

- *Product* (discussed at length in Chap. 2). That is, what are the products and services you are offering the marketplace?

- *Price.* We'll discuss pricing strategies in Chap. 5.

- *Promotion.* How will you make it known to the marketplace that you are available—and highly qualified—to execute your product and/or service strategy?

- *Place* (actually, "distribution," but the marketing gurus of long ago liked the sound of "4 Ps," so they substituted "place" for "distribution"). Place, or distribution, implies the channels that you are going to use to deliver your products and services. We'll discuss some of the alternatives in this chapter and in subsequent ones.

Those readers who may not have a formal business background may be surprised to see "price" and "product" so closely coupled with the other "Ps." This is a good example of how the many disciplines of the business world must work with one another. While pricing strategies—for example, setting your billing rate, as we'll discuss in Chap. 5—is mostly a financial issue, there are marketing implications. Set it too high, and you may lose a prospective client to a lower bidder. Set it too low, and not only may a project not turn out to be profitable, but you could even lose clients because certain clients in specific target markets may view you as unqualified *because* of that low rate you quote. "If he (or she) were really qualified, the billing rate would be much higher," might go their reasoning.

In some cases, however, you may view a specific project as strategic in nature (if you get that one, it may establish your expertise in that area or lead to other business, or whatever), and you may then adjust your billing rate downward.

Certainly, you can see the relationship between the financial and marketing disciplines. Your fee (your price) becomes not only a financial tool, but also a marketing one, to be used wisely and strategically.

Enough said; the points to remember, before we commence our discussion of the many aspects of marketing, is that (1) marketing is much more than simple advertising, and (2) marketing comprises four subdisciplines, all of which must play against the others in order to develop a successful overall business strategy.

THE BENEFITS OF MARKETING

Consultant Robert Kelley outlined four major benefits the marketing effort provides to your practice[1]:

1. *Marketing focuses your business and your efforts.* By determining the answers to your marketing-mix questions of product, price, promotion, and distribution, your resources can be directed toward your chosen services and marketing methods, rather than scattered among a haphazard range of ideas. Remember that since you are performing a variety of business functions, the fewer wasted or misdirected resources the better off you will be.

A *marketing orientation,* consisting of two critical functions, is essential for a consulting practice. You must first determine the needs and wants of your target market (as we'll see shortly), followed by an adaptation of your organizational efforts toward meeting these needs and wants. You are not the only person in the world offering computer consulting advice, so don't expect everyone to beat a path to your door begging you to help them.

2. *Marketing makes you do today what is required to secure next year's business.* By continually reevaluating your marketing mix, you can keep your efforts on track. As your marketing efforts attract new clients, your practice can survive and grow from the additional revenue.

3. *Marketing makes you visible.*   You will become very familiar to your potential clients through your marketing efforts. They will become aware of the services you offer, your prices, and your expertise.

4. *Marketing improves your organization.*   As you and your practice become well known, you can command higher fees for your services. The incremental revenue earned provides capital for additional employees, advertising, and general business expansion. Your business reputation will improve, as will the long-term survival prospects of your business.

ANALYZING YOUR TARGET MARKET

By now you should have a general idea of your target market, based on what services you will be offering. The general public is not a specific target, and a target of "current nonusers of computers" isn't limited enough. "Local real estate agencies with little or no computerization" is narrow enough to allow you to concentrate both your product and service development and your marketing efforts.

Your target should state (1) the geographic range, (2) types of businesses, and (3) computer expertise of your intended client base. Your marketing efforts will differ if, for example, you were targeting (1) accountants with installed computer systems wishing to expand usage or (2) nonautomated accounting firms.

Because you don't have unlimited resources (time, money, and knowledge) it is important that your target market be within the capabilities of your existing resources. Again, as we saw in Chap. 2, don't eliminate the possibility of adjusting or overhauling your targeting efforts as situations change; the key to survival, especially in an industry as dynamic as computer services, is flexibility and adaptability.

If revenue or the number of clients begins to decrease (or never grows), you must try to determine the reason. If it is because of inadequate advertising, a poor pricing structure, or another controllable factor, you obviously need to adjust the business strategy that is inhibiting your firm's growth. If, however, you determine that there is no longer a widespread need for your particular products and services, it is time to reassess what products and services should be marketed.

You may become aware of special problems and opportunities. A group of attorneys, for example, may express a strong desire to access legal databases and download the data into a word processing system to produce legal opinions. If enough respondents desire this capability, you may investigate the feasibility of including these systems and software among your offerings.

Additionally, you can learn what specific buying patterns exist among your future customers. Members of the consumer goods retail industry, for example, may not do much systems purchasing between mid-October and mid-January because of the heavy holiday season workload. A certain target market may be particularly cautious when purchasing computer equipment and take several months to make affirmative or negative decisions. Armed with this knowledge, you can adjust your marketing efforts to take advantage of certain features of your market segment.

You should also try to determine what may motivate your potential clients. Several times I have mentioned that you and your services should help your customers solve problems or exploit opportunities.

These two benefits you provide can be defined as dealing with negative and positive motivators, respectively.[2] A client's *negative motivator* could be falling behind on order processing, causing customers to cancel orders rather than wait for delivery. Another would be a backlog of correspondence, also resulting in lost customers. Negative motivators imply that a problem exists.

A *positive motivator*, however, is a potential incremental benefit to the client rather than the solution to a problem. His or her current procedures may be able to process all customer orders with minimal delay, but a computer system could allow a doubling of orders without a corresponding increase in clerical workers. Similarly, a word processing system could provide mass mailing capability with minimal effort, increasing that company's advertising and promotion efforts.

It is important that you know what motivates your potential clients because this provides directions for your marketing and advertising. A client base strongly motivated by solutions to critical problems will not likely be stirred by advertisements catering to positive motivators.

I also mentioned in Chap. 2 that you may find your mix of products and services changing over time. In addition to finding new opportunities, this may also be due to changing markets. All markets, those you target as well as others, are unlikely to remain static. Because of changing demographics and other factors you may find your own clients losing interest or formerly unprofitable markets becoming attractive. Through a perpetual marketing effort, including periodic market analysis, you can be forewarned of these shifts and react accordingly in a timely manner.

MARKETING AND YOUR FEES

In Chap. 5, we'll look at various methods used to calculate your consulting fees, based on salary and expense requirements, utilization rates, and so on. As we mentioned at the beginning of this chapter, however, fee setting does not take place in an isolated environment, and must take into account a number of marketing factors.

You may determine that your billing rate should be $60 per hour for basic evaluation and development services, with slight variations made for long-term contracts. Despite all of the processes that go into your calculations, however, you may find that:

- The local economy is so bad that your competitors will consistently underbid you by half (approximately $30 per hour). Are they as good as you? To many clients that doesn't matter—only the bottom line does.

- Your areas of specialization are getting a bit stale, and the demand is slacking off; therefore, your utilization rate (the percentage of time you're billable) is dropping; in theory you should require a higher billing rate to compensate for the loss. However, the market just can't support a higher rate.

- A nationally known expert in your area of specialization begins operations in your geographical target market charging the same billing rate as you. To compensate, you may need to lower your own rate.

And there may be hundreds of other possibilities, any one of which could arise at any time. It's important to constantly keep in touch with the marketing aspects of your fees—and those of your current and anticipated competition—and utilize your fees as a marketing weapon whenever possible.

PROMOTING YOUR BUSINESS

There are three principal ways to attract clients for your business. These include (1) using friends or associates as your first customers, (2) explicitly advertising the products and services you offer, and (3) establishing a reputation for excellence in your field. All play an important role in developing a comprehensive market plan.

The first and third items constitute components of the somewhat overused term "networking." When I hear that term—outside of the context of computer communications, of course—I can't help but picture cocktail-like parties with nattily dressed professionals exchanging business cards at a furious pace. In reality, though, networking merely means that you must be constantly reaching out to new people and companies, often through friends, or friends of friends, or friends of someone's barber who knows the owner of the florist around the corner who...well, you get the idea. The point is, you should constantly strive to meet new people in a variety of settings. Even if they may not be potential clients, chances are that a firsthand or secondhand contact will be.

Bernie Jordan entered the consulting profession with his first client almost contracted; many consultants are not that fortunate. Your immediate operational goals (as contrasted to the support goals of planning your product, financial, and service strategies) should be directed toward attracting clients and establishing your business reputation.

One of the most important assets any business can have is name recognition. When you think of fast-food hamburgers, automobile rental agencies, or television sets, one or two companies usually come immediately to mind. When legal offices desire advice about computerization options, Bernie Jordan would like Jordan Business Computer Systems to be the first consulting firm to come to mind.

Because a consultant is a professional (akin to a doctor, dentist, lawyer, or accountant), certain media may not be suitable for advertising. Television and radio, for example, tend to detract from the professional reputation you are trying to develop and brand you a "mass marketer." Even though some physicians and lawyers choose to advertise their practices, the majority don't, relying instead on references and walk-in business.

Newspaper advertisements tend to be more appropriate for your intended clientele. A firm specializing in real estate applications could advertise periodically in the local newspaper's real estate section. The type of advertisement is also important. Boldfaced headlines screaming **"SPECIAL: THIS WEEK ONLY"** are also inappropriate for a professional firm.

You do, however, want to follow the basic rules of advertising: attract the customer's attention, explain the product and how it will be of benefit, and provide a point of contact (address or phone number). Newspaper advertisement rates are usually based on the number of column inches involved. One word of caution: at the beginning, stay away from "special" rates with a lower per-inch charge but a high minimum number of inches per year. These special rates are more appropriate for larger firms employing several consultants with a substantial advertising and promotion budget.

Another forum for advertising is trade publications of your targeted industry. The local or state board of realtors, for example, may have a monthly newsletter that would provide an excellent advertising medium.

Many national magazines also offer regional advertising instead of or in addition to their national advertising. You could, for example, place an advertisement in the west coast edition of a magazine that research has shown members of your target market read frequently. This may be a bit much when you are just starting out, but as your business expands (and with it your geographical target) you may consider this option.

Of course, there is the Internet, a key facet of any consultant's marketing and advertising strategy. Seeing who visits a professional-looking home page is a good way to find out who might be looking for the types of services you provide. Here are some tips on Internet advertising and marketing:

- Include white papers, reproductions of articles you've written and other informational content; not just advertising.

- Use it to recruit as your business grows.

- Regularly update the contents so that someone who has previously "hit" the page will want to come back because of the updates.

- Keep up-to-date concerning advances in Internet technologies that might enable you to provide electronic commerce capabilities (e.g., metered service or pay by download content) to the general public.

A final medium you should consider is the local *Yellow Pages*. Mentioned in Chap. 3 as a minimum starting business expense, this form of advertising informs anyone with a phone book of your business services. As with regional magazine advertising and bulk newspaper advertising, you should shy away from quarter-page display ads during your firm's early growth period. A bold-faced business name and a two- or three-line statement of services surrounded by a quarter-inch box (see Fig. 3-2) will serve nicely for the first year or two at far less expense while still providing you with visibility in the *Yellow Pages*. Monthly costs average between $10 and $20, depending on location.

Because the 1980s brought competition among companies for local *Yellow Pages* books, you may often find yourself advertising in more than one company's *Yellow Pages*. The choice is yours as to whether or not you want to be listed in more than one book.

STRATEGIC RELATIONSHIPS

Often a joint effort with another institution can provide a means of gaining customers. If you have demonstrated to a local computer store your expertise in certain areas on prior contracts, it may refer you to customers who need custom programming, general consulting, or training that the retailer doesn't provide. This is especially true in the computer retail environment of the 1990s, where small shops have given way to mass merchandise-driven "superstores" who typically don't keep a programming or development staff on hand.

It is important to build your reputation and contacts with as many local computer stores as possible; as your reputation grows they may want to impress their customers by consulting with you, the expert, on particularly difficult problems. This provides you with future clients as well as another important feature; someone else is assisting you with marketing your services. For every other person, store, or organization who recommends you as a successful implementor of computer solutions, the pyramiding effect of referrals is that much more powerful.

Another joint effort that can assist you with both marketing and producing revenue is working with (and eventually receiving endorsements from) a professional organization. The local board of realtors, for example, might have a computer committee to assist members with their automation efforts. Providing consulting services to this committee may lead to myriad contracts as individual members attempt to computerize their operations. Educational and informative seminars for board members are another possibility.

Again, this strategic relationship is of great benefit to your practice: you are providing expert advice to your clients, and they are providing you with highly reputable marketing services.

Another relationship that can benefit you is working with a national or regional main office, such as a national realty organization. Under contract to the organization as a whole, you can be recommended to the member branch offices by the main office when computer services are needed. As with professional organizations, you are utilizing the reputation and credibility of the sponsoring agency to assist you with your marketing.

Finally, keep in mind joint ventures with other consultants or consulting companies. Your specialties may be database and CASE; someone else's might be LANs and networking management. Together, you could bid, win, and develop a system which takes advantage of both of your specializations in a synergistic manner. You can build these types of strategic relationships through membership in consulting organizations (that's right, networking!) or similar professional societies and groups.

MARKETING TO YOUR FORMER EMPLOYER

Often, a new full-time consultant may be able to sell his or her expertise back to a former employer. Armed with intimate knowledge of a company's plans and projects, both current and future, a consultant may be able to utilize a good working record and interpersonal relationships to obtain consulting contracts in a variety of forms. These contracts may range from short-term technical advising based on information acquired since leaving the organization, to long-term programming assignments.

As we discussed in the first chapter, very often organizations handle downsizings poorly, and dismiss critically needed people, so very often an involuntary severance can turn into an immediate consulting opportunity with your supervisor or manager. He or she may not have been the decision maker with respect to your termination, and may be sympathetic to your plight and give you a chance for immediate work. Other times, you may find consulting opportunities with other divisions or groups of that employer.

HOW MUCH TIME DO YOU SPEND MARKETING?

As soon as you begin your first contract it is likely that you will devote almost all of the time to your consulting activities (whether full- or part-time) completing this task. You may not have the time to perform the marketing functions we discussed in this chapter: speaking, advertising, meeting with prospective clients, and generally building your reputation. Once your first contract is completed, however, you may find yourself with no following assignment. The first rule of consulting is "No job, no income" (with the exception of royalty cash flow, which most beginning consultants don't have). You then begin your marketing efforts to find a client. That assignment ends, you have no future contract, and the cycle repeats.

A better plan is to allocate a certain percentage of your time and effort to executing a comprehensive marketing plan, simultaneously working on your contracts. Remember that as an independent consultant, you have no marketing department (as in a large organization) to attract future clients while you concentrate on business operations; that is another one of the many functions that you must perform simultaneously.

For example, a one-month project (based on eight hours per day, five days per week) could be extended by just over 1 week if an average of two hours per day is spent on marketing and related functions. The type of job a beginning consultant would work on is unlikely to be of such a critical nature that a five-and-a-half-week completion time frame rather than four weeks would be disastrous for your client and cause you to lose the project. Naturally, when planning a project you wouldn't tell your client, "Well, this will take five-and-a-half weeks rather than four because I want to spend time marketing my services"; that is a quick way to turn a prospective client into a former prospective client.

This also doesn't mean that you will spend exactly two hours each day on marketing efforts; you may attend a half-day meeting with the computer services subcommittee of a local accountant's group one day and perform no marketing functions the next day. You should just allocate your time appropriately to meet your tasks.

You may even find yourself involved in a long-term contract on a flat-fee basis. In this case, the sooner the contract is concluded, the sooner other projects may be started. Under these circumstances, you may decrease your marketing efforts to maybe three to five hours per week to speed up completion of the current job. The key is to be flexible in your approach to marketing (and all business) functions.

THE PERSONAL SELLING TOUCH

Just as any well-designed plan must actually be implemented in order to achieve desired results, your total marketing effort must be capped off with successful personal selling. The main focus of your advertising and personal contracts is to attract potential clients' interest in your services; once they do show interest, it is up to you to successfully close the sale.

Sounds a bit more like a retail salesperson than a professional consultant, doesn't it? If you were working in a large corporation as a computer programmer or systems analyst, you wouldn't need to be concerned with any type of selling; the organization's marketing department or sales division has that responsibility. However, it is up to you as a consultant to take a client's interest in what you have to offer and cement those ideas by convincing him or her of exactly what benefits you can provide.

Most people have a natural fear of rejection, and this brings on great amounts of stress in a selling situation. You *must* get over this phobia in order to succeed as an independent consultant. If a client ultimately rejects your proposed services, it is normally not a dismissal of you as a person but rather of the services themselves. As long as your behavior has been businesslike and you don't do anything to obviously cause any personal distaste, your personal characteristics shouldn't be the deciding factor.

The fear of rejection can sometimes be associated with the fear of failure; failing to win a client contract becomes a personal defeat. Consider this: if you were a baseball player, you could fail to hit safely two-thirds of the time and still be considered very successful with your .333 batting average. The same principle is true of consultants; not every meeting you attend will result in a contract, but your goal is to obtain sufficient projects to make your practice successful.

How then do you go about selling your services to your prospective clients? The most critical portion of this plan is your initial interview. Both you and the prospective client should have "creative tension" at this first meeting; he or she is assessing your understanding of the immediate needs as well as your professional competence, while you are determining if you can help solve the problems as well as the probability of winning that contract. You should also be assessing any possible competition you may have.

You should attempt to put the customer at ease, and at the same time demonstrate your competence. Don't brag about your skills, your "infinite, instinctive understanding of the problem," and your "fantastic solution," or anything else; if you've worked on a similar project in the past, mention that project and that client's name (if reference permission had been granted). Perhaps the prospective client knows your former one and a good reference will be the sales clincher.

Another goal is to assess the other person's readiness to award the contract. Naturally, he or she should have the authority to do so; if you are speaking with a store manager but a division director is necessary to approve any computerization contracts, little subsequent time should be devoted to meeting with the store manager *in the capacity of project approval,* especially if your first meeting is to assess the project at hand and isn't being paid for (more on this later).

Naturally you should not rudely dismiss any further conversation with the store manager, especially if assessing project requirements, but don't waste valuable time attempting to sell the contract if you determine that he or she possesses little influence in the purchasing decision.

If you receive a verbal commitment at the first meeting that is contingent upon some other action by you, such as submission of a written proposal, you should complete this action as soon as possible; a prolonged delay may cause a decision reversal by the client.

If your verbal commitment is contingent upon some action by the client, such as obtaining either permission from a regional manager to proceed or sufficient funds, you may find yourself in limbo. That may have merely been a ploy to avoid giving you a direct no, or the prospect may simply be unconvinced at the present. You should, by all means, continue selling your services through subsequent phone calls or other means—not three times each day, but at whatever interval you feel is appropriate. If a long series of unreturned calls or "We're still waiting for the main office's go-ahead" speeches convince you that the likelihood of putting the contract into action is remote, a generic letter or noncommittal proposal stating your availability for X, Y, and Z services at a given rate may be submitted, followed perhaps by one more phone call. If no decision is in sight, it may be better to file any paperwork for future reference and redirect your efforts. The contract may eventually come through, but you shouldn't divert scarce resources from viable and promising projects toward dead ones.

In short, then, you need to be a persistent and confident salesperson without being a pushy one. Your final task prior to actually beginning work on a contract is to convince prospective clients that they actually want to become clients.

"YOU KNOW IT DON'T COME EASY"

It looks so easy; the instant channel to consulting success. Numerous classified ads scream out to you, begging you to be an instantly successful consultant, to IMMEDIATELY act on just one of the hundreds of opportunities that beckon you each day.

- HIGH $$$$ NOW!...
- IMMEDIATE CONTRACTS AVAILABLE!...
- CONSULTANTS WANTED NOW!...

Scan the Sunday classified sections of most major metropolitan newspapers and you will see dozens of ads with these or similar eye-catching titles. Dozens more can be found electronically through information services bulletin boards. Independent consulting success is merely a phone call away, just around the corner, right? Why bother with all of the marketing strategies and networking and communications we've discussed in this chapter; why not go right for the immediate long-term, high-paying contract, and worry about that other "stuff" later...or maybe not at all?

Not so fast...I could tell you stories. Oh, the stories I could tell you. In fact, I believe that I *will* tell you some stories.

First, let's set the stage, from my personal point of view. I moved from Colorado to the East Coast after nearly nine years in the Rocky Mountain state, all of which had been spent doing either full- or part-time consulting. When I initially started my practice back in the early 1980s, I had followed most of the guidelines discussed earlier in this chapter: I networked, I built strategic relationships, I gave seminars—basically, I pursued the entire "package approach" to marketing that I advocate in this chapter.

Upon moving to the East Coast, however, I spent the entire first year doing full-time writing, authoring or coauthoring six books. Because of time pressures, I neglected the business building aspects of consulting and focused instead on the immediately available revenue sources.

Eventually, it was time to pursue local consulting business, and I became intrigued by the numerous advertisements, repeated Sunday after Sunday, in *The New York Times* and *The*

Philadelphia Inquirer, among other papers. Similarly, one of the national information services to which I subscribed had a computer consulting bulletin board, and a dozen or so companies regularly advertised their "client's immediate openings," urging subscribers to send their resumes along for immediate consideration. Between the newspaper and electronic sources, there were literally hundreds of companies clamoring for my services; just the thing to jumpstart a consulting practice in a new area, right?

As I said above (actually, as Ringo Starr said over 25 years ago), "it don't come easy." I could fill an entire book with less than six months' worth of anecdotes, but of course it would get somewhat repetitious and the point can be made with just a few of these events. Here are some examples:

"You have to assure me that you'll be ready to start next week," I was told on a Wednesday afternoon in early December, "my client needs someone immediately." Short notice, but the project sounded interesting, and I figured I could do the last chapter or two of the book I was completing in evenings and on weekends, so I assured the "consulting headhunter" that I indeed would be available, and I would await his call of confirmation by the end of the week. Thursday passed, and my calls to his office on the Friday of that week were received only by an answering machine. The following Monday the answering machine was still the only interface to the office, and it wasn't until Wednesday that I actually reached a live person at the office, who answered my query as to the project status with "Oh, we filled that one; someone started there on Monday." Strike one.

EXPERIENCED CASE CONSULTANTS WANTED NOW (or words to that effect): A New York consulting headhunter responded to my resume with a phone call telling me that his client had an immediate need for someone with a high level of expertise in CASE. Having used and developed CASE tools since 1981—before it was commonly called CASE—and having just finished a book on integrated CASE environments, I was reasonably certain that I had a "high level of expertise." Rather than focus on a broad range of CASE experience, the single question I was asked was "what is your experience with [a specific CASE design tool]?" When I began explaining that I had had exposure to that particular tool in the context of my broader range of CASE experience, I was interrupted with "wait...my other line is ringing; I'll call you right back." As you might guess, I never heard from him.

I was out of town when I received a call in my hotel room around 10:00 P.M. one night. I was told that a consultant to whom I had sent a resume in response to an advertisement for an experienced database consultant (perhaps my strongest computing area) had called that night, frantically saying that he had an immediate need. The next day, I tried calling the phone number he had left, but found only an answering machine. He called back again the same night, again missing me since I was still out of town, and he reiterated the absolute urgency of his request: his client needed twenty people, he only had ten, and not only did he need me NOW but did I know anyone else who could work on the project?

Following some exchanges of information, absolutely nothing happened for over a month. Then I received a call telling me to report for an interview the next day (hey, buddy, I've got a life too, ya know?). When I discussed my schedule conflict, I was told that he would check for an alternative day, and get back with me the next day.

Still waiting...

I received a call one day in response to a resume I had submitted to a consulting firm at a job fair. "We have the perfect position for you," the person began, and then cited the name of a product I had never used. When I took a direct approach and immediately told the person that I hadn't used that particular product, his response was "Hmmm...I wonder why your name came up in our database?" He then proceeded to quiz me about my experience and background, information easily obtained from my resume, and when I told him that in recent years I had been primarily a writer, he responded with "What kind of books? You mean novels?" How closely did you say you read my resume?

And the list goes on and on. Intrigued by the trend that developed from the first couple of inquiries, I conducted an experiment from late 1992 through early 1993. I contacted nearly every single consulting headhunter who advertised for products and technologies in my skill set, most of whom prefaced their on-line or print advertisements with "IMMEDIATE OPENINGS" (or a variation on the theme).

We'll disregard the 70 percent or so that didn't even respond to resumes and, sometimes, follow-up phone calls, despite my perfect match with their "immediate needs." The rest of them—*every single individual or company*—ended up like one or another of the above situations I have described.

Anecdotes are one thing, but the purpose of this book is to learn as much as possible about the consulting business, so let's try to understand *why* this seemingly easy road to consulting success is, for the most part, a mirage.

There are at least six different reasons that the "answering the ads" approach to consulting is likely to be a failure. One source for this book, who formerly worked at a consulting headhunter company and who spoke to me about the subject on the condition of anonymity gave me these reasons:

1. A significant proportion of the print and online advertisement for consultants, as well as job fair booths, including those which claim immediate openings, are merely for the purpose of collecting resumes from prospective subcontractors.

2. Even the more successful consulting headhunters, those which acquire contracts from their client companies, tend to have a favored set of subcontractors—typically a dozen or so— who are regularly placed with their clients. Others merely wind up in their consulting database, acting mostly as "filler." That's especially true for COBOL programmers...what, you C and Pascal programmers don't get the joke? You see, in COBOL you have a reserved word FILLER used for space padding in record structures, and...oh, never mind. Seriously, just because you send your resume to a headhunter does not mean it receives equal treatment with others already in their database, regardless of how exemplary your abilities and experience are.

3. These headhunting companies basically act as body shops, filling positions that have a stringent set of matching criteria of years and types of experience. In many cases these requirements come from the client companies, who specify that they want "two-plus years of Oracle Version 6 on VAX/VMS—that's a firm requirement!" The most experienced database consultant, perhaps one with ten years working with every other relational DBMS product on the market *except* Oracle, does not qualify. (Recall our discussion in Chap. 2 about consulting and the "whole person concept.") To make matters more difficult, nearly every one of these headhunters promotes the body shop concept by maintaining a database of all the resumes it has received, with entries by product. Unless your resume explicitly states every single DBMS, CASE tool, spreadsheet, and other software system with which you have had experience, it's likely you won't even pop to the forefront during a resume search by the headhunter, even for a project for which you are extremely qualified.

In fact, items that can't readily be quantified, yet are as important or more so than "n number years of experience with x" are rarely even considered. Of the 25 or so companies with which I had personal contact (not just sending a resume in response to an advertisement), only one broached areas such as successful completion of projects, and that was in response to a statement on my resume noting that I had successfully managed over twenty software development efforts. Even then, the company's interest in the subject was prefaced by, "Please provide a list, because our client will most likely ask us to provide more detail."

Think about it...if you were hiring a consultant, even a subcontractor, for a PC database project using the Xbase language (note: Xbase is the generic name for the dBASE language as used by dBASE, FoxPro, Clipper, and other PC database products), which of the following people would you consider more likely to succeed in your environment?

- Person A, with two years of FoxPro programming experience, all of which consisted of converting existing specifications and designs into code modules; this person has very little data modeling and database design experience.
- Person B, with ten years of dBASE-specific Xbase programming experience, all of which involved the entire development life cycle (requirements through maintenance).
- Person C, with four years of FoxPro experience, but who also has a spotty track record of success (or lack thereof).

At first glance, Person B would appear (at least to me) to be the most qualified database developer, even if your environment were to be implemented in FoxPro; following the logic of our discussion of Chap. 2, a good consultant is adaptable and for an experienced dBASE programmer to learn the nuances of FoxPro is a rather trivial task, much less complicated than turning a "pure coder" into a qualified analyst and designer. In the world of consulting headhunters that we're discussing now, Person B would most likely not even be a serious candidate for a contract, and with some of the recruiters Person C will have an edge over Person A, despite his or her lack of regular success, simply because of the additional two years of "experience." Most recruiters, if faced with a requirement for "three years of FoxPro experience" won't try to aggressively promote Person A because he or she is viewed as not meeting the requirements, though arguably his or her skills may far exceed those of Person C.

In short, factors such as past success and breadth of experience often do not come into play when pursuing consulting business in this manner; it's important to keep that in mind.

4. Many of these search firms keep an excessive proportion of the fees received from their clients, often up to half. While it is reasonable to expect them to make a profit and to meet their overhead requirements from the fees they collect from clients, in many cases they attempt to retain far too high a percentage of the total revenue *for your work*.

5. Partially due to the fee gouging described above, their primary goal is to find the contract labor to whom they can make the lowest outlay. Often their per-hour fee is negotiated with their client before they attempt to fill that position, and then they look for what might be termed the low-cost supplier. Factors such as exceeding the minimum requirements (example: eight years of working with a specific CASE tool instead of the two years specified), a broad range of IS experience, and the other factors that separate high-quality consultants from run-of-the-mill contract labor are summarily ignored. Faced with a choice between SuperConsultant (you) at a moderately higher rate than AverageConsultant (the other guy), odds are that they will go for the other guy because of the greater profit margin, especially for long-term, full-time contracts.

6. Finally, there is another factor we should consider; just as with those of us who go straight to the source (e.g., the clients) when seeking business, these headhunter firms, also, lose a significant portion of business they pursue and occasionally are "jerked around" by their clients. "Guaranteed" projects are delayed or canceled, their phone calls to their clients are often ignored and unreturned, and so on. Basically, they operate in the same constrained environment as consultants.

When you take all of these factors into account, and couple them with the anecdotal evidence I raised earlier in this section, you can come to only one conclusion. In the interest of maintaining a complete marketing strategy and pursuing all types of leads in your quest for business activity for your firm, it may be worthwhile to check out the advertisements and opportunities that look promising and appear to be "the perfect match for your background and abilities," but keep in mind what we've discussed in this section; be forewarned that to base your entire marketing effort for your consulting business on this narrow and haphazard way to get business, as easy as it may look on the surface, is a dangerous step to take.

The reason I'm spending so much time on this subject is that it appears tempting and easy to channel your marketing efforts exclusively into this arena rather than doing it the hard way. This is especially true for beginning or inexperienced consultants, but do not use it exclusively. Remember I said that I fell victim to this seemingly easy trap, and I spent a tremendous amount of time and money (faxes, internetwork electronic mail, trips, and so on); it achieved little more than wasting my time (even though there was the corollary activity of conducting research and testing my premise for this book, which was indeed valuable). This headhunter-based channel wasn't very prominent in Colorado, and I made the mistaken assumption that, even in a depressed economy (New York–New Jersey, 1991 to early 1993), there was business available and this was the way to pursue it. It just goes to show you: even experienced consultants sometimes make mistakes when confronted with something new.

Summarizing, there are no shortcuts to consulting success; you *must* remember that, even in terms of your marketing activities. In the full-time employment world you most likely won't even get a "We received your resume and will keep it on file" response card from most of the newspaper advertisements you answer even if your skills and experience are a perfect match to those stated in an ad; you can expect the same degree of success if you try to take shortcuts to reach your potential client base. There is no substitute for the personal touch in marketing. To the headhunters you are little more than a potential body to fill a slot for a short period of time, if even that; to many you are nothing more than an additional incremental counter so they can tell their prospective clients that they have a subcontractor database of 100 or 200 or 1000 consultants.

SUMMARY

I wrote the preceding paragraphs for the Third Edition of this book, and decided to leave them in this edition verbatim. At first, given the boom in consulting activities over the past four or five years and the increasing use by consultants of brokers and recruiters as the source of their work, I thought that I would delete those paragraphs. Instead, I decided to retain the material as a reminder that as economic and business fortunes shift, there *still* is no substitute for hard work in the marketing world. Though finding work through others might be easier today (circa 1998) than in the early 1990s, the next economic downturn could tighten that channel for many consultants, and those who neglected marketing and business development on their own may find themselves unpleasantly suprised when "easy" work dries up.

Looking in on Bernie Jordan, he decides to place a small but distinguished-looking advertisment in the monthly *Phoenix Law Review*, the most commonly read publication among local attorneys. He also creates a Web site (mentioned in the advertisement) that highlights the services and specialities he offers. He has also spoken with acquaintances in the legal profession about speaking at the Arizona Bar Association monthly breakfast in the near future. He is in the process of preparing a "statement of capabilities" for his firm.

Feeling that this effort will be sufficient and very cost-effective for the near term, especially since he is still consulting part-time, Bernie will review the marketing plan periodically to see what changes must be made to meet shifts in target markets, increasing competition, and other situations.

END NOTES

1. Robert E. Kelley, *Consulting: The Complete Guide to a Profitable Career*, Scribner's, New York, 1981, p. 105.
2. Herman Holtz, *How to Succeed as an Independent Consultant*, Wiley, New York, 1983, p. 84.

FINANCIAL CONSIDERATIONS OF CONSULTING

Regardless of whether you or your accountant does your firm's books, you must still understand some important financial and accounting principles. We saw before that your business skills are as important as your computer skills in building and maintaining a successful consulting practice. This knowledge is also useful in understanding many of your clients' business problems.

In this chapter we will discuss some financial topics of concern to you as you begin your business. We will review revenue patterns and their effects on your business operations. We will look at cash flow analysis and budgeting as a tool to aid in your financial planning.

We will also discuss the basics of financial statements and their importance, as well as ways to obtain further information from their numbers. We'll look at how an understanding of different categories of business costs is essential to business analysis and planning. We'll talk about different ways to obtain initial business capital. Of course, you need to know how to compute your consulting fee. Finally, we'll see how scenarios can be used to try to predict the future status of your business.

REVENUE PATTERNS AND CASH BUDGETING

Your revenue patterns will depend on the types of products and services you will be offering. *Revenue spurts* will occur when you depend primarily on single-service, short-term contracts such as designing specific computer systems or contract programming. Your contracts are not likely to come at regular intervals, and dead times, with little or no revenue, can happen. *Revenue streams,* however, tend to result when you depend primarily on royalties from commercial software or books, or long-term contracts for business earnings. One example of a long-term contract would be a two-year weekly seminar series about various computer legal topics for the American Bar Association at many locations around the country. Another is a long-term system development contract where your client is billed monthly for services rendered.

If you rely primarily on services that provide spurts of revenue, you should try to balance the active and inactive billing periods with some royalties or other revenue streams. This will provide capital for business and living expenses when other revenue producers temporarily slow down. By devoting your early inactive periods to developing commercial software or writing a book (as I did), the deferred income will hopefully provide you with enough business and personal capital to prevent cannibalization of your personal and business assets.

An important tool to help you plan your income and expense timing is the *cash budget,* illustrated in Fig. 5-1. The cash budget's purpose is to help you recognize and plan for your cash needs and determine if sufficient cash will have been collected to meet these needs. For example, it is unlikely for any business to earn and collect $1.50 for every $1 that it spends, in perfect synchronization. Revenue could have been earned but if it is not collected yet, you may be forced to borrow or dip into your personal and business savings to cover the expenses. Peter Drucker, a well-known business and management professor, once stated that the "whole secret of financial

Cash Budget
Jordan Business Computer Systems

	JANUARY	FEBRUARY	MARCH	APRIL
Projected revenue collections	3000.00	500.00	1000.00	500.00
1st month (70%)	2100.00	350.00	700.00	350.00
2nd month (30%)		900.00	150.00	300.00
Total	2100.00	1250.00	850.00	650.00
Receipts				
Total collections	2100.00	1250.00	850.00	650.00
Bank loan	1000.00			
Total	3100.00	1250.00	850.00	650.00
Payments				
Letterhead	75.00			
Business cards	25.00			
Post office box	15.00			
Accounting services		50.00		
Answering machine	150.00			
Office supplies	25.00	10.00	5.00	7.50
Phone (business)	10.00	10.00	10.00	10.00
Yellow Pages ad		12.50	12.50	12.50
Miscellaneous advertising			75.00	60.00
Total	300.00	82.50	102.50	90.00
Beginning cash balance	—	2800.00	3967.50	4715.00
Net cash gain loss for current month	2800.00	1167.50	747.50	560.00
Ending cash balance	2800.00	3967.50	4715.00	5275.00

FIGURE 5-1   Cash budget.

management [is to] know when you'll need money and make sure of it before you need it."[1]

A cash budget covers a number of periods, usually monthly, and examines known and projected cash inflows and outflows for each period. The projected revenues and expenses must be estimated as closely as possible. If revenue doesn't meet expectations for a particular month, the future periods being examined must be adjusted to reflect the lack of cash carrying over into the next period. This is where an electronic spreadsheet on your own computer system will come in very handy; changes can be made and the results can be shown instantly.

The cash budget displayed in Fig. 5-1 is a simple one: basic projections of revenues and expenses are made. The first section shows the estimated revenues for each of four months, as well as the time period in which these amounts will be collected. An assumption is made that 70 percent of all revenues are collected in the month earned, while 30 percent is collected in the subsequent month. An existing business could make this determination from sales and collection histories, while a new firm would have to rely on estimates and research.

Also note that receipts for January include a $1000 bank loan; even though this amount is not considered revenue, it still is cash inflow, which is what we are concerned with.

The bottom section contains the beginning cash balance, net cash flow, and calculated ending cash balance for each month. Jordan Business Computer Systems should not have any cash flow problems if actual revenues and collections are on target with the estimates; each month shows a positive ending cash balance. If any ending cash balance were negative (including insufficient cash to meet the month's obligations), borrowing or other financing would need to be arranged. If Bernie were planning to purchase a $6000 computer system in March, additional capital would be required.

FINANCIAL STATEMENTS

If you have studied accounting or finance while in school, you know that financial statements can present a useful picture of your firm's financial health. An *income statement* displays the income, expenses, and net earnings (or net loss) for a particular period of time, such as a three-month interval (fiscal quarter) or an annual period. Income statements can become extremely detailed and complicated as the information reporting requirements increase, but a simple one (as illustrated in Fig. 5-2) will probably serve your own needs.

An income statement contains three sections: (1) the *revenue section,* which lists a summary of income and adjustments to income (such as refunds and allowances for uncol-

Jordan Business Computer Systems

Income Statement for Year Ended
December 31, 1997

Revenues			
Consulting revenues	$15,350.00		
Less: Uncollectable accounts	2,000.00		
Net consulting revenue		$13,350.00	
Interest revenue		55.00	
Total revenues			$13,405.00
Less expenses			
Office and postage		175.00	
Miscellaneous supplies		125.00	
Depreciation		300.00	
Insurance		125.00	
Advertising		350.00	
Telephone		150.00	
Total expenses			1,225.00
Pretax income			12,180.00
Less income taxes			1,500.00
Net income			$10,680.00

FIGURE 5-2   Income statement.

lectable accounts); (2) the *expense section,* showing the business expenses incurred for that period divided into various categories; and (3) the *net income section,* a summary of the total adjusted revenues less total expenses. Income taxes are included in this section.

A *balance sheet* provides a "snapshot" of a firm's assets, liabilities, and net worth at a given instance. When the amount of a firm's *assets* (what it owns) is greater than its *liabilities* (what it owes), the firm has a positive net worth; the company could be dissolved today and if all assets could be sold for *book value* (the stated value on the balance sheet) all debts could be paid off and there would be money left over for the owner.

Similarly, a negative net worth (liabilities greater than assets) could cause problems; for example, the owners would

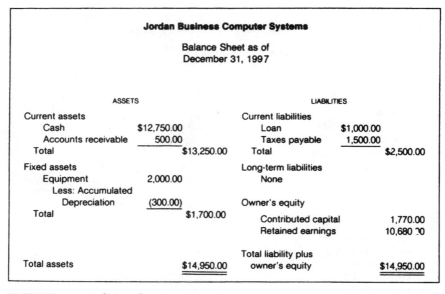

FIGURE 5-3   Balance sheet.

not be able to recoup their initial and subsequent investments following business dissolution or they might face possible bankruptcy for not being able to pay debt installments. A sample balance sheet is shown in Fig. 5-3.

Both assets and liabilities are divided into two categories: current and long-term. *Current assets* are (1) cash and (2) other assets that are expected to be converted into cash within 1 year from the date of the balance sheet. *Current liabilities* are debts that will be paid within 1 year from the balance sheet date. *Long-term assets,* such as land, buildings, and equipment are those that will be on the books past the next year. Similarly, *long-term liabilities* are those that will not be paid off within the next year.

If you operate your business under the *accrual basis* of accounting (discussed further in Chap. 11), you recognize revenues on your books at the time earned rather than when cash is collected. It is possible that a large contract completed at the end of the year would show a large amount of revenue that hasn't been collected. Anyone reviewing your company's financial statements may see a year with high net earnings and substantial net worth; if your client were to default on payment and it couldn't be collected, the revenue then would not really exist (barring successful recovery through a collection agency or lawsuit). At some future time the revenue will be subtracted from that future year's revenue as uncollectable.

The *statement of changes in financial position* helps you and anyone studying your firm's finances recognize these situations by showing changes in your company's individual accounts and the overall effect on either your cash balance or your *working capital,* the amount of assets you have at your disposal to meet expenses. Working capital is defined as the difference between current assets and current liabilities. Figure 5-4 shows this statement.

Bernie's statement of changes is an extremely simple one to prepare and understand. Since his business has not undergone many financial transactions during the past year, he has not had to use his working capital to purchase equipment (he already owned his computer), retire long-term debt, or increase inventory (since he doesn't have any inventory).

```
┌──────────────────────────────────────────────────────────┐
│              Jordan Business Computer Systems              │
│                                                            │
│           Statement of Changes in Financial Position       │
│                 Year ended December 31, 1997               │
│                                                            │
│                                                            │
│      SOURCES AND USES OF WORKING CAPITAL                   │
│                                                            │
│      Sources                                               │
│      Net income                    $10,680.00             │
│      Add back noncash expenses                            │
│         Depreciation                   300.00             │
│      Total operational cash sources          $10,980.00   │
│      Proceeds from long-term debt                —        │
│      Total sources of working capital         $10,980.00  │
│                                                            │
│      Uses                                                  │
│      Acquisition of equipment                    —        │
│      Net increase in working capital          $10,980.00  │
└──────────────────────────────────────────────────────────┘
```

FIGURE 5-4   Statement of changes in financial position.

Naturally, if you are operating on a part-time basis, only maintain a few clients, and don't have many business expenses, you should instinctively know how well your firm is doing financially. As your operations expand and more contracts are handled, however, the financial statements take on added importance in helping you comprehend your firm's financial health.

RATIO ANALYSIS

Large operations often need financial analysis over and above that which could be determined from the financial statements we have seen. This is to isolate problem areas that otherwise may remain hidden. If you feel additional financial information is required, ratio analysis of your firm may be necessary.

INITIAL CAPITAL

Once your initial expenses are defined, as we saw in Chap. 4, you must determine how much capital is initially required and where this money will come from.

The most common capital sources for a consulting business are savings withdrawals, loans, and capital investment. Loans may assume many forms: bank loans, home-equity loans, borrowing from friends or relatives, or Small Business Administration loans. Capital investment may also be from many sources, such as friends, relatives, or venture capital firms.

The primary difference between a loan and capital investment is that you are legally obligated to repay a loan but do not give up partial ownership of your business, while investors are "subordinated" to creditors but gain partial ownership of their investment target (i.e., they are purchasing stock in the firm).

Most consultants, if they follow the guidelines for starting slowly, should have minimal capital needs, easily met from savings or minor bank loans. During your firm's conception stage, at least, there should be minimal need for venture capital or other forms of equity investment.

COSTS

An understanding of the various types of costs involved in a business's expenses is important. You must distinguish between *fixed costs* (those that exist whether revenue is earned or not) and *variable costs* (those that are a product of the revenue-earning activity). Your goal should be to earn enough income to reach the break-even point.

The *break-even point* for a financial period is when all costs have been covered by revenue earned and no net loss will occur. For every income-producing activity, the difference between the revenue earned and the associated expenses is known as the *contribution margin,* or profit resulting from that activity.

When the sum of the contributing margins for all activities is equal to the total fixed costs for the period, your net earnings will be zero and the break-even point will be reached. Any revenue after the break-even point will contribute toward the firm's net profits. This assumes, of course, that each activity will contribute more revenue than the associated variable costs. It would be a rare job you would accept that produces a net loss from that contract.

Examples of fixed costs are *Yellow Pages* advertising (a yearly contract), annual business licenses, post office box rental, answering service, and, if you don't work at home, office rent, phone, and utilities. Any salaries you pay to employees other than on a "when-used" basis will also be fixed costs.

Variable costs may include subcontractor payments for specific jobs, photocopying services for seminar materials, and seminar room rental. These variable costs would not be incurred if the contract weren't accepted.

For example, Bernie Jordan has calculated the fixed costs for the upcoming year, as shown in the table at the top of p. 100. His goal is to ensure that over the next year his contracts provide enough net income (i.e., total contribution margin) to pay for these fixed costs. If every contract were to fall through, he still would incur these minimum expenses.

Yellow Pages advertising	$180
Business cards, 1-year supply	30
Business stationery, 1-year supply	40
Voicemail	100
Post office box rental	30
Total	$380

Another way to classify your business costs is as either direct or indirect. *Direct costs* can be defined as those that can be allocated to a specific contract, while *indirect costs* could be defined as "supporting expenses."

If Bernie signs a contract with a brokerage firm to conduct a seminar about investment software, the costs of printing workbooks would be considered a direct cost of that assignment. His *Yellow Pages* advertisement that attracted that contract is an indirect cost; it can't be directly allocated to the seminar in any identifiable portion.

At the end of the year, he could allocate a portion of his total indirect costs to each contract in proportion to the relative revenue of each job. Such allocation, however, is similar to an allocation of a portion of fixed expenses to each contract.

Speaking of fixed costs, it seems that the distinction between direct and indirect costs is similar to that of variable versus fixed expenses. An indirect cost could be a variable one, though, just as a direct cost could be fixed. Variable costs are not synonymous with direct costs, nor do fixed costs always imply indirect expenses.

In our seminar example, Bernie has calculated the following data:

Revenue per attendee	$100
Cost of handouts per attendee	10
Conference room rental and coffee service	75

The contribution margin per attendee, again defined as revenue minus variable costs, is $90 ($100 − $10); the only variable cost involved is the expense of handouts.

The conference room rental, however, is both a direct and a fixed cost; it can be identified as an expense of this particular seminar, and is fixed in the sense that once the seminar is held, the $75 will be paid whether one person or thirty people attend.

Finally, the advertising, postal box rental, and other items listed previously are both indirect and fixed costs; they can't be designated to any specific assignment and are incurred despite the number of contracts undertaken or revenue earned.

General newspaper advertising (as opposed to that for a particular seminar offering) would be considered an indirect and variable cost. Unless you have contracted for a minimum number of column inches per year, you can vary this advertising expense as you see fit; it can't, however, be allocated to any particular contract as a direct cost would.

The key is to be able to identify any expense you face as either a variable or fixed cost, as well as direct or indirect. In order to intelligently manage the financial operations of your consulting firm, a close hold should be kept on any costs. Knowing how to calculate contribution margins, break-even points, and contract profit potential is extremely important. Your financial statements, as mentioned before, present a picture of your firm's financial health, but only after the fact; fading "vital signs" on a balance sheet or income statement may appear too late for you to salvage your practice. Closely controlled costs help prevent problems from occurring in the first place.

A final type of business cost, though different from the above ones, is the *opportunity cost* you face with every decision you make. If you decide to conduct the brokerage firm seminar we just examined, your opportunity cost is the revenue (if any) you pass up from *not* conducting some other seminar or accepting a client contract.

Determining opportunity cost can often be tricky. It is easy to see that if you refuse a contract in order to work on your six-month commercial software project, the opportunity cost is the revenue you would have earned from the contract. But what about the reverse situation? If you take time away from your software project (or book project, as I did while writing this volume) to conduct a seminar, how do you determine what your opportunity cost is? If the time away just means submitting your software or book to the publisher two weeks later than anticipated, you don't really have any opportunity cost (assuming you don't go over a submission deadline and lose a portion of your advance or incur some other financial penalty). The best approach is to determine approximately what revenue you will lose, if any, and use that figure as your opportunity cost.

Often, you may choose to accept one contract at the expense of losing another even though the refused contract would provide more revenue. This may be because the first job will lead to a series of subsequent contracts that, over the long term, provide much more revenue than the second one. In this case, you are choosing the project that has the least opportunity cost over the long term, rather than looking at just short-term projections. The lesson: Be sure to look at both current and future revenues when making any opportunity cost decisions.

SCENARIOS AND PLANNING

If you could exactly forecast all future revenues and expenses you should consider a career in fortune-telling rather than computer consulting. The rest of us need to make predictions based on market research, knowledge of business capabilities, and similar managerial tools.

Since the future is obviously uncertain, you should establish various scenarios (situations) to estimate various outcomes. What will happen if a "sure" job falls through at one of several points during the contract's duration? How will actual seminar attendance that is half (or double) the planned registration affect revenues (both from the seminar itself and potential future clients)? How do you determine what your future revenue will be for opportunity cost decision making, as we saw in the preceding section?

The important point here is that you should be prepared for the unexpected. Any business operation must always have contingency plans to invoke when situations change or don't develop as planned. The more complete your scenario planning is the more likely you will be able to adapt to unexpected situations.

The scenarios developed form the basis of *pro forma* financial statements. A pro forma income statement is a projection of revenue and expenses over the scenario's period, while a pro forma balance sheet projects a snapshot of the firm at a future point. By analyzing the financial outcomes of the scenarios a realistic picture of the likelihood of success as a business operation can be determined.

Your own computer again comes in handy here. By using a spreadsheet analysis program, just as with your cash budget, pro forma statements can be automatically adjusted to reflect the outcome of different business strategies and situations.

DETERMINING YOUR CONSULTING FEES

In each of the previous editions of this book, I had material in this section that discussed the formula-driven, "mechanical" way to establish your consulting fees. You would figure out various components of the revenue you expected to generate, figure out your targeted utilization (the percentage of time you expected to be billing rather than spending on marketing and other activities), work out various scenarios to cover your overhead, and so on.

The past few years have altered my thinking regarding fee setting, and now I believe that there is one simple rule to guide you in making this determination:

Take into consideration the going market rate for your specialty and your level of expertise, adjust if necessary for special needs of your prospective client or that engagement, and you have the rate you should be charging.

For example, if you're a data warehousing consultant at the time this is being written (early 1997), the marketplace wants your services! Following the mechanical approach and applying formulas might yield (for example) a $65 per hour suggested billing rate, based on your specific financial and business circumstances. However, the market conditions might say that $125 an hour in the metropolitian New York City area was, well, just about right. If market conditions support your charging this rate—that is, if clients are willing to pay it—then charge it!

If for example, you have a specific client who balks at $125 per hour but is willing to contract with you for a nine-month, full-time basis, you may find it well worth your while to reduce your overall rate to $115 or $120 per hour because of the contracted steady work. For certain types of projects on which you are absolutely certain of the scope and effort, you may be willing to provide a fixed-fee proposal (but be very careful that you have the scope of the effort and the guidelines of the engagement well defined so that you don't have any suprises awaiting you!). Negotiate, negotiate, negotiate!

In certain circumstances, you may even find it to your advantage to play the "professional day" game that many independent clients abhor. Basically, a professional day rate is a flat fee paid for "an average day's work," almost as if you were a salaried employee. This is pitched to consultants as, "The average day's activity is eight hours; occasionally you might have an hour or two extra, but other days might be only six hours." Well, you can guess what happens a lot of the time—a lot of client-mandated ten-hour days for basically eight hours of compensation, with no six-hour days anywhere in sight. An unpleasant situation that should be avoided at all times, right?

Not necessarily. A few years ago, while living in central New Jersey, about a two-hour commute (each way) from New York City, I took a six-month engagement for a Wall Street brokerage firm through a consulting firm that offered me a professional day contract. The agreement, though, among all parties, including the client, was that I would be able to work at home the majority of the time, thus saving four hours of commuting time (which would be nonbillable). Therefore, days when I worked an extra hour or two weren't a problem, because I was spending less overall time—with travel included—on the project. When everything was taken into consideration, the pay-per-day approach worked just fine for me, without my having to go through any calculations or formulas.

Part of the reason I believe that the market rate approach is really the only way to set your fees is that since the consulting market is changing so rapidly these days, requiring you to adjust accordingly, your fees should be adjusted as well. Clients are well known to lower rates when market conditions favor them, but of course they usually complain and carry on if you, the consultant, try to raise your rates. My philosophy has always been that which was expressed in Mel Brooks's movie *Young Frankenstein* back in 1976. Igor (Marty Feldman) meets Dr. Frankenstein (Gene Wilder) for the first time, and says: "My grandfather used to work for your grandfather—(pause)—of course, rates have gone up!"

PERSONAL FINANCIAL CONSIDERATIONS

So far, we've focused on the financial aspects of consulting in a business-only sense. We've looked at income statements, cash flow analysis, and fee setting from the business perspective, without any consideration of personal financial needs.

While this is a proper context—as we'll discuss in Chap. 11, your business and personal financial records and transactions ideally should remain separate from one another, or you should at least formally document any transfers for tax and other record-keeping purposes—it is important to understand that for many consultants, there *are* ties between their personal and business financial situations.

For example, let's take the cash flow analysis document shown in Fig. 5-1. Often it is helpful, to determine whether you can meet both your personal obligations (rent or mortgage, car loans, utility bills, etc.) and your business expenses to expand the formal business cash flow, to take into account these types of regular and irregular personal expenditures. Even though this has little to do with your business, it can help give you a complete picture of your combined business and personal financial situation, and possibly prevent nasty surprises like running out of cash.

SUMMARY

In this chapter we saw how important the financial aspects of a consulting business are. We briefly looked at many types of financial statements, analyzed the different types of costs a consultant can incur, and discussed some of the different ways to determine your consulting fees. As we discussed in Chap. 4, though, there are market and competitive forces that must be considered in determining your fee structure.

Now, back to Bernie Jordan. Based on his projected concentration of services, Bernie expects to receive most of his income in spurts as various contracts are negotiated and executed. He is considering a series of seminars like "Open Systems for the Legal Profession" which, once in full swing, will provide some steady income (revenue streams) to balance his revenue flow as he moves toward full-time consulting.

After determining his initial expenditures, Bernie developed the cash budget shown in Fig. 5-1. Because his expenditures will be modest, he will be working from his home, and will be still working full-time elsewhere, no borrowing is projected.

Bernie is familiar with accounting and financial statements because of his business degrees. Since his consulting operations are just beginning, there are no historical data from which meaningful financial statements can be developed. However, he develops several scenarios for the upcoming year's business, with various levels of business activity. This way, he can see the effect on the bottom line of different situations. After studying the pro forma statements Bernie is further convinced of the likelihood of success as a computer consultant.

END NOTE

1. "How New Entrepreneurs Are Changing U.S. Business," *U.S. News & World Report,* March 26, 1984, p. 68.

CHAPTER
SIX

PUTTING IT ALL TOGETHER: THE BUSINESS PLAN

INTRODUCTION

So far we've looked at a variety of decision factors in your consulting activities—financial, marketing, product and service, organizational, and personal—but only as individual entities. Just as we discussed in the relationship between the financial and marketing aspects of setting your fees, though, all of your business decisions must fit together as though they were pieces of a jigsaw puzzle. No decisions should be made in isolation from one another.

The point at which you bring all of these decision points together is in your *business plan*. The business plan is a document that contains the specifics of what services you will offer, to whom and through what channels they will be directed, how the operations will be financed, and many other decisions; in short, it is an overall plan for your business (and hence the name).

The most important use of the business plan is arguable. It would be very difficult, if not impossible, to obtain financing for your business without presenting a business plan; anyone investing in or loaning funds to a firm wants a realistic projection of that business's chances of success. Perhaps more important, though, is that a business plan forces the consultant to think through all aspects of his or her strategic plans, and to conduct any necessary further research. It's one thing to have the brilliant idea to conduct hands-on training in PC technology for displaced defense workers. You must know, however, exactly what hardware and software is required to conduct these services, how to finance this equipment, and whether a market even exists for your divinely inspired plan. It is much better to discover during the planning stages that your ideas aren't feasible than to invest time and money in an ill-fated business operation. At the very least, you should be able to avoid unpleasant surprises like unexpected competition and unforeseen expenses.

COMPONENTS OF A BUSINESS PLAN

There are many different sources (books and magazines, for example) that discuss business plans and the recommended contents of the documents. A typical business plan might include the following:[1]

1. A *cover page* containing your company's name, address, phone number, and document date
2. An *executive summary* (or *introductory summary*), which explains the major points presented in your plan
3. A *table of contents* for lengthy documents, including page number references
4. *Information* about your company, describing your industry classification and what products and services you intend to provide
5. Information about your company's *industry classification* including its history, current factors, and estimated future prospects
6. *Market research* including estimated market size, trends, and competition
7. A *market analysis* that covers your customers and the estimated market share and sales you hope to capture

8. A *marketing plan* that discusses marketing strategies, pricing decisions, advertising methods, and other promotional means

9. What *professional assistance* you will use, such as attorneys, accountants, bankers, financiers, and other help

10. A *general operations plan,* including geographical business location and strategy

11. Any applicable *research and development programs,* especially concerning consultants who develop commercial software

12. The *time schedule* for implementing your plans

13. Any *critical risks and problems* you may face, such as competitive responses, unfavorable industry trends, and failure to achieve revenue projections

14. A *financial plan,* including forecasting profits and losses, a pro forma balance sheet, applicable cash flow analysis, and break-even charts

15. Plans for *financing* your firm's options

16. Your firm's *legal organization* (sole proprietorship, partnership, or corporation)

I'd also suggest that you add appropriate references to the above list and, for firms that already have outside investments, a list of investors and the capitalization structure of your business.

FORMATTING ISSUES

A business plan prepared with the intention of seeking $5 million in second-round financing for a software products company inevitably will be more comprehensive than one completed by a potential solo practitioner consultant. The business plan presented later in this chapter was prepared from the latter viewpoint, with less emphasis on external financing and financial projections than would be required by a potential investor (though business revenue projections and initial expenditures are included). Bernie Jordan, our new consultant and the plan's preparer, is more concerned with integrating his random thoughts and numerous scratch-pad sketchings into an organized business blueprint than submitting the plan with the intention of seeking capital investment or loans. That business plan, however, can form the basis of subsequent ones targeted toward outside investment.

Let's look at some general guidelines for preparing and presenting business plans, particularly if your target is investment in your business or the plan is intended for other outside sources (as opposed to being for your own use):[2]

1. A business plan should be no more than 1/4- to 1/2-inch thick and loosely bound in a clear plastic cover. Some investors receive 500 to 1500 business plans each year so in order to have your submission considered seriously, it should be concise and readable. (*Author's note*: While working for a large computer vendor, I was responsible for an investment analysis project in which a multi-million-dollar investment in a software company was being considered. That company's business plan was approximately 75 pages long, and provided more than enough detail in the appropriate portions.)

2. A business plan submitted for financing should be preceded by a phone call or letter of introduction or, more desirably, a referral from a respected friend or business contact. If you don't have much business experience prior to submission, your accountant, attorney, or a satisfied (and influential) client may pave the way for serious consideration of your plan.

3. Investors tend to fund only certain types of businesses, sometimes limited to certain geographical areas, and at certain business life-cycle stages (e.g., start-up, first-stage or second-stage financing, operating at break-even or at a profit, etc.). Sources and listings of investors, including venture capital firms, can provide guidance to help you avoid submitting a plan to an inappropriate investor.

4. While small business consultants and others can professionally prepare a business plan for you, investors are less interested in a highly polished document than one that is well-thought out and contains essential information. Your business plan is a reflection of your own organizational ability and skill in expressing ideas, and you should know your business plan as intimately as your business itself.

5. Your competition, both current and projected, should be detailed and realistically evaluated. If you are proposing a nonproprietary product or service, such as educational seminars and PC software training classes, how quickly could a local computer superstore or other consultant cut into your market share? What are your relative strengths and weaknesses as compared with those of your competitors?

SUMMARY

The business plan is the document in which you tie all of your independent decisions together, ensuring that they mesh with one another. Your operations, financial, product, and marketing plans should come together as a well-researched business plan to act as a blueprint from which you can build and manage your consulting firm.

The complexity and size of the plan will vary with the intended readership; one that is meant to convince a venture capitalist to invest $750,000 in your firm will be more complex than one meant as a guide for the preparer alone, such as a full-time or part-time consultant. Regardless of the user, the plan should be detailed enough to be useful to that reader.

END NOTES

1. Robert E. Kelley, *Consulting: The Complete Guide to a Profitable Career,* Scribner's, New York, 1981, pp. 45–46.
2. Sabin Russell, "What Investors Hate Most about Business Plans," *Venture,* June 1984, pp. 52–53. This list has been revised slightly by the author from its original version in the First and Second editions of this book, to reflect the changing times since the mid-1980s.

SAMPLE BUSINESS PLAN

The following pages include a sample business plan. For the previous edition of this book, I updated the sample plan from the edition before that to touch on what was still, in the early 1990s, a shaky economy in the Phoenix, Arizona, area. At first, I planned to update the business plan yet one more time for this edition, but instead I decided to leave it as is, with this guideline to you, the reader:

Carefully read this plan which only a few years ago was a perfectly valid one for a small consulting firm in that area. There is mention of "turmoil" in the marketplace, modernizing "antiquated personal computer systems installed in the early and mid-1980s," and so on. *Any consultant who tries to run his or her business on an out-of-date business plan is in serious trouble*. Examine the structure of this relatively simple plan, but I strongly recommend that you also look at the content and think about how much has changed and how it would be rewritten if Bernie Jordan were preparing it now.

As an exercise, you might even want to take a crack at updating the business plan yourself, for one very important reason: If you have difficulty crafting a valid business plan for this scenario, then you may be in for some rough times as you try to do so for your own business. Look at this as an early test of the viability your own consulting practice.

JORDAN BUSINESS COMPUTER

SYSTEMS BUSINESS PLAN

JANUARY 4, 1993

PREPARED BY:
BERNIE JORDAN
7300 N. 27TH AVE.
PHOENIX, AZ 85000
(602) 555-8675

TABLE OF CONTENTS

I. EXECUTIVE SUMMARY

Jordan Business Computer Systems is a computer software and consulting firm being formed by Bernie Jordan. The firm will begin operations in the Phoenix metropolitan area and eventually expand to other Arizona markets such as Tucson and Flagstaff.

Jordan will concentrate its efforts on small and medium-sized businesses that are currently not being served by the established consulting organizations in the Phoenix area (this issue is explored in the market overview in the next section). Jordan will target businesses that may require only standalone personal computer systems or small networks of computers. These small business clients typically don't provide sufficient returns to large consulting firms that have full-time employees and other high-overhead items to be supported. By utilizing careful cost control and a low-overhead structure, Jordan can offer clients personalized service at an attractive cost.

II. THE INFORMATION SYSTEMS CONSULTING MARKET IN PHOENIX

BUSINESS CONDITIONS

The information systems consulting market in the Phoenix area has undergone some degree of turmoil since the 1988–1989 time frame. Some large (*Fortune* 500–class) firms had opened "exploratory outposts" in the area to capitalize on the area's economic growth that was projected for the Sunbelt.

The economic slowdown in Phoenix that began in 1989 forced most of these large, highly capitalized but high-overhead consulting operations to terminate local operations. Their niche market—software development and consulting services for large manufacturing-oriented companies in the area—was filled by firms that had formerly targeted small business operations such as real estate agencies, construction firms, and similar businesses. Some of the smaller consulting companies were unsuccessful in making this market-oriented transition, while others succeeded and have experienced modest operational and revenue growth.

The result of the dynamics described above has been that a large portion of the client base in the area currently is not served by the existing consulting and software firms; this client base comprises the large number of small and medium-sized businesses that currently either have no automated information systems capability or desire to expand and modernize antiquated personal computer systems installed in the early and mid-1980s.

The reason that this market is often ignored, or at least downplayed, by the existing consulting firms is that the return from work in these areas is likely to be insufficient to support an expanding consulting business operation. A typical consulting or software development project in a small business might only return $2500–$3500 (the per-project business model is discussed further in the General Operations Plan); while several projects of this type may be suitable for an individual consultant or a single-person firm such as Jordan Information Systems, this return typically is insufficient per-project income for a firm with several partners or owners and additional employees.

The market for professional software and consulting services for small businesses has been somewhat filled by "moonlighters," computer-literate individuals with full-time jobs elsewhere who recommend and install systems, write software, and resolve problems on a sporadic basis as their own work schedules permit. Some of these individuals do good work, others don't. As a result, potential clients must navigate many obstacles in acquiring adequate professional assistance. Chief among these obstacles is concern whether the moonlighting consultant will be available to maintain (modify and/or upgrade) the client's system, an issue much less relevant to a full-time consulting firm with an established local presence such as Jordan.

TECHNOLOGY TRENDS

In addition to the economic and business condition scenario discussed above, there are a number of technology-related trends that are accelerating the need for small business consulting and software services.

The personal computer market underwent dual revolutions during 1992—one in the area of technological performance, the other related to pricing. The tremendous increase in the power and performance of the "typical" personal computer (powerful processors, such as the Intel 486; tremendous capacity for disk storage; large amounts of computer memory; etc.) was accompanied by cutthroat pricing on the part of major system vendors as well as "clone" manufacturers. As a result, an extremely powerful standalone personal computer running a graphical user interface (GUI) can be purchased for around $1200, or about $400 less than a much less powerful system cost four years earlier.

The combination of rapidly advancing technological capabilities (not only in the computers themselves but also in peripherals such as network devices and laser printers) and highly competitive and attractive pricing has brought two types of small and medium-sized business operations into the target market for consulting and software services:

- Companies that previously didn't have any computer systems due to cost and other issues

- Companies desiring to modernize or expand their computing capabilities by replacing old systems, adding new computers and network capabilities, or adding advanced peripheral devices such as laser printers, fax modems, and scanners

- Companies whose key personnel previously had been afraid of computerization, but who now wish to take advantage of new levels of user-friendliness (through the use of graphical user interfaces)

Television newspeople and the written press (both general and business) continue to tout the growth of service industries, and some reluctant companies in those industries may gain increased confidence due to those continuing reports, and implement or expand automation capabilities.

MARKET CONCLUSIONS

As a result of the issues discussed in this section—the economic dynamics of Arizona and those trends related to technological capabilities and pricing—the market for a firm such as Jordan Business Computer Systems, which specializes in computer systems for small and medium-sized businesses, is not only growing, but is unlikely to be filled by the consulting firms that currently serve the area. As business conditions slowly improve in the area, these established firms are likely to target large companies that have expanding information systems needs but are reluctant to take on full-time employees. Most long-term, contractual modernization and development efforts will continue to be handled by the established firms, who in turn will continue to bypass the small businesses.

III. INFORMATION SYSTEMS INDUSTRY EXPERIENCE

Jordan Business Computer Systems is owned by Bernie Jordan. Mr. Jordan has been in the computer industry since 1985, working in several capacities. He not only has experience with all classes of computer systems (mainframe, midrange, and micro) through his full-time position as a software engineer at ABC Manufacturing, but has also functioned as a part-time consultant since 1989. Working with Walters and Associates, he was responsible for a number of consulting projects, performance systems analysis, and applications programming in the dBASE III Plus programming/database language, as well as troubleshooting systems, installation and upgrade, documentation, and other consulting tasks that Jordan Business Computer Systems will handle for its clients.

IV. GENERAL OPERATIONS PLAN

PRODUCTS AND SERVICES TARGET MARKETS

Jordan Business Computer Systems will serve the following primary target markets:

1. Small and medium-sized businesses in the target geographical area that are exploring automated information systems for the first time
2. Small and medium-sized businesses in the target geographical area that currently have some degree of computerization and seek to modernize and/or expand their capabilities.

Examples of the *types* of businesses Jordan will target include (but are not limited to):

- Home health care
- Veterinary and medical offices
- Business service providers (beauty salons, restaurants, etc.)
- Local, state, and federal government

The products and services offered by Jordan will include:

1. *Evaluation of small business information needs,* as well as recommendations for best-choice solutions such as selection of desktop computers, software, network topologies, and peripheral devices.
2. *Custom software development*—for specialized business applications (accounting, inventory management, customer management, etc.) that can't be adequately met by commercially available software products. All custom software development will utilize "platforms" (such as

dBASE IV) or code generators; the purpose of this is to improve development productivity by using tools and languages that alleviate a great deal of the tedium such as file management and record access.

3. *Migration and transition services.*   These include rewriting or moving commercial and custom applications from one environment to another (example: standalone personal computer to a local area network).

4. *Desktop publishing*—for clients who need professional quality output for newsletters, advertising brochures, and other material.

5. *Seminars and training sessions in specific products and technologies.*   Seminars will be used primarily as a marketing tool and secondarily as a revenue source.

PRICING

Client contracts will typically be performed on a per-hour cost basis. Because Jordan will have extremely low overhead and can afford to be flexible on the profit component of the fee structure, projects initially will be performed at a rate in the $30–$35 per hour range. This structure will be extremely competitive, falling below that which can be supported by high-overhead competitors. On occasion, fixed-price contracts will be considered, but only for proj-p
125   125
ects with which Jordan is very familiar and can accurately gauge the level of effort.

The rate structure will be evaluated in mid-1993 and be adjusted accordingly if the market can support higher rates.

BUSINESS ORGANIZATION

Jordan Business Computer Systems will be organized as a Subchapter S corporation, affording corporate liability protection with relatively simple record-keeping and tax-filing requirements.

OFFICE STRUCTURE

An existing structure will be modernized to be a home office and demonstration and training area for clients. The capital improvements necessary to bring this structure to office suitability are described in the Financial Plan.

V. MARKETING PLAN

Jordan Business Computer Systems initially will concentrate on marketing activities outside the realm of paid advertising (discussed next). The primary exception will be *Yellow Pages* advertisements for several local cities and towns.

Tentatively, display ads will be placed in all directories, along with entries under the headings of *both* "System Designers and Consultants" and "Computer Software." Pending initial budgets, this *Yellow Pages* plan may be adjusted accordingly.

The bulk of the marketing activities will be of the following nature:

1. *Networking at organizations such as the Phoenix Business Association or industry-specific lunches, dinners, and meetings.* These sessions will include distributing material about technical and business-related topics, with a slant toward utilizing the services of Jordan Business Computer Systems. When possible, speeches will be presented to establish professional competence.

2. *Building associations with local computer retailers whose customers desire software development.* This was a highly successful channel for Mr. Walters's (Jordan's technical and business advisor, as mentioned in Section VII) consulting business operations in Tucson, some projects of which were completed by Mr. Jordan.

3. *Building associations with other professional service practitioners in the area.* Examples are accountants and attorneys, whose clients are likely to require computer consulting and/or software development.

Initially, the activities noted above and similar ones will be focused in the Phoenix area. As new geographical areas are targeted (as described earlier in the business plan), similar activities will occur in those cities as well. Local phone numbers or an 800 number will be acquired in each new market. The calls will be automatically forwarded to the Jordan Business Computer Systems office in Phoenix.

VI. FINANCIAL PLAN

INITIAL EXPENDITURES

The following start-up expenditures are anticipated for Jordan Business Computer Systems:

Computer systems, peripherals, office equipment, and communications

- Two 486 PCs with local area network $5000
  connections: $2500 ea. (*Note:* The reason for
  two PCs is to be able to develop network-based
  software for clients. The intercomputer connections can be developed and tested at Jordan's
  office. Also, each system will be equipped with
  large amounts of main memory and disk storage
  both for development purposes and to mirror
  client systems, including file servers.)
- Additional business management software: 2000
  spreadsheet, file management, etc.
- Accounting software   1000
- High-resolution laser printer   3500
- Fax machine   1000
- Personal copier   1000
- Multi-line phones: 2 each at $100. (*Note:*   200
  Multiple-line phones will be necessary to permit
  connections to on-line information services such
  as Compuserve as well as for having lines free for
  client calls.)

Total estimated equipment and software costs $13,700

Office

An existing room in Mr. Jordan's home will be converted

into a home office. Since this office will serve as the primary business and work location for Jordan Business Computer Systems, it is anticipated that the office will qualify for the home office deduction under the new more restrictive Internal Revenue Service rules.

Mr. Jordan has elected to receive a voluntary severance lump-sum amount of $38,000 from ABC Manufacturing. This will be used for the initial business expenditure and for personal living expenses during the business start-up period.

1993–1994 BUSINESS FORECASTS

The business forecast model is based on the following assumptions, which in turn are based on past experiences coupled with extrapolations about current business and economic conditions and technology.

1. *The "typical" client project is 100 hours*; assume an average of one month (25 hours per week billable) to complete. This typical project includes tasks such as system analysis and design, software development or integration, installation, training, and troubleshooting, equipment evaluation, purchase, and testing.

2. *The average billing rate is $35–$40 per hour per project.* As stated earlier, Jordan intends to keep the hourly rate at the low end as a competitive advantage, and since overhead will be kept to a minimum.

3. *Based on the above two figures, each project will generate an average of $3500–$4000 revenue.* A "full" schedule—one involving very little downtime between projects and the one month per project duration—would generate $42,000–$48,000 revenue. Since 25 hours per week is allocated on average toward billable work, sufficient time is available for marketing, business development, and retroactive work such as problem resolution for former clients. Additionally, unlike competitors who are

moonlighters, client work need not be planned around "full-time work" at another job, thereby allowing far more total hours and potential billable hours for Jordon than for many of its potential competitors.

Based on the above assumptions, the following job and revenue estimates are projected:

1993.   5 jobs; $17,500–$20,000 revenue (this assumes a 4–5 month "ramp-up" of business operations). While it is possible that simultaneous projects may occur, a conservative estimate is provided.

1994.   12 jobs; up to $48K revenue. This is a conservative estimate, which can be greatly expanded through the use of subcontract help for simultaneous projects (discussed next).

Financial plans and estimates will be revised at least every quarter during the first two years, based on project data to date in that fiscal year as well as work backlogs at those points.

EXPANSION

No full-time employee hiring is anticipated for at least the first two years of business operations. When specialized skills that Jordan doesn't possess are required (example: programming skills in a specific language, or experience with a given operating system or networking environment), or when multiple jobs occur simultaneously, subcontractors (programmers and other consultants) will be utilized. Typical candidates include interested local college students or those consultants who have worked with other local consulting firms. When subcontractors are used, the billable hours will reflect an appropriate hourly wage to the subcontractor plus overhead and a profit portion for Jordan; the appropriate proportion will be judged at the time.

VII. PROFESSIONAL ASSISTANCE

BUSINESS AND TECHNOLOGY ADVISORY

Mr. Richard Walters of Tucson will function as the business and technology advisor for Jordan Business Computer Systems. Mr. Walters is an expert not only in computer technology but also in consulting operations. He has worked with advanced technology for over 20 years. Mr. Walters has volunteered his time in this matter, and also will assist with advice for Jordan client projects on as-needed basis.

LEGAL

All legal matters for Jordan Business Computer Systems will be handled by Mr. Mike Michaelson, an attorney with offices in the Tempe and Glendale suburbs. Mr. Michaelson has handled personal and business legal matters for Mr. Jordan in the past.

ACCOUNTING

Initially, all financial records will be handled internally and online, using accounting software; this will be sufficient for the level of revenue and initial capital and operational expenditures anticipated for 1993. During the business planning cycle for 1994, the need for external accountants will be evaluated and, if business activity warrants, one will be retained.

PART TWO

YOUR
PRODUCTS
AND
SERVICES

DEVELOPING INFORMATION SYSTEMS

For many of you, the primary manifestation of your consulting activities will be through developing computer applications for your clients. Those of you with some experience in developing information systems (likely, most of you) are no doubt familiar with one or more of the many development methodologies and modeling techniques widely used to manage and control the development and implementation processes.

In the world of consulting, the term that most commonly applies to development methodologies and techniques is "situational." That is, many of the characteristics and attributes of the development process that would apply to one consulting client—say, a *Fortune* 500 corporation—are *not* the same as those of a seemingly similar situation for a small local retail business. This dissimilarity is true even if the systems you are developing appear on the surface to be nearly identical (example: internal financial accounting systems).

In this chapter we'll explore the various aspects of developing client computer systems, from your first attempts at acquiring a contract to do so, to the various methods you can use during the development process. Much of our discussion will be from the perspective of what steps are the most appropriate for which situations and what types of clients.

PROApOSALS[1]

One of the most important types of document you will write during your consulting is the proposal. This is no overstatement; you can establish a direct cause-and-effect relationship between effective proposals to clients and the resulting consulting and development work.

There are many different characteristics and variations of proposals, and this section discussed the major attributes of a good proposal. Proposal formats, contents, and other characteristics differ, sometimes radically, based on the characteristics and other factors of the information systems—and the clients themselves—discussed in this chapter. Therefore, *each proposal should be treated as a unique entity that is prepared in conjunction with a unique situation.* Extremely subtle distinctions, such as how you present your company's capabilities in a particular situation, can often make the difference between success and failure in the proposal process; I wish to emphasize the importance of carefully examining each and every component of a proposal during its preparation and revision.

THE PURPOSE OF PROPOSALS

A proposal is a written statement of your (1) intention, (2) willingness, and (3) qualifications to accomplish a particular mission. In the context of this chapter, missions include:

- Developing a computer system
- Responding affirmatively to a request for proposals (RFP); that is, that you or your firm will accomplish the task requested

It's important to note, though, that you may submit a proposal to a current or prospective client for consulting activities outside of the realm of computer systems development; for example, for conducting training seminars or performing advisory services. Therefore, the principles presented in this section can be adapted to many other consulting situations and business opportunities.

A proposal provides a *written record* of your (1) intentions, (2) willingness, and (3) qualifications; *the very act of putting these three categories of items into writing signifies a commitment on your part above and beyond any verbal statements.* It is one thing, for example, to listen to someone describe a series of tasks that must be completed, and to respond with, "Yeah, we can do that." As with buying automobiles, real estate, investments, and other items, the absence of a *written* commitment to perform or provide some items at a specified price leaves too much room for misunderstanding and contention between the parties involved in a transaction. Not only is the recipient of the proposal protected by having a written record of specific commitments, *but you—the proposal writer—are also protected from claims that you committed to perform some set of tasks that in actuality you didn't commit to do.* All in all, the presence of a written proposal forms the basis for written contracts of performance, so the more items in writing the better for all parties involved.

Proposals also function as a *sales and marketing tool* (Chap. 4). When submitting a proposal to another company or organization, you are giving it a document which, if properly prepared, contains a great deal of information that is part of your consulting sales and marketing strategy. Statements of qualifications and capabilities; references; presentations of creative, innovative solutions; and other components tell the recipient that you *know* what you are doing, and in fact *are very good at* exactly what they would like you to do.

Proposals also serve as a *demonstration of your communication abilities,* both written (the document itself) and verbal (through follow-on briefings to and meetings with the recipient). While this may appear superficial, your professionalism and your consulting organizations are represented by your communications. In some cases, your proposal to a particular firm may be to work with them to prepare a proposal for another company (e.g., a joint consulting venture). In these cases, your demonstrated communications abilities may have a direct bearing on the success and acceptance of your proposal.

Your proposal serves as a demonstration of your *organizational abilities*. Not only is the content being evaluated, but the manner in which the content is presented is also being considered by the recipient of your proposal. Intangibles such as the time frame in which a proposal is submitted (five seconds before the deadline? seven weeks after an informal request?) provide implicit statements as to your overall technical and professional capabilities.

For those of you who are primarily software developers and who have little or no experience with proposals—yet are embarking on consulting adventures in which you must frequently prepare and submit proposals—preparing a *good* proposal has much the same distinction as the difference between developing software using structured techniques versus developing a GO TO–laden series of spaghetti programs. Both programs (or proposals) may work, but the well-structured one is more indicative of your capability to handle complex tasks than a poorly structured one.

Finally, and maybe most important, a proposal serves as the written extension of your *business or technical strategy*. A proposal should be prepared *after* (or at least iteratively with) a situation-specific business or technical strategy—in our context, a development project—and should reflect that strategy throughout each and every sentence, paragraph, and page. Nothing is more confusing to a reader of a proposal than seeing inconsistencies in implicit messages, technical material, or other facets of a proposal. If your business strategy, for example, is to win a client's business at all cost in hopes of pursuing future work, your pricing strategy should reflect that goal. Similarly, if your technical strategy is to avoid risky, unproven technologies, be cautious about proposing products that are barely announced and may or may not be commercially available in your required time frame.

Characteristics of Proposals

Proposals may be solicited or unsolicited. Solicited proposals often are in response to a request for proposals (RFP), a document in which a prospective client formally requests proposals to be submitted by prospective bidders (consultants). In other cases, a written proposal may be provided in response to an informal request. Even in informal situations (discussed next), your proposal should take a written form for the reasons discussed earlier in this chapter.

Proposals may also be categorized as formal or informal. The primary distinctions between proposals that fall into one or the other of these two categories are size and format.[2] Informal proposals tend to be smaller in size, often taking the form of a long business letter.[3] Many of the "overhead" components of proposals are reduced in size or even eliminated in informal proposals, given the likely familiarity of the parties involved with one another. For example, the section dealing with the proposal writer's capabilities and qualifications may be eliminated if prior work had been done by one party for the other.

As we mentioned earlier, proposals should be tailored to each and every situation. Assume that you are preparing proposals in response to two solicitations, one each from two different companies. One is for the installation of a local area network (LAN), along with custom development of a number of software systems that must interface to the LAN. The other is to develop a long-range strategic plan for a *Fortune* 500 company; the plan will include a five-year pro forma cost analysis, a long-range migration plan toward client/server technology, and staffing recommendations during the period under analysis—more of a "pure consulting" project rather than one oriented to development.

Your statement of capabilities and qualifications should be written differently for each of these proposals. While both forms should include items such as how long your firm has been in business and refer to a demonstrated record of success, the format for the LAN project should stress *hands-on* LAN experience and software development, and list many or all of the similar projects you have completed successfully. The other proposal, however, should stress your background in strategic planning and business-related issues, and list your references for similar types of projects and programs.

Marketing messages, proposal format, and all other aspects should be similarly adapted to each and every situation.

Given that proposals represent you, your company, or organization, *appearance* is very important. As with business plans (Chap. 6) and other documents, the wide-spread usage of laser printers and graphical software provides everyone with the capability to produce attractive, professional documents. Graphics, charts, and tables should be used in conjunction with text. A caution: there is sometimes a tendency to overuse fonts, text sizes, textual attributes (shadowing, outlining, etc.) and other capabilities that are available with modern document-preparation tools; these should be used intelligently, but rapid changes in fonts and other attributes actually can detract from your proposal. Be careful not to overuse such capabilities.

Finally, proposal *size* should be determined by the situation. If your proposal is in response to a request for prices for specific software packages and some simple installation work, it should be shorter than one detailing highly complex software development tasks. Many RFPs specify a maximum length for responding proposals; these specifications should not be violated.

FORMATS OF PROPOSALS

As with most of the other documents we discuss in this book, the *formats* of proposals should be adapted according to individual situations. One recommended format, as discussed in *The Consultant's Guide to Proposal Writing*, by Herman Holtz,[4] is discussed below.

Section I: Introduction
1. *About the offerer.* An introductory portion that provides some lead-in to Section IV.
2. *Understanding the requirement.* This portion is intended to demonstrate *up-front* that you have a clear understanding of the prospective client's needs and opportunities.

Section II: Discussion
1. *The requirement.* This portion expands the previous subsection into a detailed explanation of the requirements.

Together with the next two portions, this section would, for example, form the bulk of the technical response to an RFP or comprise the technical marketing presentation for an unsolicited proposal.

2. *Analysis.* This subsection describes your analysis of the client's environment.

3. *Approach.* This is where you tell *how* you will satisfy the requirements at hand.

Section III: Proposed Project. The subsections of this section detail a number of project-specific organizational, staffing, and procedural management items with respect to the project. These include:

1. Project organization
2. Management
3. Plans and procedures
4. Staff
5. Deliverable items
6. Schedules
7. Resume(s)

Section IV: Qualifications and Experience

1. *Relevant current and recent projects.* This is the situationally adaptable portion about which we wrote earlier; you or your organization's most relevant successes should be emphasized here.

2. *Resources.* All of your available resources, including employees, subcontract assistance, development environments, etc., should be detailed here.

Miscellaneous

Front matter. An attractive title page and other introductory material.

Appendices. As necessary.

DEVELOPMENT LANGUAGES AND PLATFORMS

OK, let's assume you get past the proposal stage, your client accepts your offer, and you are to begin work developing some type of computer-based information system. In some situations your development environment—the hardware, operating system(s), language(s), and other building blocks—already have been preselected for you, and your proposal has reflected your expertise in those areas. You may be contracting to do software maintenance on or to make enhancements to an existing system, and all of those decisions were made long before, during initial development. Alternatively, there may be organizational edicts such as "Thou shalt develop on Unix" or "Thou shalt use only Brand X LAN environments."

These types of situations in which you have little or no say in your development environment tend to be more common in medium and large companies, those with an entrenched information structure. This isn't to say that new technology is never introduced into these types of companies, for we're all familiar with the downsizing trends and accompanying interest in new platforms, languages, and so on. You may find yourself being responsible for the first pilot program using some relational database X or a particular fourth-generation language (4GL). For the most part, though, you are likely to have less freedom in platform and language selection in these types of environments than with a small retail business first exploring automation.

Given the freedom to make a choice of language and platform, consultants typically select those with which they are most familiar. Not coincidentally, platform familiarity is a direct component of managing the risk on a given development-oriented engagement. In the optimal situation, there is some degree of convergence among

- Familiarity
- Client acceptance
- Market acceptance

This means, for example:

- You are very familiar (that is, "an expert") with Visual Basic 4.0 and Microsoft SQL Server 6.5 programming
- Visual Basic 4.0 either is a formal standard or is widely used at your client for developing client-side applications to interface with Microsoft SQL Server 6.5—also a client standard
- The marketplace considers these products and platforms to be "acceptable," if not leaders.

The reason for including marketplace acceptance in the mix has to do with countering some of the resistance you are likely to meet as you pursue application development projects. Examples of this resistance include the following:

- You are finishing up a six-month design project at a client, and you are asked to put together a development plan for the implementation of this application—basically, the project is yours subject to acceptance of your proposal (that is, it's not a competitive situation). You personally feel that the XYZ programming language, using Company ABC's compiler, is a far more productive development platform than any of the "leading" alternatives on the market today, but your client is wary of this language because of its abysmal market share and corresponding concerns about long-term support issues.
- You submit a proposal for a development project in which you will (again) use the XYZ programming language, this time in response to an RFP and in a competitive situation. Your rates are better than any of your competitors'; your proposal is professional and clearly communicates your expertise at working in similar situations; but at the same time, the prospective client is very wary about the against-the-grain, almost cultlike fervor of those who use XYZ.

The point is that for better or for worse, you should at least have a good sense about what is "acceptable" in the marketplace—

and among your prospective clients—in terms of development platforms. It is unarguable that different applications require different programming languages, and this has been clear since the early days of computing (COBOL for mainframe and minicomputer business applications, FORTRAN for scientific ones; dBASE or FoxPro or Clipper for simple, PC-based business applications, C for more complex PC applications; and so on). This is one more decision you need to make regarding your service offerings and specialties (Chap. 2).

METHODOLOGIES AND LIFE CYCLES

There are literally hundreds of books, and thousands of articles and papers, written about methodologies and life-cycle models used to develop computer systems. Our purpose here is not to discuss the relative merits of each, but rather to discuss the situational aspects of different ones.

The "traditional" life cycle, sometimes known as the "waterfall" life-cycle methodology, is one in which one distinct process feeds into the next with little or no iteration. Figure 7-1 illustrates the various states in this methodology. Note that different versions of the methodology have slightly different steps.

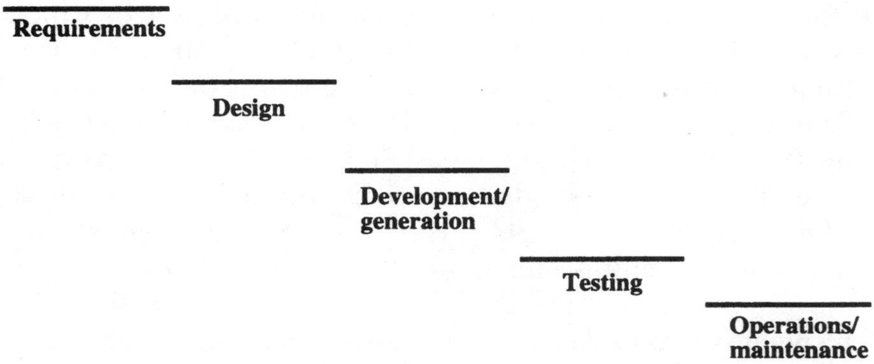

Requirements

Design

Development/ generation

Testing

Operations/ maintenance

FIGURE 7-1   The traditional life-cycle methodology.

Later in this chapter, we'll look at a system development example that utilizes this methodology.

Other methodologies are built around rapid prototyping and "throw-away code," in which a set of user requirements is gathered and a quick prototype is developed to get user feedback on-screen and output formats, processing, and other characteristics of the information system, *before* full-scale development occurs. Variants of this methodology are gaining popularity in recent years, though sometimes it may be difficult to convince a small business client that you aren't simply churning billable hours as you go from one prototype to the next. Again, we have an example of the situational nature of consulting and systems development. A multiyear project at a large company may be the appropriate environment for a prototype-based methodology, while a small business owner may have the view, "Cut this 'prototype' stuff; I need a system by next month."

CASE

Computer-aided software engineering (CASE) may or may not be appropriate for a specific development project. A general rule of thumb is that larger clients may be more interested in CASE-based development, but when cost savings are involved it's possible to convince a smaller client that a design-automatic system-generation CASE environment may provide cost savings over traditional hand-coding development.

Contrary to popular opinion, CASE is *not* an artifact of the 1980s gone forever from the software development and productivity scene. There are still numerous modeling and design tools—some integrated packages, others specially tailored toward a specific area such as data modeling—and while the "CASE will do everything, including replace programming" fervor is gone, many organizations have done an admirable job of integrating CASE capabilities into their development practices.

Here's a brief rundown of some CASE issues relative to consulting and software development:

1. *Have a clear goal in mind for CASE usage.*   Don't use or recommend CASE just for the sake of using CASE, as the use of various CASE tools and products initially often *increases* development time the first time around until some level of experience is gained with the tool and accompanying modeling techniques. As we mentioned before, clients, especially small business owners or managers, are not going to be too pleased when the tools that are supposed to justify any incremental cost through time savings actually result in a longer development cycle.

2. *Thoroughly analyze any CASE tools before "real life" usage.* Watch out for vendor hype! Of course, this applies to end-user software products as well as development tools and environments, but since CASE is often a hard sell with your clients, you don't want to have to explain at some future point why the tool(s) you fought so hard to use really don't work as well as claimed.

3. *Consider pilot program introduction of CASE.*   CASE applies to many different stages of the development life cycle, uses many different methodologies and modeling techniques, and in short can become a discipline all by itself. If you personally don't have a great deal of experience with CASE but, say, your rather sophisticated client views CASE usage as a plus, consider taking a specific life-cycle stage—say, requirements collection or database design—and using that as your initial introduction to a specific product or CASE discipline.

PROTOTYPING

There are a lot of advantages to the use of prototypes in consulting-based systems development efforts. Many users, particularly those with little or no computer system background, often change their mind about the "look and feel" of their applications after viewing sample screens and reports. In other situations, proof-of-concept issues can be determined through the creation of prototypes—for example, verifying the standards compliance of a particular communications protocol driver your client wishes to utilize.

The premise behind prototyping is that a consultant (or any developer) can *quickly* generate a shell of key components of a computer system that can then be used to get feedback from the eventual users as to their relative likes and dislikes about the formats, organization, and some of the processing of the system. The general premise, "Spend a little time and money now, save a lot of time and money later," can be a cost-effective approach to systems development, as it is easier to make changes following a small investment of time rather than after intensive and complex coding, database design, testing, and often multisystem installation. *The key is to convince your client of this.* As we discussed earlier, some clients will be receptive to the use of prototypes during their system development, others more reticent.

INTEGRATION AND COMMERCIAL SOFTWARE

So far in this chapter, our focus has been on systems development that involves software development by you, the consultant. There are likely to be situations—many of them, in fact—where off-the-shelf software solutions will solve specific client needs. Some extreme examples are word processing and spreadsheet management. If your client specifies a need for these functions, you *aren't* going to develop those functions from scratch, writing the code to do these functions, when hundreds of commercial solutions are available. Even if you were capable of doing so (and keep in mind that many applications programmers and developers fail miserably at developing system software, so that would not be a given anyway), you won't find any clients willing to pay for the development time to create customized versions of those commonly available applications.

There are many "vertical"—industry-specific, to overgeneralize—applications that are also commercially available, which may be more cost-effective for your client to implement than a customized solution. In some cases, a client may require only a single application around which his or her business operations are based (example: inventory management for a construction company). In most cases, however, one or more commercial applications need to be integrated with one another, or with custom software that you develop. In these situations, a large portion of your "development" will likely consist of making different applications work with one another: communicate, share data, and otherwise cooperate in meeting business needs.

In some of these environments, the applications and their components will be "open," meaning that they comply with certain standards designed to make interoperability and connectivity easier. In even more cases, though, you may find yourself writing "glue routines" to exchange data, establish and manage communications connections, and generally try to make things work together that weren't designed to do so.

Therefore, your creation of information systems for clients may involve more than just the designing and coding with which you have had past experience. Those consultants with prior experience in integrating applications with one another will inevitably be using those skills in the course of their consulting activities; the rest will certainly learn how.

A DEVELOPMENT EXAMPLE

Let's look at a development example to give you an idea of a representative development project on which a small business consultant would work. The methodology used for this example is the traditional one illustrated in Fig. 7-1, ranging from the beginning stages of analyzing business needs and requirements, through the implementation.

BUSINESS AND REQUIREMENTS ANALYSIS

The starting point in developing any computer system is *knowing your client's business*. Many clients we have worked with have related stories of retail computer salespeople or computer vendors' sales representatives recommending specific computer hardware or software without attempting to determine the customer's needs and problems. In order to establish your reputation as a knowledgeable and competent consultant you must serve the needs of your client base and recommending ill-fitting computer systems is the same as a custom tailor designing a business suit that is three sizes too large.

There are several reasons why understanding a client's business is essential. Most important is that no one understands a business and its problems like its owner or manager. You are not being hired as a management consultant to analyze the operations of the business with an eye for change. Rather, you should make recommendations where necessary as a service to the customer, but the primary emphasis should be on understanding current operations and problems to match the best possible computer system to the business.

Additionally, involving the client as much as possible provides a measure of protection for you, the consultant. As your client checks off requirements that you agree upon together, you are less likely to have an irate customer insisting that the completed system doesn't meet his or her needs.

The first step in the business analysis phase is the *interview*. A two- to three-hour interview should be scheduled with the client. The site of the interview is unimportant; it may be the customer's office, your office, a restaurant, or any other place conducive to exchanging ideas and information. Both you and your client should prepare for the interview prior to the actual meeting. The client should bring copies of important reports, invoices, often-repeated form letters, and other documents to the meeting. For each document, the client should note (1) the time involved in preparation of the form, (2) how frequently the document is generated, (3) the amount of retyping or re-creation required, and (4) how many employees currently work with the document type. The client should additionally consider why he or she is contemplating a computer system. Is it because of an increasingly backlogged work load, which results in overtime by present employees or the hiring of temporary help to keep up with the work load? Or is it to allow for planned future growth of the business? Your client should also attempt to analyze backlogs in current operations in addition to paperwork problems.

The consultant also needs to prepare for the first meeting. You should familiarize yourself with the client's type of business through reading, talking with friends and other customers in the same business, and any other sources available. Even though you want the client to describe his or her business situation, the interview will be of greater value if you are prepared than if you depend on your client to supply you with all background information. Less time will be spent attempting to understand details of the business operations that you should be able to investigate on your own. This serves a dual purpose. You and your client can start discussing problems and situations without regressing through as much background discussion as you would if you weren't prepared, and it serves to increase your esteem in the eyes of the client; you consider his or her business important enough to perform background investigation. You should also conduct a preliminary analysis of software and computer systems that have been implemented for the application being investigated, including systems you have designed for other customers in the same or similar businesses. This will acquaint you with the area under study so you will have a general idea of current efforts. Keep in mind that you are not limited to current software or hardware configurations, but you should be aware of what has been done in the area, along with any successes and failures.

These topics should be addressed in the preliminary interview:

1. Why is the client investigating a computer system?
2. What are current problems as the user sees them?
3. What is the volume of transactions performed in daily operations and periodic and special reports that must be produced?
4. What amount of information is currently stored in file cabinets or other media form, and what is the projected growth of transaction and storage volume? How many people perform similar tasks and how much time is spent working on the various functions?
5. What current communication of information takes place among various business sites (warehouses, branch offices, suppliers and customers, etc.)?

A sample evaluation form that I've utilized during client interviews is illustrated in Fig. 7-2. This form provides a convenient checklist to ensure that relevant topics are covered.

You should let the customer lead the discussion, but keep in mind the topics to be discussed and ask questions or inquire further at appropriate times. Having a written checklist as well as a mental one aids you in keeping the discussion on track. Don't be afraid to let the conversation drift to related topics, but make sure the main points discussed here are covered.

Back in Chap. 4, we discussed positive and negative motivators that lead toward computerization. The answer to question 3 in Fig. 7-2 will provide you with the reason your client wants a computer. Depending on whether it is to exploit opportunities or solve problems you have a clue to how to proceed with the negotiations and subsequent development.

For example, Ms. Johnson of LTA (Looking to Automate) Building Supply Company, a Tucson, Arizona, building materials warehouse, asks you to design a computer system for her business. Using the above interview guidelines, you determine the following information:

1. Ms. Johnson is interested in a computer system because she expects her business volume to double in the next 12 to

1. Name _____

   Address _____

   _____

   Phone _____

2. Application(s) _____

   _____

   _____

   _____

3. Reason for computerization: _____

   _____

   _____

4. Client's computer background (include current systems): _____

   _____

   _____

5. Existing hardware, if any (include internal and external memory sizes): _____

   _____

   _____

6. Number of system users: _____

7. Multiuser/network requirements (include number of simultaneous users; type and location of other nodes) _____

   _____

   _____

   _____

   _____

8. Installation time frame: _____ Desired   _____ Mandatory
                               (if mandatory, state why)

   _____

   _____

   _____

   _____

FIGURE 7-2   Requirements analysis form.

9. Desired/budgeted system price range: _____
    _____

    Is amount a fixed budget requirement?   _____ Yes   _____ No

    Is hardware included in above price?   _____ Yes   _____ No

10. Desired user interface: _____ Menu _____ Command/query _____ No
                                                                       preference

11. Custom programming desired: _____ Yes   _____ No

    If yes, state why: _____
    _____
    _____

12. Software already reviewed (include comments and reactions): _____
    _____
    _____

13. Is there a projected need for subsequent add-on applications?

                         _____ Yes   _____ No

    If yes, what interaction with existing or proposed applications is desired?

    _____ None _____ Data sharing _____ Windowing/applications switching

    _____ Other (state) _____

14. What degree of postinstallation training and support is desired?

    _____ None   _____ Operational instruction   _____ On-call support

    _____ Other (state) _____

15. Projected data storage volume: _____
    _____
    _____
    _____

16. Special requirements that *must* be met (not already mentioned):
    _____
    _____
    _____
    _____

FIGURE 7-2   (*Continued*)

18 months. Invoice preparation for builders is taking much longer than before due to increasing transaction volume, and three employees must now spend their entire work shift preparing invoices.

2. LTA currently processes 75 to 100 invoices per day, and each one takes approximately 10 minutes to prepare. When a builder calls LTA requesting building supplies, the employee must search the file cabinet for the appropriate inventory sheets. Each sheet contains product information (part number, size, estimated quantity in stock, price, and reorder point), manufacturer information (which vendors can supply the product, addresses, and wholesale prices), and which of LTA's customers use the material in their building.

It takes about 2 minutes to find each inventory sheet, and each invoice is normally for three different products. Once the file forms are pulled, the in-stock count is decremented by the number of parts ordered and the invoice is prepared with appropriate information (part numbers, quantity ordered of each part, price per unit, and total sales price for the invoice). A desk calculator is used by the invoice preparer to total dollar amounts.

3. LTA divides its product line into three main categories: windows, doors, and fixtures (kitchen and bathroom cabinets, countertops, etc.). There are approximately 2000 different windows in stock, 800 different doors, and 1500 fixtures. Though the quantity of invoices is expected to double, the number of different products will remain fairly constant in the foreseeable future.

4. If a clerk tries to fill an order and insufficient stock exists in the warehouse, he or she must call the main warehouse in Phoenix to check if they can loan the Tucson division stock to fill the requested amount. If so, the Phoenix office enters the amount requested on their local computer and a special interdivision transfer form is produced for next-day shipping of goods. If the Phoenix office needs to inquire about Tucson's availability of a product, an employee will call Tucson and a manual search will be performed on the inventory supply sheets.

5. When employees update the inventory sheet, they are supposed to check if reordering is necessary. Because of the growing backlog, however, LTA's clerks often forget to perform the check and on-hand inventory is usually below the safety-stock level. This has caused more frequent shipments from Phoenix than are necessary (along with increased transportation costs) as well as missed sales when builders purchase the supplies from a competitor rather than wait for LTA to restock.

6. When there is breakage of windows and other spoilage of goods the respective inventory files must be updated. Ms. Johnson has noticed that breakage reports often pile up for several days before the actual updates are performed, and often the reconciliation takes place after normal working hours, forcing overtime pay for the union employees.

After the interview, you compile facts from your notes and come to the following conclusions about LTA's business situation:

1. LTA is losing business because of untimely filling of orders. This situation will probably deteriorate as invoice volume increases.

2. Despite the projected increase in invoice volume, data storage requirements (either manual or automated) will remain relatively constant because of the stability of LTA's product line.

3. Having a quicker method of filling invoices will allow LTA's business volume to increase without a corresponding doubling in employees to process orders. This will provide greater operating leverage; that is, the same amount of fixed costs (salaries and equipment that do not change with increasing units sold) can produce a greater amount of revenue, thus increasing the net income of the business.

4. A means to automatically search Phoenix's inventory (and allow Phoenix to search local inventory) would be desirable.

Once you have conducted the preliminary interview, a short report containing original notes and the above conclusions should be presented to Ms. Johnson for her feedback and approval. Again, this is important because when the client is involved in the project from the beginning there is less risk of having a dissatisfied customer when the final system is delivered. Assuming that no major corrections are necessary or omissions are discovered, you are ready to proceed to the next step.

Preliminary System Design

The traditional development life-cycle concept allows for several stages of system design. The early stages, often called *conceptual design,* allow design decisions to be made without regard to the specific hardware, software, and communications interfaces used. The process concentrates solely on the relationship among proposed system components and, during software design, among software modules.

The conceptual design stage utilizes modeling techniques such as entity-relationship diagrams (Fig. 7-3) for data design and data flow diagrams (Fig. 7-4) for process design. In recent years, object-oriented design techniques have come into favor among many practitioners, replacing or supplementing traditional modeling methods. As with the overall methodology you choose to employ, different projects and systems may be more suited to different methods of modeling.

In some life-cycle instantiations, conceptual designs are then transformed into *logical designs* in which some degree of decision is made as to the form of the resulting system, but not necessarily to the level of specific product features and capabilities. An example would be a conceptual data design, which is then transformed into a generic relational database model.

Finally, designs should acquire some *implementation-specific* characteristics, such as the aforementioned general relational database model being further transformed into one with features of Oracle or Informix or dBASE IV.

Capacity Analysis

Even though it's not a formal life-cycle stage, an important step in refining your designs prior to development or product

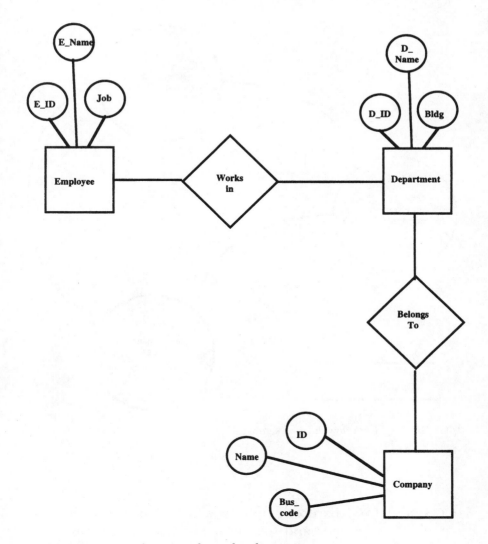

FIGURE 7-3   Sample entity-relationship diagram.

selection and hardware platform selection is *capacity analysis.*
Simply stated, capacity analysis is the process of determining
storage and processing requirements for system components.
Ms. Johnson has provided the following information regarding
LTA's data. For each part in the inventory (2000 windows, 800

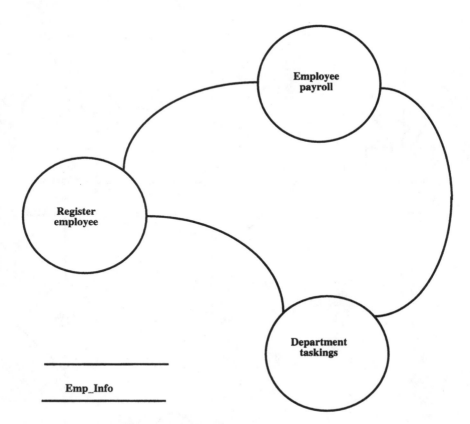

FIGURE 7-4   Data flow diagram sample.

doors, and 1500 fixtures), there is a five-digit part code (one alphabetic character and four numbers), a quantity in stock that is never more than 500 for any one unit, a part name that is ten characters or less, a price between $10 and $500, and a reorder point (somewhere between 50 and 150). Similar information produces the manufacturer and customer data used in the calculations.[5]

By simple mathematical calculations, we can roughly determine computer storage requirements. For simplicity, assume that we are dealing with 8-bit ASCII characters: 1 byte equals one 8-bit character.

Part data
Part number	5 bytes
Quantity	1 byte (integer number)
Price	4 bytes (room to store 1 floating point number)
Reorder point	1 byte
Part name	10 bytes
Total	21 bytes

21 bytes per record × 4300 records = 90,300 bytes

Manufacturer data
Name	15 bytes
Address	45 bytes (including city, state, zip code, and phone number)
Cost	4 bytes
Minimum order	1 byte
Total	65 bytes

65 bytes per record × 100 suppliers = 6500 bytes

Customer data
Name	15 bytes
Address	45 bytes
Rating	1 byte
Total	61 bytes

61 bytes per record × 200 customers = 12,200 bytes

Total bytes of permanent storage: 109,000 bytes

We already have seen that the number of different parts is not expected to increase substantially. Assuming a 50 percent growth rate in new customers over the next 18 months, 6100 bytes can be added to the total, giving 115,100 bytes.

An important decision must now be made: What other storage requirements exist? For example, if LTA must keep the past 18 months' invoices online (immediately accessible), it is easy to see how storage requirements will increase drastically. However, Ms. Johnson decides that since past invoices are referred to infrequently, they may be stored in file cabinets. She can make this determination because all accounts receivable are controlled from the Phoenix office. They currently reconcile all payments against outstanding invoices on their own computer system and wish to continue this practice. If it were determined that Tucson's LTA warehouse would handle their own accounting functions (payroll, accounts receivable and payable, etc.) additional storage would be needed to allow for the extended online data. Note that we are not dealing with a question of technology here. It is certainly technically feasible for Ms. Johnson's new computer system to handle these accounting functions, but the *political* decision has been made to keep these functions in Phoenix. Again, you need to design a system to meet the requirements of your clients, not your own ideas of how their business should be operated. You should make your clients aware that certain capabilities exist that they are not utilizing, but the final decision is up to them.

HARDWARE SELECTION

You can now make a preliminary decision on what class of hardware is needed. Owing to the data storage requirements calculated, a microcomputer would probably be sufficient for LTA. If storage of 5 million bytes had been calculated a microcomputer could still be installed, but you now know that a hard disk (or some other storage medium capable of handling large amounts of data) is required. However, if 80 million bytes of data were to be put online, you should start considering a machine in the minicomputer class.

Similar logical design criteria can be superimposed over LTA's communication requirement. Ms. Johnson has two major options in connecting the proposed computer system with the Phoenix office's hardware. If a search for a part determines that insufficient stock exists locally to fill the order, an *automatic* search (no human intervention) of the remote data can be performed. This requires natural or imposed compatibility between the two computer systems. If both systems run the same inventory software, automatic searches can be performed chiefly through the communications software. If, however, different software is used in Tucson than that which is currently used in Phoenix, some type of front-end program is required to translate data interrogations from one software form to another. We have now entered the realm of distributed databases, a complicated and expensive system design criterion.

Ms. Johnson's other option is for the local software to notify the operator of the insufficient stock condition. The operator must then access the remote computer (through dial-up lines, for example) and, using the remote software, access the inventory system.

Several complications arise because of this decision. If Ms. Johnson prefers option number 1 (automatic search), LTA must either use the same software (and possibly hardware) in both cities or provide for an expensive front-end program to handle the dissimilar accesses. Phoenix's existing software will probably need to be modified (or totally replaced) because of the system changes.

After studying these findings, Ms. Johnson determines that owing to the improved reordering system resulting from the new system, LTA will not be out of stock as frequently as now, causing less inquiries of Phoenix's system (Phoenix calls Tucson only five to ten times per day despite handling three times as many transactions as Tucson). For such infrequent remote access, you should recommend option number 2, manual intervention to access the remote computer system, which may be more cost-effective despite the slower access. Now a modem and simple communications software can allow access to the other system.

Another advantage of this decision is that LTA is not limited to certain hardware or software systems. During the physical-design stage you are free to explore the full range of hardware and software available.

Together with Ms. Johnson you decide that two employees would be able to handle all current and projected invoice processing and other inventory preparation. Ms. Johnson would also like one terminal to be free for correspondence, memos, and other word processing functions. A simple diagram of the proposed system is shown in Fig. 7-5. Notice the lack of detail because we are at the early stage of design.

One word of caution: If you determine that storage, communications, political, and other requirements that surface during the interview and preliminary design stages are far beyond your capabilities, you should seriously consider referring your client to another consultant specializing in that class of systems. For example, a nationwide distributed database covering 50 nodes over a packet-switched value-added net-

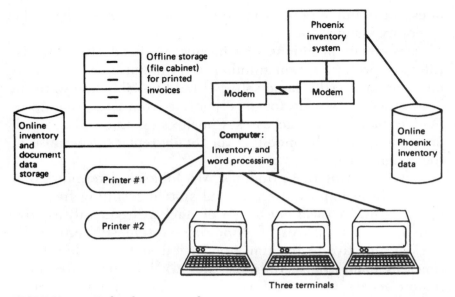

FIGURE 7-5   Refined system configuration.

work may be a bit too much for a consultant experienced in installing simple microcomputer-based information systems. No doctor, lawyer, or accountant is an expert in *all* areas of his or her profession, and computer professionals are no different. Rather than damage your business reputation (and your image) by undertaking a task that you are not experienced enough to complete successfully you should direct the customer to the appropriate specialist. You may be able to work with the other professional in an apprenticelike relationship on the consulting contract and increase your knowledge of that area; after all, you sent business to him or her. The other consultant may also direct clients looking for services in your area of specialty to you. This way, good professional relationships are created and nurtured.

TRAINING

In the next chapter, we'll discuss general training methods such as conducting seminars. During the course of systems development, however, you will likely have a period in which the users, maintenance staff, and/or others involved in the new system familiarize themselves with their new hardware and/or software. This may be a relatively simple task for menu-driven or GUI-based environments with only one or two applications, or may be more complex if many different applications will be included, especially those which interact with one another.

All training should be, to the greatest extent possible, hands-on, with sufficient supervision to ensure correct use of the system. It's important to remember that you can develop the most elegant, productivity-enhancing computer system possible, but it can be sabotaged by inadequate user training.

MAINTENANCE AND SUPPORT

When a computer system is designed by an in-house programming-analysis staff it is usually assumed that they, with assistance from the vendors and possibly third-party contractors, will maintain the system, including program modifications and implementing additional applications. As a consultant, your obligation normally ends when you have successfully installed the system and trained the users. This should be specified in the contract between you and your client.

Some clients, however, may desire continual modifications of their system, especially if the software was custom written. In these cases you should negotiate some type of retainer fee or additional hourly rate for continued postinstallation support.

OVERVIEW OF DOCUMENTS

During the course of your consulting-based systems development, you may find yourself needing to write many different types of documents. In *The Computer Professional's Guide to*

Effective Communications we discuss these many types of documents in detail, giving examples of many of them.[6]

REQUIREMENTS

There are two primary categories in which requirements documents can be included: *High-level documents,* which focus on general statements of need, and *refined documents,* which take the validated requirements from the high-level documents and further refine them prior to embarking on the specifications process. High-level documents often go by such names as *Statement of Needs,* and include such items as those discussed in the preceding section. A refined document is one often referred to as a *System Requirements Document* or a *Statement of Product Requirements.*

Many organizations have formal design methodologies with corresponding formal structures for these and other documents. For example, those government employees or contractors operating within the U.S. Air Force's development process develop high-level and refined requirements documents according to the structure specified in whatever the current formal methodology is (currently the 2167-A methodology). In these types of situations, and their parallels in the corporate world, the structure of the documents you would prepare is predefined. In other situations without such a rigorous structure to which your writing must conform, you are free to develop documents in the manner you see most fit. Such documents might include the following items:

1. *Introduction and overview.* This section should describe the current information systems environment, whether manual or automated, and the purpose of issuing this requirements document (such as "upgrade the entire corporate accounting system" or "automate the entire chain of video stores"). Mention should be made of major shortcomings in the current mode of operation.

2. *List of requirements.* This section should contain one or more lists of the requirements, or *needs,* similar to the exam-

ples shown in the previous section and illustrated in the sample document later in this chapter. Items which aren't essential to the mission of the organization may or may not be included, but should be designated as such with a lower priority or under a separate heading.

3. *Document review and comment procedures.*   The format of comments, deadline dates, and submission criteria (to whom, at what office or organization) should be stated explicitly.

The primary distinction between the format of a high-level requirements document and one oriented toward the refined list of requirements is the amount of detail among the items listed, as was demonstrated in the previous section's examples.

If possible, requirements should be prioritized. One way is to assign a multiple-level priority distinction (example: 1 through 5, with first priority items being those that are absolutely mandatory to continuing business operations, priority 5 items being desirable but not mandatory, and priorities 2 through 4 on a linear scale between the two end points). This prioritization will help give reviewers a good understanding of the needs of the information system and, for example, not cause them to reject the overall concept outright because they feel too many "nice to have" items are being included as real-life requirements.

In general, the more formal your consulting environment is (which might be translated to "the bigger the customer") the more levels of detail you are likely to be providing in your requirements documents.

SPECIFICATIONS

Following the validation of these requirements, it is the responsibility of those involved in the development life cycle to translate each requirement into one or more specification items. As with requirements, a definition of "specification" is in order to put the process in context.

A specification can be viewed as *a general statement of what must be accomplished in an information system.* Caution should be taken to ensure that prospective solutions, whether generic or implementation-specific, not influence the form of the specification statement. For example,

> Employee processing should utilize a client/server architecture, using an object-oriented database as the data storage layer.

is a statement that is likely to be far too restrictive to be of much value in a specifications document. Rather, the above statement is oriented more toward the design stage and corresponding documents for that process; these are discussed later in this chapter.

One way to look at specifications is to see them in the context of requirements. For example, a sample requirement of:

ITEM	PRIORITY
Customer checks out a tape	1

This requirement might be refined into a specification as follows:

1. *Customer checks out a tape.*   When a customer checks out one or more tapes, his or her customer file is accessed and checked for positive and negative items. Negative items include overdue tapes and outstanding payments owed. Positive items include membership in the *Frequent Renter* program. This transaction history must be checked against activity at all stores. Any current in-store specials or customer discounts are applied to the amount due. Following payment for the rental, the customer's file is updated with the tape or tapes checked out and their due dates.

The specification lists the individual components and items that must be accomplished to meet the requirement it represents. Note that no mention is made of the sequence in which the processing is executed, the programming language in which code might be written, underlying databases or table formats, program flow control, or any other issue which deals with the *implementation* of that specification. Rather, the specification concentrates on stating *what* must be done, not *how* it will be accomplished.

DESIGN DOCUMENTS

Design documents are completed at the point at which you switch your orientation from "what must be done" to "how it will be done." Correspondingly, design documents should be heavily graphically oriented. Including entity-relationship database designs, data-flow diagrams, structure charts, context diagrams, and other graphical tools can help tell others *how* a particular process should be accomplished when the actual development begins.

Other tools, such as pseudocode (English-like instructions without having to worry about programming language syntax) are also valuable in the lower-level, implementation-specific design documents.

CONTRACTS

Except for rare occasions, any software developed for a client should be *licensed* to the client, with ownership and copyright retained by you. This ensures that your customer doesn't turn around and resell your program to others, recovering his or her costs and profiting from your efforts. Your client should sign a nondisclosure agreement to prevent leakage of your source code (if you choose to provide it) and your contract should clearly state the terms of license (exclusive, nonexclusive, etc.).

An exception to the licensing and nondisclosure agreements may occur when your client and you agree to develop a software package for the client's use but also to jointly market the program to other potential users. In this case, your client may recover his or her costs by making an investment in the software development and sharing the proceeds of resale to others. If this situation occurs, the resulting software may be marketed on a limited basis to the client's business associates and contacts, or developed as a commercial package to be self-published or licensed through a software publisher (discussed later in this chapter).

Your contract should state that the only applications and features to be included in the completed software are the ones previously and mutually agreed to by your client and you. This will prevent confusion and disagreement at a subsequent time if your client were to say "Oh, by the way, I'd like this feature added also, within the cost provisions already provided."

Sample contracts are available through a number of sources, such as the Independent Computer Consultants Association (ICCA; see Chap. 12).

PRICING

A task almost as difficult as determining total implementation time is setting a price for your contract software. Should you charge a flat fee? How about charging on a per-hour basis? Should you place a ceiling on the number of hours?

While many consultants may use different methods, an approach I favor is to take your estimate of development hours (with a buffer to handle unexpected difficulties), attach an hourly rate, *and* place a ceiling in the contract on the number of hours (as described in Chap. 5). I favor this approach because you are guaranteed a fair wage based on the number of hours estimated for the project. Since you have a reasonable estimate (hopefully) of the development time with built-in protection for overruns, the total development process is handled in much the same manner as a normal consulting contract: your compensation is based on the time and effort you devote to the project.

Your client also benefits in two important ways. First, the possibility exists that the project may be completed in less time than projected, resulting in some (or substantial) savings. Second, he or she is protected, in case you have made miscalculations of the time involved, by the ceiling of hours. There is no reason the client should pay substantially more because your estimate, based on mutually agreeable specifications, was inaccurate.

How do you benefit from this type of arrangement? Remember our marketing lesson: A satisfied client usually leads to many more satisfied clients. If a project is brought in under budget or a client realizes that he or she is protected by your "outstanding" sense of fairness in the form of a price ceiling, your reputation as a fair business person (as important as your reputation as a knowledgeable professional) will spread among prospective customers.

If, however, you find unsuspecting (or gullible) clients, contract on a straight hourly basis, and consistently complete the project at double or triple the original cost estimate, it won't be long before your reputation also spreads, and I don't mean as a fair businessperson. Even though you can legally collect these exorbitant fees (if your contracts are structured so), in the long run you will end up as the loser.

What hourly rate should you use? Remember, there are several forces at work here. The first is the competitive nature of the particular function you are doing. For example, basic PC programming is a skill possessed by many more professionals, and "non-professionals" as well, than it was a decade or so ago; therefore, premium pricing for such contracts should be carefully considered since they may turn into competitive bidding situations.

Another situation is what might be termed the "volume purchase" issue. Just as the unit cost of nearly any commodity or item is lower if you "purchase in bulk"—that is, buy 15 cases of something rather than just a case or two—the same might be true for the price per hour of consulting and development. If a contract is expected to take, say, between 750 and 1000 hours over a fairly regular schedule, you should consider pricing the hourly rate lower than if it were for a shorter duration. For example, if your regular consulting rate is $50 per hour, a long-term development contract might be priced at $40 or $45 without too much hardship (assuming that that allows you to operate at a profit), if you are given a commitment to a minimum number of hours.

Finally, you should allow yourself some type of contingency for long-term contracts in case a project is suddenly canceled or scaled back. These typically are negotiated individually, but include items such as "kill fees" (cash payments in lieu of an early contract cancellation) or a higher (and perhaps retroactive) hourly fee for scaling back a significant portion of a system development effort.

WARRANTIES

A *disclaimer of warranty* should be included in the contract of any software development. This indicates that your software is sold without warranties as to performance or merchantability; no express or implied warranties are included with the program, especially if you provide source code to your clients; you don't want any experimentation with your source code to cause the software to break and find yourself liable.

Your contracts should state explicitly the limitations of warranty as a means of protecting yourself. As we discussed earlier, closely check the language you use in your contracts against model contracts (or by using an attorney to review those contracts).

SUBCONTRACTING

In Chap. 13, we'll discuss the use of subcontractors in more detail. For now, let's just say that it's important to *carefully* choose the people with whom you work. This doesn't necessarily mean, though, following a checklist of "x years of ABCD programming," if you recall my...well, discussion from earlier chapters. In many cases, you may hire a "quick learner" who in the space of 2 or 3 days can outperform people with more direct experience with a particular system.

It's always best to keep in mind that ultimately you are responsible for the people you hire and their work. Passing blame "don't cut no slack" with most customers and clients, so choose carefully.

COMMERCIAL SOFTWARE

The first two editions of this book devoted an entire chapter to the development and marketing of commercial software as a key revenue channel. Today's smart money, however, says that commercial software is an extremely difficult—some would say too difficult—market to try to exploit. The reasoning is that the growing sophistication of desktop environments, with graphical user interfaces (GUIs) and LAN-based applications, requires far too much "overhead" programming to even come up with a competitive product with the necessary set of basic features.

While this is true to some extent, there is still a growing market for "home grown" commercial software which could be produced by a consultant as part of a full-service line of offerings. Martha Page, principal of Gates Phoenix, a software agent (discussed more in a moment), categorizes the market for commercial software as:

- *Software aimed at the "computer itself."* This includes the traditional horizontal applications (word processing, spreadsheets, etc.); these are more likely to require LAN-based and GUI environments, large development teams, and heavy marketing dollars, and are likely to remain the province of the major software houses.

- *Vertical market software.* This is still a relatively young industry (particularly for those programs with a relatively low list price). Examples include collector or hobby software, those applications which are oriented toward functions such as record keeping or similar tasks.

Most examples from this latter class of software typically are stand-alone PC-based (either Microsoft Windows or Macintosh as the primary user interface model, on respective hardware platforms) and perform a set of very specific functions. They are typically distributed by small software publishers with relatively small marketing budgets, but who still have inroads into distribution channels.

As with books (Chap. 10), one possibility to reaching the *appropriate* publisher is through the use of an agent (an example being Gates Phoenix, in Phoenix, Arizona). We use the term *appropriate* because smaller publishers tend to limit themselves to a certain subset of the overall commercial market (due primarily to limited budgets and other, similar reasons). Agents, good agents, that is, try to keep on top of the overall software market and know which firm is looking for what types of software.

Another similarity to the book business is that a great deal of the return for your work tends to be somewhat down the road, in the form of royalty streams. Advances tend to be rather small, so even a software package that eventually becomes a big seller will likely have a prolonged period until payoff. Therefore, as we discussed in Chap. 5, any consideration of commercial software among your offerings should be considered in your overall cash-flow planning with near-term needs.

SUMMARY

In this chapter, we've discussed many different topics relating to the development of client systems and software, and we took a brief look at the commercial aspects of software offerings as well. Perhaps the most important thing to remember is the situational nature of each development project. In some, such as those oriented toward initial development for a small business, you are likely to have a high degree of flexibility in the choice of development platforms and methodologies. In others, such as contract work for a large corporation, you may find yourself with a development language, hardware, operating system, developmental methodology and models, and other aspects rigidly specified.

It's also important to remember that before you can have a system to develop, you must first acquire that business, and this is typically done through a proposal. There are also other written documents you may find yourself completing during the development process, from requirements analysis forms to design documents.

Finally, ensure that all development is done in accordance with appropriate contractual and legal protection.

END NOTES

1. The information in this section is adapted from Alan R. Simon and Jordan S. Simon, *The Computer Professional's Guide to Effective Communications*, McGraw-Hill, New York, 1993, Chap. 7.
2. Herman Holtz, *The Consultant's Guide to Proposal Writing*, Wiley, New York, 1986.
3. Ibid.
4. Ibid., pp. 13–17.
5. The data format that is presented is a result of normalization of the filed data. That is, data redundancy has been reduced by formatting the data to facilitate cross-referencing rather than repeating common material. The data normalization process is discussed in many database management books.
6. Alan R. Simon and Jordan S. Simon, *The Computer Professional's Guide to Effective Communications*, McGraw-Hill, New York, 1993. The information in the following sections is adapted from this source.

CONSULTING SUCCESS PROFILE: CHRIS DATE, DATABASE SPECIALIST

CAREER AND CONSULTING HIGHLIGHTS

B.A., Mathematics, Cambridge University

M.A., Mathematics, Cambridge University

IBM, 1967–1983

Author of numerous database textbooks, professional computer books, and papers

One of world's best-known specialists in database technology

Chris Date describes himself as an independent author, lecturer, and consultant; most practitioners in the computer profession, especially those heavily involved in the database arena, refer to Mr. Date as an expert, a description he humbly downplays. ("Experts are supposed to know all the answers," he says, "which I certainly don't.")

Regardless of what descriptive phrase one uses to describe Chris Date, he nevertheless is recognized as one of the world's best-known specialists in database technology, especially relational technology. Prior to leaving IBM in 1983, he was involved in technical planning and externals design for the IBM products SQL/DS and DB2. His book *An Introduction to Database Systems: Volume I* (currently in its fifth edition) is considered the de facto standard for database textbooks; it has sold nearly 450,000 copies and is used by several hundred colleges and universities worldwide. He also is the author of several other books on relational database management and well over 100 technical papers. Mr. Date is in demand worldwide as a lecturer on database technology and has consulted with numerous organizations, particularly many of the leading DBMS vendors.

Chris Date's career in the computer field began in 1962 with Leo Computers Ltd., London, U.K., as a mathematical programmer. He quickly moved into education and training, teaching computer system fundamentals, assembler language, and high-level languages. He was also involved in planning for "next-generation" computer systems, developing courses, and leading a team of instructors on an IBM System/360 clone machine.

In 1967 he joined IBM Hursley in the United Kingdom as a programming instructor, developing and teaching the basic training program at that site (system fundamentals, assembler language, PL/I, and other subjects). From 1969 to 1974, he was one of the principal instructors in IBM's European education program for the European software labs, developing and teaching courses in many different subjects, particularly database technology. Thus began the themes which have brought Mr. Date to prominence in the computer consulting world in the past decade: database technology and education.

In 1970, concurrent with his education and training activities, he worked with Paul Hopewell of IBM in trying to define a set of database extensions to the PL/I language. For this activity,

Chris Date spent many hours studying different aspects of the database arena, from IBM's IMS hierarchical DBMS product to the Database Task Group (DBTG) network database model…and the relational DBMS model, which had recently been described in Ted Codd's original *Communications of the ACM* paper in June 1970, and which would start what arguably could be called a revolution in the data management world. The mathematical foundation of the relational database model was one of the things Mr. Date remembers being attractive about his studies in that area, given his academic background in mathematics from Cambridge University.

In mid-1971 Mr. Date went to the United States to present findings on his database extensions for PL/I to IBM insiders, helping Mr. Codd to champion database technology (specifically, relational technology) within IBM—a lone battle in those days, as Mr. Date recalls.

Through 1974 Mr. Date continued his dual track of "relational database evangelist" and education and training specialist within IBM. At the ACM SIGMOD* meeting in 1974, the "great debate" occurred between relational proponents and those of the CODASYL/DBTG network database model. The original lineup was to have been Ted Codd and Chris Date speaking in favor of the relational side, with Charles Bachman and Jim Lucking speaking for the network model. Visa problems prevented Mr. Date from attending, and a stand-in was found. By this time, however, Mr. Date was beginning to gain a worldwide reputation in the database field as a leader in the relational world.

Also in 1974, Mr. Date moved to the United States, initially for a two-year assignment with IBM in California, and he decided to remain in the United States as a permanent resident. Part of the reason was his career path at IBM; the major database work at the corporation at that time was taking place in California, and a move back to the United Kingdom would

---

*Association for Computing Machinery Special Interest Group for the Management of Data.

have meant switching to a field other than databases, which was increasingly becoming his true calling.

While at IBM in California, he was involved in the development of database language extensions for high-level languages—COBOL, FORTRAN, PL/I, and others—for a new IBM computer system that was eventually canceled. He also developed the Unified Data Language (UDL), an "onion layer" language designed to allow support for relational, network, and hierarchical databases. His original purpose was to have the relational component—the "center of the onion"—implemented, but his UDL was so "all-purpose" that plans were made to implement the entire system, and several prototypes were built in the late 1970s.

In 1975 Mr. Date took another gigantic step toward prominence in the database consulting arena by writing his first book, the best-selling *An Introduction to Database Systems: Volume I,* a book that many of us in the computer field have used as a textbook (and which I've used several times when teaching database courses). He wrote revised editions in 1977 and 1980, plus a companion volume in 1982.

During the late 1970s and early 1980s, a series of reorganizations and management changes at IBM, coupled with strategic product decisions, began to give Mr. Date thoughts about a career change. The success of his books, plus an ever-increasing demand for him as a speaker at IBM user groups, professional conferences, and universities, coupled with strained relationships within IBM about his outside activities, prompted Mr. Date to leave IBM and become an independent consultant. He still remembers the exact date and time— "Friday, May 13, 1983, at about 2:30 P.M.," he recalled in the interview for this book.

Mr. Date spent the next few years working for himself, writing more books, teaching, and working under a long-term contract with RTI, the makers of the INGRES DBMS product. Mr. Date, like many prominent consultants, made a conscious decision as to the types of contracts he'd accept, those with which he felt most comfortable. In his case, "database consultant" meant working with vendors on product and research issues, writing, and teaching—but not necessarily working with user organizations to design and fine-tune their databases or inspecting application code for optimization possibilities. As Mr. Date says, he thinks of himself primarily as a teacher.

Interestingly, apart from the RTI contract, Mr. Date was never the initiator with any other client with whom he became involved; all the others were "cold calls" to him, primarily due to his reputation in the field. He also was careful to avoid contracts which (1) had the potential for a conflict of interest with his RTI arrangement, (2) caused concerns about whether he could deliver in a timely or effective manner, or (3) conflicted with his own sense of social responsibility. In short, ethical guidelines were just as important to Mr. Date during his early days as a consultant as revenue and profitability were.

In 1985, he joined forces with Ted Codd, also recently departed from IBM, and Sharon Weinberg, forming Codd & Date International and several sub-companies. At that time, he also withdrew from his RTI contract to ensure that the consulting firm would not appear to have a special relationship with an individual vendor, that is, a conflict of interest.

For the next six years, Mr. Date's consulting and teaching activities were channeled through the Codd & Date firm (though his writing activities remained an independent activity, many of them in conjunction with Hugh Darwen, Colin White, or David McGoveran). In 1991 he left Codd & Date and returned to independent status, the primary impetus being that the management aspects of an international consulting company—hiring employees, directing activities, and so on—took time away from the activities he most enjoyed, the actual teaching, writing, and research.

Among his more recent consulting activities in the database arena are a regular monthly column in *Database Programming & Design* magazine, a seminar course in "Advanced Aspects of the Relational Model," and further investigative study into relational and object-oriented database technology.

When asked about advice for a beginning consultant, particularly one wishing to acquire a worldwide reputation in a specific computer or IS technology, Mr. Date offers the following suggestions for success:

- Luck! In his own case, he happened on a field, relational databases, during the "ground floor" stages, which led to a number of strategic partnerships and relationships, and activities, such as his writing, all of which have fostered his career.

- Be prepared to work even longer hours than when regularly employed elsewhere. Mr. Date's average work week is 60–70 hours, and more when writing a book. Weekends turn into fertile work times due to the fewer number of telephone interruptions (except from other self-employed people doing the same!).

- Assuming one has the necessary skills and expertise, the problem then is becoming known. Teaching courses or seminars through national organizations like those we discuss in Chap. 8 does two things: It gets one's name into "circulation," and can lead to follow-on consulting work. The same is true for writing. In short, the teaching-writing-consulting cycle can all feed off each other for sustained activity in each area.

- Look for outlets overseas as well as in the United States. Such diversification might help buffer you against changes in local or regional economies.

- "Be true to yourself" by not accepting work that you don't feel good about. This of course must be balanced against personal commitments and needs, but when possible you should view consulting as the opportunity to pick and choose among projects based on such factors without being forced into accepting ones with which you aren't comfortable.

Like most of us in the computer industry, employees as well as consultants, even a consultant with a world-class reputation such as Mr. Date, have felt the economic bite of the past three or four years. As he recalls, "My specialty is education, and education is one of the first things to be cut in a recession." His public classes, those that are widely advertised and that anyone can attend, are "way, way down—less so in Europe, but very much so in the United States." Fortunately, his private course business (single-client requests, which usually are taught at a client site) is still adequately in demand.

Likewise, book sales are way down, basically for the same reason. As Mr. Date says, though (and this is seconded by this author),

> I feel bound to add that I feel short-changing education is very shortsighted, and some clients are smart enough to realize this. If you think education is expensive, consider the alternative. So...even in times of recession, you should be able to find a market for your services. It just might be more difficult, that's all.

When asked to give advice to consultants in their quest for success (and Mr. Date cautions that each consultant should have a personal definition of "success," whether it be money-motivated, recognition-oriented, barely squeaking by while still being independent, or something else), he includes:

- A consultant *must* want to be independent, because of all the ups and downs that come with the business.
- Be honest.
- Behave ethically and with integrity.
- Pay attention to detail.
- Be efficient and keep good records.
- Be humble—*don't* be arrogant—and be willing to say you don't know when you really don't know.
- Don't be greedy; overcharging for work leads to overly high expectations, and if you don't deliver, the word will soon get around.
- Have an in-depth knowledge of your chosen field, and keep current (or, preferably, *set the trend yourself*).
- Pay attention to communications skills, both verbal and written: even if you won't formally be teaching seminars and classes, you will find yourself making numerous presen-

tations, many in the course of business development or presenting findings.

- Be willing to work hard.
- Be willing to work long hours.
- Be willing to work unusual hours.
- Be willing to travel.
- Drive and tenacity are essential.
- Make sure you and all others concerned understand the implications of your activities on personal relationships; things like the effects of travel, strange hours, etc. have their impacts on everyone, including young children. A support system and stable base at home are highly desirable!
- Exercise self-discipline; if possible, have a home office dedicated to work activities, and watch out for distractions; be able to set and meet deadlines; be organized (plan ahead, but don't be event-driven); and be flexible (despite the previous point, always be ready to switch to Plan B, as we discussed in the first chapter).
- Take good care of yourself; despite the long hours, balance your work load; eat properly and take time for exercise; have other interests and make sure you can switch modes for mental refreshment; get good medical and disability insurance.
- Maintain a good list of contacts.
- Finally, hope that good luck comes your way.

As with Mr. Date, those of us in various areas of the computer field often owe our success to others, very often to those we have never met. Mr. Date says:

> Let me inject a tribute to Ted Codd. Many people in this field owe their careers and very livelihoods to the work that Ted Codd did in the late 1960s and early 1970s, and this is more true of me than perhaps it is of most people. I was very fortunate in meeting up with Ted so early in the game and becoming his disciple, as it were (some might say evangelist).

TRAINING AND SEMINARS

Financial planners, stockholders, realtors, and other professionals have long used seminars as a means to create and build a client base. Offered at little or no cost, these seminars have provided a means for professionals to demonstrate their skills in various areas of business. Additional sessions between the client and the professional can be scheduled to arrange a working relationship.

Seminars have also been a way for people in all businesses to learn the latest methods and technology in their areas in a short period of time. In the computer field programmers, analysts, and others have been able to stay current in a rapidly changing environment.

The explosive growth of microcomputer use has been accompanied by a growing pool of computer owners and operators with little or no previous experience with hardware or software. Many of these people are categorized as "technophobiacs," or those afraid of the new technology. With the mass media's increasing coverage of computer-related topics, however, the general population is being inundated with the idea that the information age revolution currently underway will rival the industrial revolution in changing our business and personal lives. The desire for computer literacy is and will continue to be a strong motivator for business people.

SEMINAR GOALS

Before you begin planning a series of seminar offerings, you should determine exactly what your goals are. Are you planning on using the seminars primarily as a revenue producer, with little expectation of gaining future clients from the attendees? Or are you using the sessions mainly as a marketing tool, with little substantial resulting revenue?

Your own objectives will determine your marketing and pricing strategies. A seminar meant to be a profit center will have to provide enough revenue to justify your efforts and costs of producing the class, while the objective of attracting future clients for individual consulting services can provide less earnings. Be sure that you have clear objectives in mind when planning the course contents, pricing, and marketing means.

TARGETING YOUR MARKET

The rule presented in the first section of this book applies here as in all other areas of your consulting business: choose a target market and concentrate your efforts there. You could conceivably conduct seminars in the following areas:

1. *General computer knowledge for both business and home applications.*   These seminars have been extremely successful and have proliferated in number. However, many universities, colleges, community or junior colleges, and technical schools have been adding classes of this type to meet the increased public demand. In order to compete, your seminar should be differentiated somehow from the multitude of offerings. Follow-on clients may be somewhat sparse unless you gear your advertising toward businesses rather than home and general use.

2. *Specific applications area.*   Many owners or managers of businesses studying computerization of their transaction processing and other business functions consider attending

an introductory-level computer seminar that specifically discusses their business area prior to purchasing a system. They often consider this a small investment in the front end of the computerization process. Many realtors, insurers, and other business operators become increasingly frustrated and confused as they journey among the many retail computer outlets in their region only to hear every salesperson recommend a different computer and software package as "the ultimate solution." A seminar conducted by an independent consultant, with no affiliation to any hardware or software brand or a specific computer store, might be seen as a forum for objective information.

3. *Intermediate topics.* These may include general computer knowledge for the experienced user (such as latest developments in certain applications software areas), computer language instruction (Visual Basic, C, etc.), or crash courses in microcomputers for the mainframe computer professional. One word of caution: Many attendees of intermediate-level courses often like to demonstrate how much they know, so you must thoroughly understand your topic. (This is also true of all seminars and classes you conduct, of course.)

4. *Teaching specific software packages.* A large seminar market in the personal computer field has been instruction in specific software bestsellers such as Excel, WordPerfect, Microsoft Access, and Lotus Notes. The virtues of word processing, spreadsheets, and database managers have been extolled in the computing and general media and people would like to learn how to use these systems. The novice user usually seems more comfortable learning from an "expert" rather than from self-paced instruction (including on-line interactive tutorials).

5. *Computers for children.* These sessions could cover elementary programming, graphics techniques, general principles, or educational software. Throughout the 1980s and into the 1990s, computers have become a fixture in schools at all levels, providing opportunities for consultants who specialize in educational systems.

6. *Specific aspects of computer technology.*   In Chap. 2, we discussed many of the "hot" areas of computer technology such as open systems and client/server computing. Seminars about one or more of these topics are likely to appeal to a growing number of both computer professionals and end users. Seminars in these areas also tend to command a much higher enrollment fee—often $1000 to $2000 for a 3- to 4-day session—than that for seminars in many of the previously mentioned areas. There are two cautions, though. First, the lagging economy of the early 1990s has caused something of a drain on attendance at these high-priced seminars due to corporate cutbacks (but that provides opportunities for consultants who can "undercut" the market). Second, many of these seminars may best be conducted in conjunction with a national or regional seminar company who can target a widespread market with direct mail and other advertising. We'll discuss these types of strategic seminar company relationships later in this chapter.

CO-SPONSORING A SEMINAR

Several options exist for planning, organizing, and conducting a seminar. Many consultants prefer to work alone; that is, the seminar is sponsored and conducted by the consultant and the firm's partners, if any exist. When you want to stress your independence and nonpartisanship to your potential audience this is normally the desired route.

When your business is in the early stages, however, communicating your competence to your potential clients may be difficult. Over time, a satisfied client base coupled with strategic advertising can establish your reputation. In the seminar business, however, you need credibility from the beginning. Why should someone pay $50 or more to hear you speak about or teach computer topics if you are an unknown entity? Endorsement from a local, well-established computer store, hardware vendor, or software publisher may be the key to making your first gains in this area. You should be careful not to become too dependent upon or intertwined with your co-sponsor. Your clients deserve the open mind and wide search range that an independent consultant provides, and you should do nothing to tarnish that reputation. However, the initial endorsement and sponsorship may be beneficial to the success of your business.

You will be sharing the revenues from the seminars, of course, but you will also be sharing the expenses and are likely to attract a larger attendance than if you attempted to start on your own. It is possible, therefore, that in addition to the increased potential clientele, your net income will also be greater than from a solo effort.

Why, then, should a retail computer store co-sponsor a seminar with you or any other consultant? After all, they are supplying the legitimacy to the overall seminar package. Presumably, their reputation as a solid community business will attract customers.

The answer is simple: Computer stores often do not have the expertise that you offer. Many store owners, managers, and sales personnel have a limited knowledge of computer hardware and software. They are primarily sales people with a lack of experience in such critical applications areas as real estate, insurance, and accounting. Some associates are extremely knowledgeable about computers, of course, but may not understand the business applications. You can provide them with a service, just as they provide you with one. A store conducting a seminar in conjunction with a computer consultant is less likely to be perceived by the public as conducting the seminar solely to sell attendees on a specific computer system. They are now providing an educational service to a target market and are one step closer to being a full-service store rather than just a retail outlet.

Additionally, many computer stores that are just beginning operations have limited resources. You are providing them with publicity and professional services just as they are performing the same function for you. By working closely with you, they are building their resources of local consultants who may bring customers to them.

Another advantage that you enjoy from working with a computer store is access to hardware and software, particularly if your seminar will involve hands-on experience (seminar techniques will be discussed later in the chapter). When your consulting operation is in the early stages of its life you are usually constrained by a somewhat limited budget. Even if you have a large capital pool from which to spend, making the substantial investment in hardware and software necessary to support hands-on seminars, or even those with demonstrations of different software packages, is a questionable action given the volatility of the computer industry. Why purchase hardware and software for demonstration purposes when it will probably be obsolete within 6 months? By then new stars of the computer world will have appeared. Computer stores usually can provide enough hardware and software to provide hands-on training for 10 to 20 attendees, increasing your maximum supportable audience.

As stated earlier, you must be careful not to become labeled a front person for your co-sponsor. One of the simplest ways to avoid this is to work with several co-sponsors. You may start with one computer store and conduct a seminar in general computer principles, and then you might hold the same session with a second computer store along with a real estate seminar. A third store could co-sponsor a BASIC language class and a medical system seminar.

You need to be honest with all parties in this relationship. The computer stores or other co-sponsors should be aware that you intend to maintain your independence when dealing with any clients on a postseminar basis. You should not be expected to favor your co-sponsor over other stores just because they worked with you on a particular seminar. For those clients you do recommend to a particular co-sponsor, you should not be relied on to recommend a high-priced system just to boost the store's revenues. Any co-sponsors expecting such treatment should be avoided.

SPONSORSHIP AND ENDORSEMENT

In addition to possibly working with a partisan store or vendor, you should strive for another form of sponsorship, especially for seminars covering specific applications. Few things will attract a computer-shy realtor to a real estate computer system seminar more than endorsement by the local board of realtors. Similarly, the state bar association or local chapter of the American Medical Association lends an image of reputability to your presentation. Just as with any seminar when you are starting out, gaining this sponsorship may be difficult. You do have an advantage over advertising a general computing seminar in the local newspaper and hoping for a large turnout. You can submit an agenda and proposed list of demonstrated software to the governing organization and sell the idea. You have the opportunity to hold a demonstration session to prove your competence and knowledge of their industry. You should stress to your contact on the committee or board that you are interested primarily in endorsement to stress to members of that profession that you can fill a valuable role for them. Monetary sponsorship is not your primary goal (but you should think twice before turning away any funds!).

You should initiate contact with the sponsoring organization (let's use the local board of realtors as an example) through a contact you have in that profession: the realtor who sold your last house, for example. If you don't know anyone personally in that profession, ask a business acquaintance or friend of a friend. Eventually you will be in contact with someone who serves on a subcommittee of the board of realtors and can connect you with the president of the board or someone else of influence. Some organizations have a computer resources or education subcommittee that would be your first official contact. Once you gain subcommittee endorsement your program may then be voted upon by the full board of directors.

After gaining board endorsement you should attempt to get publicity for the seminar in any local newsletters or other professional publications. For example, a real estate seminar may be publicized in the beginning advertising pages of the local multiple listing service.

Another potential co-sponsor is a "free university" or similar continuing-education program. These groups offer a wide range of classes and meetings to the general public in athletics, arts and crafts, health, business, and personal finance. Many also offer beginning computer-education classes. In exchange for their share of the registration fees these organizations offer wide distribution of class schedules (and thus a large potential audience at little or no advertising cost to you) and the umbrella of endorsement, which again can be valuable if you are just beginning your seminar programs. An advantage over working with a computer store is not having to worry about conflicts of interest, but you are less likely to attract a high-paying professional clientele from these classes.

WORKING WITH SEMINAR COMPANIES

So far, we've discussed working with computer retailers for "local type" seminars, as well as acquiring sponsorship for industry-specific sessions. There is a third type of strategic relationship which may be worth pursuing, especially if you plan to conduct seminars or training sessions on a national basis or in a high level subject such as open systems or distributed databases; that is, through working with a national seminar company.

We've all gotten their brochures in the mail, the glossies advertising technology-specific sessions or seminars conducted by internationally known experts (including those by our Consulting Success Profile studies from this book). For those of you readers who have aspirations of achieving national or international recognition in specific technology disciplines, these companies may be a valuable partner for reaching a wide market for these types of sessions.

Terms vary from company to company, and often are negotiated on a case-by-case basis to include flat fees, percentages of revenue, or various combinations of compensation alternatives. Some companies specialize in specific technology types (example: LANs and communications) while others sponsor sessions in a wide variety of subjects. Therefore, it always pays to shop around among companies for one or more that meets your needs for a specific seminar offering.

LOCATION

The location of your seminar can be critical to successfully attracting the desired target market. If you are conducting a seminar to discuss computer systems with members of the legal, medical, or similar profession, a session conducted in a hotel conference room is more likely to be perceived as a professional offering than one held in an unused elementary school classroom on Saturday morning. A class teaching children elementary programming, though, would be better suited to that classroom than a conference room. Be flexible in your locations. No two seminars are exactly the same and location should be carefully considered for each offering.

A third alternative is to hold the session in your office (assuming you have one). The major problem here is that space often limits you to a certain number of attendees (assuming you don't have an on-site educational facility). The advantage, of course, is lower fixed costs for room rental and miscellaneous services.

Seminars offered in conjunction with a computer store can be held at the store's educational facility if access to a wide range of computer equipment is needed. Otherwise, your impartiality will be enhanced by a conference room or other site offering.

When you decide to schedule a seminar in a hotel conference room, you should look for:

1. *Price.* Wide variation exists in the price of hotel conference services, sometimes depending on the time and date chosen. Be sure to shop around. Prices also vary among major cities.

2. *Services.* Are coffee, water, and other beverage services available? Will your room be configured as you desire?

3. *Advertising and publicity.* Does the conference have a publicity service listing their upcoming classes and seminars? If so, what charges, if any, are added to your bill?

4. *Rooms.* If your seminar will be lasting longer than 1 day and will be attracting clients from other cities, they will

need sleeping arrangements, preferably at the same hotel where the conference is located. You should obtain information about guaranteed reservations and group discounts, if any exist.

5. *Flexibility.* Can an alternative room be scheduled if attendance will be greater or less than anticipated? If so, what are the additional charges?

TIME AND DURATION

The time, season, and weekday can affect the success of your seminar. The session should be scheduled for a time when most members of your target market are likely to be free to attend. A seminar for retail merchants conducted between Thanksgiving and Christmas, regardless of the weekday and time, will likely be unsuccessful because of inconvenient scheduling. Saturday mornings may be convenient times for children's sessions, while evenings may be better for members of certain professions.

The duration of the seminar is also important. Some people like to "take a big gulp" and attend an all-day session (6 to 8 hours), while others prefer short meetings (1 or 2 hours) for several consecutive weeks. The best guideline here is to try one method, and if your attendance is low you may want to switch tactics for your next offering. Certain seminar topics are better suited to one form than the other, of course. A class teaching BASIC to beginning students is better suited to several hours per week for 8 to 10 weeks, while "Advanced Features of System X Database System" for current users may be better received as a 1-day session.

SCOPE OF MARKETING

When entering the seminar circuit, at least during the beginning of your offerings, you should limit your marketing efforts to local businesses and the public. Advertising costs and other expenses will be reasonable and you are at a stage when your main goal (aside from producing revenue, of course) is to build both your client base and your reputation. As you become an acknowledged expert in your specialty areas you can then begin targeting markets on a regional or national basis.

PRICE

The big question every consultant must ask is "How much should I charge?" The answer is an unshakable "It depends." A seminar dealing with general computer knowledge readily available in the mass media (if someone wants to look for it) should be less expensive than a narrowly targeted topic, such as property management applications.

You can pursue one of two different strategies in determining your price: *price penetration* or *price skimming*. Price penetration means setting your fee low enough to attract many customers; the high volume will offset the relatively low margin. Price skimming is when you set a high price, hoping to attract the select few able and willing to pay for your services and knowledge. Which strategy you choose is dependent on your target market *and* your available resources.

For example, you specialize in medical and dental applications and operate your consulting business alone. Therefore, each client who hires you should contribute enough revenue to cover your expenses and provide enough net income to compensate for your entire resources being concentrated on his or her project. In other words, you need to make every dollar count. Assuming that you want to attract new clients through a medical system seminar, you should probably pursue a price-skimming strategy because doctors can be perceived as willing to pay more for your services than grade school children attending an elementary programming class. While you could offer a relatively low-cost seminar with follow-on consulting services priced at $60 per hour, you might then be perceived as baiting your clients with a low-cost enticement, rather than as a professional consultant—not exactly the reputation you hope to convey.

A class discussing general computer knowledge, however, would probably not be too successful with a price-skimming strategy. Many of the attendees who later become clients will be looking for simple computer systems or general advice. These services will require relatively little of your time and resources while still producing enough revenue to make the effort spent with the client worthwhile. As mentioned earlier, general computer knowledge is available through many sources, so a high price tag is not likely to attract a large audience; you are just throwing away potential revenue.

These pricing strategies also apply to other aspects of your practice; you can calculate an hourly rate (Chap. 5) and analyze whether your market can support this price (Chap. 4), but the skim-versus-penetrate strategy pervades your overall business and marketing goals.

You should also offer group discounts for several people from the same office, family, or organization enrolling at the same time. This is likely to increase attendance. Early registration discounts, such as a $100 seminar being reduced to $90 if registration is received prior to 1 week before the seminar, encourage people to commit themselves to attending. If a potential attendee hasn't paid and the seminar day brings 2 feet of snow (or 85° temperatures and bright sunshine) your class may fall victim to environmental factors. Once someone has already paid a fee of $125, however, the snow suddenly becomes surmountable and the sunshine less attractive than if the fee had not been committed.

BREAK-EVEN ANALYSIS

Each seminar arrangement should be preceded by a break-even analysis. You should know how many attendees are necessary for you to meet all of your costs. The concept we introduced in Chap. 5 of variable and fixed costs will be reexamined.

Assume that you plan a seminar to introduce local dentists and physicians to the medical office billing systems commercially available. You will be conducting the seminar by yourself at a local hotel's conference room. Based on your research and past seminar experience, you arrive at the following revenue and cost figures:

Fixed costs	
Conference room rental (20–30 attendees)	$150
Coffee/water service	25
Newspaper advertising	300
Direct mail advertising (300 mailings)	
Postage (32 cents each)	96
Letter photocopies (5 cents each)	15
Envelopes	3
Total fixed costs	$589
Contribution margin per attendee	
Seminar price	$75
Less: Handout materials	
(40 pages per person, 5 cents per copy)	2
Total margin	$73

The following assumptions have been made here:

1. The attendees must preregister; no at-the-door registration will be allowed. Therefore, the exact number of handout packages can be printed. If preregistration were not required, a handout reserve for last-minute registrants would be included under fixed costs.

2. One price is applicable to everyone; if multiple-pricing strategies were used, an average price per attendee must be estimated and used in your calculations.

3. No calculations are made for future revenue from registrants who become clients; the seminar will be viewed as a stand-alone profit center.

Based on the previous figures, 8.06 people must attend for you to break even and cover all fixed costs ($589 divided by $73 net earnings per registrant). You would round this to have your break-even (or near-break-even) registration at eight people.

What do you do if registration is not sufficient to meet your fixed costs? Some costs may be recoverable, such as room rental (possibly after subtracting a small charge). Advertising costs, however, cannot be recovered and you will be faced with a loss whether or not you cancel the seminar.

Even though your time involved in seminar preparation may be substantial, no allowance for that cost has been included, since you don't pay yourself. However, the opportunity cost (Chap. 5) should be considered in your decision making; if you spend 50 hours preparing a seminar that does not have enough registrants and therefore is canceled, those 50 hours could have been spent on software development, magazine article writing, or some other revenue-producing activity. Naturally, the number of preparation hours will depend on whether this is the first time you have developed this seminar. If you are using a seminar package that you have presented before, most of your time will be spent on revision and updating, substantially reducing the preparation time over that of initial development. When considering opportunity cost, determine if your *projected* attendance will cover both the actual fixed costs and the revenue that likely (not wishfully) could be otherwise earned.

ADVERTISING

There are many ways to advertise a seminar. The key to choosing your method is what will attract your target market. A real estate systems seminar should be advertised in the real estate section of your local Sunday newspaper, while a general computer information course would be out of place in the same location. You should consider the following media:

1. *Newspaper.* This is the preferred choice for most locally marketed seminars. The business section of the Sunday newspaper is excellent for business applications and other sections may be used for narrowly targeted applications (for example, the sports section for "Use of Computers in Coaching"). Many newspapers also have free columns such as calendars of upcoming business events, local business

news, or general-interest classes open to the public. Check your local newspapers to see if they contain similar features and contact the appropriate editor.

2. *Direct mail.* You should only use direct mail for a narrowly defined target market, such as local accountants. Mailing lists can often be obtained from the professional organizations discussed earlier; if not, the *Yellow Pages* provides a convenient reference to your market. Letters should be professionally written on your letterhead and contain pertinent information regarding price, date, time, location, and most importantly, how the addressee will benefit from attending.

3. *Professional journals.* For specific applications seminars, especially those endorsed by a professional organization, you may be able to promote your session in the local or regional (or even national) newsletter or journal publication. If your seminar carries the endorsement of the local board of realtors, for example, your notice should state that fact, as it is a *strong* selling point.

4. *Speaking engagements.* Organizations often have periodic breakfasts, brunches, or other social-business events. Speakers are sometimes desired for these occasions. While you probably won't earn much revenue, if any, from these speaking engagements, a well-delivered and appropriate speech may promote your seminar (and your firm) to your audience more than all other advertising combined. You should check with the endorsing organization and watch the appropriate events calendar in your newspapers to learn which events frequently occur.

5. *The Internet.* Developing a "training and seminars" home page for your consulting business, with appropriate links from other sources, is a form of advertising that you should also consider.

Timing is a critical factor in your advertising. An initial newspaper advertisement appearing 3 days before a seminar will be of limited use in attracting clientele who must preplan a busy schedule. Generally, initial newspaper advertising should appear 3 weeks to 1 month before your seminar date, with following announcements at periodic intervals continuing until the seminar. If direct mail is used the letters should also arrive with 3 to 4 weeks of lead time. The letter will coincide with the newspaper advertising and the lead time will give busy managers time to read the letter.

PREPARATION

Few events are as embarrassing as a presentation where everything goes wrong, especially when presented to an audience of clients offering potentially lucrative business. All spoken material should be rehearsed and criticized by a sample audience. *Do not* read your material, but don't expect to speak from memory during the entire session. You should be comfortable enough with your subject to use simple note cards or an outline.

All software demonstrations should be tested for correct operation and results. If sample data files are needed they should be created before the actual seminar. You may want to demonstrate data-entering techniques of several software packages, but don't force your audience to watch while you enter large amounts of data.

You should also verify arrangements with your seminar location contact (such as hotel conference staff) several days prior to your seminar. It is difficult to convince an audience of your competence when you and they are standing outside a locked conference room door waiting for the janitor to bring the key.

SUPPLIES

You should arrive early on the seminar day to configure all hardware and software and make at least one more trial run of any demonstrations. You should also ensure that beverages (coffee, tea, water), condiments (sugar, artificial sweetener), and supplies (glasses, cups, saucers, spoons, stirrers) are set up by the hotel staff or whomever has that responsibility. For a small group (20 or less) doughnuts or sweet rolls may be offered for a morning session, or snacks (nuts, coffee cake) for an evening class.

Name cards (large index cards bent in half work nicely) should be supplied for all attendees along with markers. Extra pens, pencils, and paper can be furnished. Receipts for the amount paid should be already prepared for prepaid attendees and created for same-day audience members.

All visual aids should be set up before any clients arrive. This allows time for you to meet informally with your audience. Visual aids could include a slide projector, chalkboard (don't forget chalk!), easel, and flipcharts, or overhead projector. If possible, you might even conduct your seminar using multimedia techniques: a big-screen projector for computer demonstrations, audio and video material, and so on. Be careful, though, not to overdo the presentation aspects of your session at the expense of your material.

A reference material packet should be given to each member of the audience; it should contain (1) an outline, (2) appropriate textual material, (3) copies of important slides or other visual aids, (4) references for further information, (5) a critique sheet to provide you with feedback, (6) a form for the attendee to fill in name, business, address, phone number, and current computer equipment for you to arrange possible follow-on services, and (7) your business card clipped to the front.

LECTURE TECHNIQUES

One short section of this book cannot teach you how to speak to an audience, but you should be aware of several important points.

1. *Give your audience what it wants.*   At the beginning of the presentation goals should be established to provide you with guidelines. By asking the audience what they expect to learn from the seminar, you are establishing an interactive dialogue between you and them and at the same time narrowing your range of topics. If you have prepared a general real estate seminar equally covering finance, investment, and property management but the audience appears to be heavily interested in property management to the exclusion of the other two topics, you may be able to adjust the emphasis of your topics more in the direction of property management subjects.

2. *Use appropriate levels of discussion.* A seminar on computer applications for legal offices, with an audience full of legal professionals, will be taught at a different level than one discussing distributed database architectural issues with a group of computer professionals. In some cases, "computerese" is the appropriate language of choice for your audience; in other situations you should focus primarily on the business benefits of technology rather than the internals and the details themselves. It's important to understand your audience and set your discussion level appropriately.

3. *Encourage questions and interaction.* When your audience feels comfortable enough to ask many questions and propose scenarios, you are able to communicate more easily than if you speak nonstop for several hours on end. By the type of questions asked you will be able to determine how much of your material is being successfully transmitted to the audience.

4. *Offer hands-on experience where possible.* It will probably be difficult to provide hands-on activity for an audience of 45 people because of the probable imbalance of your computer hardware and software resources and the number of clients. If you have approximately the same amount of resources and attendees, you should allow them to use several software packages and proceed through several sample problems.

Many audience members may be touching a computer for the first time. Under close supervision and by proceeding slowly they can quickly gain confidence in their ability to operate a computer. For larger audiences that will be using machines, you should have several assistants to provide close supervision over a portion of the group. By dividing up the supervisory work you can proceed more quickly than if you must resolve all questions and problems that arise.

5. *Use visual aids.* Even if hands-on experience will not be provided, you can rent or borrow a machine that projects your terminal image on a large screen. This will allow the audience to see exactly what happens during the operation of various software packages. Other visual aids should be used, including appropriate graphs, charts, and outlines.

FOLLOWING UP CLIENT LEADS

The response forms included in the reference material package provide you with a convenient means to build your prospective client database. During any session breaks and after the seminar is concluded, several strong leads may arise from your conversation with attendees. After any services are provided for these clients, you can contact other audience members. Inquire about their current business operations; determine if they might eventually use your services. If not, you may still have created a valuable reference, provided they enjoyed and learned from the seminar. They might recommend your consulting firm to friends or others in the same business.

SUMMARY

Seminars can provide you with a valuable means of building your client base. In addition, a substantial portion of your consulting revenue can be generated from these seminars. Once you have defined your target market, you can proceed alone or join efforts with local computer businesses or other establishments. The advertising media, location, time, day, and price must be chosen with your target market in mind.

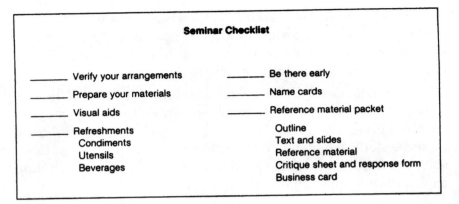

FIGURE 8-1   Seminar checklist.

You should be adequately prepared for the seminar through rehearsal and by verifying all arrangements (see Fig. 8-1). The seminar session itself should use demonstrations and visual aids as appropriate to increase your audience's understanding of the presented topics.

CHAPTER

NINE

COMPUTING AND TECHNOLOGY ENVIRONMENTS

There is a saying that all computer consultants should memorize and live by in the course of their professional work: "the right environment for the job." While this should be a statement of the obvious, it does bear some discussion, which we will provide in this chapter.

At one time, as discussed in previous editions of this book, there was a rather clear demarcation among computing environments and the types of applications likely to be hosted on each—and, therefore, the types of services you might consider offering for one or more of these platforms. Overwhelmingly, corporate data processing and "real" applications would be found on a mainframe platform, and almost always on an IBM mainframe; departmental, mid-range applications would be found on a DEC VAX or an IBM AS/400; and personal productivity applications, as well as those geared toward running small businesses (i.e., those with less than $2 to $3 million in annual revenues) would be found on standalone PCs or PC-LAN environments. You would also find specialized applications such as computer-aided design (CAD) running on high-powered workstations, other types of specialized applications requiring intensive computing power running on supercomputers, and so on.

At present, though, we have the following IT landscape as a backdrop for our discussion in this chapter:

- After a decade or so of increasing functionality and better understanding of its capabilities (and limitations), client/server computing is increasingly being used for applications that formerly would have been deployed on the corporate mainframe.

- The Internet has brought about a convergence of traditional computing functionality with other forms of communications (cable, broadcast TV, telephony, etc.), bringing forth environments that defy all previous technology classification categories.

- "Client/server computing" is no longer a set of PCs or workstation computers connected to a single server and making simple database requests; the advent of middleware, multitier computing architectures, complex distributed transaction models, etc., has changed the PC from an easy entry point for beginning consultants to an element in highly complicated environments that require just as much systems and networking expertise as more traditional platforms such as mainframes.

In this context, let's take a brief look at the computing environment landscape, circa 1997, and what it means to your consulting career.

MAINFRAMES

If you were in the computing profession in the late 1980s and early 1990s, you no doubt heard, over and over, that "the mainframe is dead." It would be supplanted by "much less expensive, much more flexible" LAN-based computing with PCs as clients and higher-powered PCs as servers. And, as a result, a frenzy of migration activity came out of nowhere as organizations raced to move applications from these "antiquated" and expensive mainframe computers into "the modern era."

So now we jump ahead to 1997. IBM has come roaring back from its well-publicized market slips, mainframe sales are surging ahead, mainframe *technology* can hardly be considered stagnant or antiquated, and many companies, prompted largely by the Year 2000 problem (Chap. 2), are engaged in a "mainframe or client/server" debate (again!) regarding their core applications.

As a computer consultant, you can only sit back and shake your head at the turnaround—and turnaround again—of the conventional wisdom concerning the mainframe and its place in corporate computing. But at the same time, a mainframe-literate consultant now has a large number of opportunities to provide consulting services. As discussed in Chap. 2, we have

- "Ordinary" application development—developing or maintaining COBOL applications on mainframe platforms, for example
- Mainframe-oriented integration—using a product such as IBM's MQSeries to develop message-enabled environments that integrate different platforms (for example, two different mainframe applications, or one application hosted on an AS/400 and another on a mainframe)
- Migration and transition services
- Year 2000–related services, including in-place patching and repair of applications that will "break" because of date-related problems

The list goes on and on.

Should a consultant whose background is PCs and LANs consider it a necessity to learn mainframe technology? Not necessarily, given the wide range of opportunities in the areas with which he or she is already familiar (discussed later in this chapter). At the same time, a consultant who wishes to concentrate on large corporate (that is, *Fortune* 2000–sized) clients *and* who wishes to do something other than develop departmental-scale applications (for example, specialize in data warehousing) will no doubt come across mainframe technology at some point. At the very least, a working *familiarity* with appropriate applications and/or core technologies (for example, DB2/MVS for a data warehousing consultant) should be considered part of your core knowledge, even if you don't plan on ever doing actual hands-on work on the mainframe; interfacing with mainframe components requires an understanding of what's happening there.

MINICOMPUTERS AND MID-RANGE SYSTEMS

Yes, minicomputers still exist, despite the well-publicized woes of Digital Equipment Corporation, Data General, and the many other formerly high-flying companies of the early and mid-1980s. For example, there are still a large number of applications hosted on Digital VAX computers. You are particularly likely to find these types of environments in the pharmaceutical industry.

You could build an entire consulting specialty around "Year 2000 work in VAX/VMS environments" or a similar offering targeting users of IBM's AS/400 systems. In any event, you are still likely to run into these mid-range systems at larger clients, and just as with mainframes, it's valuable to at least have an understanding of the capabilities—and corresponding opportunities—within these environments.

PC-LAN COMPUTING

The phrase "PC-LAN computing" encompasses an extremely broad range of alternative computing environments, but there are some common characteristics across the spectrum that are important to consultants.

First, the personal computer as a standalone platform with little or no interface to other computers has all but disappeared. The ease with which networked environments can be created and the rapid spiral downward in the cost of PC-based technology have made LAN-based environments a practical, sensible alternative for even small, family-owned businesses (if you specialize in that client base).

Accompanying this connectivity and interoperability, however, are complications that a consultant needs to recognize. For example, when I began consulting in the early 1980s, I specialized in small-scale dBASE III and dBASE III+ environments. Though I developed and deployed applications for both standalone and networked environments, those with networking had very primitive setups as compared to today's capabilities. As a result, I had to worry about issues that I wouldn't have to consider if I were developing similar applications today (such as, synchronizing users), but at the same time, I had the advantage of not having numerous configuration alternatives to worry about [setting up an Open Database Connectivity (ODBC) driver, network drive mappings, dynamic link libraries (DLLs) and incompatibilities, etc.].

The point is that as technology has changed over time, the PC-LAN environment of 1987 bears little resemblance to its descendant, circa 1997—and its further descendant in 2007 will look nothing like today's environment. True, an 80386-based PC running MS-DOS is the ancestor of a Pentium-based PC running Windows 95, but when the big picture is considered in terms of types of applications and how they're developed, overall computing architecture, and many other factors, it is imperative that any consultant be tuned into the state of the art and, more important, what it means to his or her client base.

THE INTERNET

No matter what areas you choose to emphasize, there is no escaping the Internet. From browser-based "thin client" applications on a client's intranet to the use of Internet technologies to enable cross-enterprise electronic commerce, *every* consultant should rethink his or her service offerings, specialties, marketing and advertising strategies and tactics—indeed, every aspect of his or her consulting career—in the context of what has occurred in the past few years with respect to the Internet.

As we discussed in Chap. 2, being an Internet consultant involves far more than developing Web sites for corporate clients; it requires that you consider the impact of technology, architecture, interfaces, and *opportunities* in everything you do.

Though there is no way to know with certainty, it is highly likely that over the next three to five years there will be far more change in the Internet world and the areas of computing it touches than in, say, mainframes. That is, a newly developed mainframe application, circa 2000–2003, will look *fairly* similar to one developed today, though there may be more capabilities, even better technology, and so on. An Internet-oriented application developed at the same time, however—well, who knows? Will there still be a browser interface? What role will intelligent agents play in the overall architecture? What aspects of mobile computing technology and personal digital assistant (PDA) technology will be part of "ordinary" Internet models?

SUMMARY

Change, change, change. When I look back at CP/M machines, early MS-DOS PCs, programming languages and environments seldom used today—all from a period barely 15 years ago—it's with a mixture of excitement at how far computing has come during that time and a sense of weariness at the effort required to keep up with these environmental changes and their impact on one's consulting career. In Chap. 12, we'll discuss ways to stay on top of these changes, but to conclude our discussion for this chapter, it's important that you understand that "the right environment for the job" will continue to be a watchword of consulting.

WRITING AND CONSULTING[1]

There is a common theme among the "how to become recognized" aspects of marketing one's abilities: Write books, articles, and papers. In this chapter we'll discuss the different channels for your writing, and focus on which are most appropriate for different types of consultants—the goal being synergy among your consulting activities.

WHAT SHOULD YOU WRITE?

There are several primary channels through which you can pursue professional writing in the context of your consulting practice. Within each of those channels there are further breakdowns with respect to subject matter, audience, type of writing, and other categories; these are discussed in more detail later in the chapter. As we go through these various channels, keep in mind your own particular consulting goals and try to imagine how you can use one or more of these outlets in your own business activities.

MAGAZINE ARTICLES

The "simplest" but by no means the easiest area in which to publish your writing is computer-related magazines such as *Byte*, *Datamation*, *PC World*, or similar publications. Alternatively, some subject matter may be applicable to general business or other publications such as in-flight airline magazines.

By "simple" we mean that magazine articles have far less restrictive guidelines and rules than technical papers (discussed next), yet also are far more compact, and take less time to write, than books. There is a large variety of categories from which you can draw ideas for magazine articles you can write on computer-related subjects, including:

1. *New products.*   Most computer periodicals publish articles about new hardware, software, peripheral, and support products. As new computers, printers, DBMS software, spreadsheet programs, LANs, and other products appear on the market, a corresponding need arises for articles about these products. If, say, a new product is coming to market and you want to be "the first consultant on your block" to specialize in its use, writing about it is a good way to gain recognition.

2. *Existing products.*   Even products that have been on the market for a while have the potential for appearance in your articles. An article about advanced features of a given product, programming techniques, or other "tips" is likely to be of interest to periodicals and their readers. The same is true for writing about existing products within your consulting specialties as with new products.

3. *Technologies and trends.*   Many computer periodicals also publish articles about "new" (to the general computing public) technologies, the effects of those technologies on current and future products, and related trends. If your forte is object-oriented databases, CASE, networks, open systems, or similar topics, you might query a publisher about an article on one of these or other subjects.

Unlike the orientation of technical papers (discussed in the next section), articles about technologies and trends intended for "general" computer publications tend to be of a tutorial nature. That is, an article about latest trends in distributed databases should assume an explanatory tone rather than be of an academic, "proof-intensive" nature. Later in this chapter we'll talk more about the respective types of writing most applicable to various careers; for those who feel more comfortable targeting general publications rather than technical journals, the writing style and subject matter should fit the medium and audience.

4. *Regular columns.*   Many successful writers have grown from writing occasional articles to being featured in regular (weekly, bi-weekly, monthly, or of some other frequency) columns in publications. If you have a particular area of consulting expertise, such as UNIX, open systems, or database products, you might try to follow a string of successful articles with a request for a regular column on your area of specialization. If you can find a good match between a publication's needs and your knowledge and experience, you may be able to arrange for a regular column.

TECHNICAL PAPERS

Many computer professionals, particularly those working in research environments with leading-edge technologies or in academic climates, elect to write technical papers for journals, conference proceedings, or other "intellectual" outlets. Unlike magazine articles, which tend to have a "free format" (that is, the content, style, and design are dictated primarily by commercial concerns), technical papers—even those of nearly identical subject matter to cousin magazine articles—are far more restrictive in their presentation. For example, the sample tutorial article about distributed database trends discussed in the previous section would take on a far different appearance if it were targeted for a technical journal rather than a general computing magazine. First, there would be an automatic assumption that the reading audience would be almost exclusively computer professionals (or at least students in a computer-oriented curriculum) rather than a mix of end users and computer generalists such as PC software developers with little or no distributed database exposure. Correspondingly, a magazine tutorial would likely "regress" further into discussions of applicable database and distribution fundamentals *within the body of the article itself* as opposed to a technical paper, which usually has an introductory paragraph or two with citations to previously published papers, books, or other sources; it is left up to the reader whether he or she feels the background information is worth researching.

Second, technical papers usually are governed by various restrictions with respect to the content, the proof of concepts, and other characteristics. The author of a magazine article on integrated CASE environments may be able to "free-format daydream" about the optimal, ultimate instantiation of such a platform, while a technical paper would usually be required to cite various research projects at universities and companies in this area as sources of the technical information. The journals themselves often have various established policies that govern the format, content, and required background research for papers published in their publications.

A magazine article might, for the sake of uniqueness, be written with a humorous flare or in some other manner that makes it stand out from its likely competitors in other periodicals. It is unlikely, however, that such a style would be applicable to technical papers.

With respect to your consulting practice, technical papers may serve the same purpose as magazine article writing: achieving name recognition among potential clients.

BOOKS

Many computer-related subjects—those applicable to general publications as well as technical journal subjects—can be expanded to book length. Writing a book might appear to be an intimidating prospect; though it is a time-consuming process, it is well within the capabilities of most well-disciplined computer professionals. In fact, the process of book writing is very similar to developing computer code for medium to large-scale systems.

Computer books can assume the characteristics of magazine articles; that is, they may be tutorial in nature, product-oriented, or discuss trends or other subjects of interest to computer professionals. Alternatively, they may appear to be book-length variations of technical papers, flush with formulas, proofs, and other characteristics of academic writing.

We'll talk later about choosing subject matter for computer books; in the meantime, keep in mind that there are many publishers in the computer book field, and the ongoing rapid changes in computer technology create a constant need for books about new products, technologies, and other subjects.

HOW DOES THE SUBJECT MATTER RELATE TO MY CONSULTING PRACTICE?

Getting any article or book published can benefit your career in the computer field tremendously. That benefit, however, can be maximized by careful planning that matches the subject matter to the current or future goals of your consulting practice.

If, for example, your current area of specialization is applications for computerized investment analysis, an article, paper, or book with a financial orientation provides a highly beneficial coupling with your practice, more so than, for example, a textbook about compiler theory. This is not to denigrate the latter possibility, however; your career goals might include teaching part-time, or eventually full-time, at a leading university; the textbook can provide a tremendous boost to achieving that particular goal. Regardless of how close a match there is between your consulting activities and the subject matter about which you write, remember that you still get paid for writing!

PUBLICATIONS MEDIA

Let's take a closer look at the different outlets for your writing that I mentioned in the previous section. Computer magazines and periodicals can be divided into several categories, each with its own distinctive potential for publishing your writing, including:

1. *General.*   This category includes such staples as *Computerworld, Datamation,* and *Systems Integration.* You

might target an advanced-level article that discusses, for example, how industrial companies are easing their way into using object-oriented technologies, to these types of publications.

2. *PC-oriented.*   This category contains publications that straddle the line between end users and computer professionals, given the preponderance of PC usage among non-computer types. Product-oriented articles, technology tutorials, and similar articles are appropriate to submit to these kinds of periodicals.

3. *Product-specific.*   This category may be viewed as a subset of either of the first two categories, and primarily the PC-oriented periodicals. Most of the popular computer systems have had or still have publications dedicated to their products. Articles that contain usage tips and similar product-specific subjects might be targeted to these publications, such as *MacWorld*.

4. *Technology-specific.*   Many of the leading technologies, such as database systems and communications, have periodicals dedicated to them. For example, *DBMS* and *Database Programming and Design* are two magazines that deal primarily with database issues. An article about database performance tuning would be applicable to either of these publications.

5. *Company-specific.*   The product-oriented category deals primarily with PC-level products. Large companies with many users, such as Digital Equipment Corporation, have third-party magazines dedicated to issues relating to the company and its products. An article that deals specifically with a company's hardware or software would be appropriate for such a publication.

As we mentioned earlier in this chapter, you might also find publishing success through periodicals outside the scope of the computer field. General business magazines, airline magazines, personal finance magazines, and other categories of publications often publish technical articles. Be aware, though, that articles likely to interest one of these types of publications will be more general in nature (example: a survey of laptop computers, or how open systems will affect hardware purchase decisions) rather than articles about technical trends in object-oriented languages.

Correspondingly, technical journals usually are published by and managed through a sponsoring organization, such as the Association for Computing Machinery (ACM), the Institute of Electrical and Electronic Engineers (IEEE), or a similar group. Within each organization, there are usually several journals, each dedicated to a different technology or discipline, plus a "flagship" journal. Technical papers may be oriented to an applicable journal.

An interesting thing to note is that the lead time for journal publication of a paper can often be several years, given the various editorial policies of technical reviews and other actions. It is not uncommon to see a paper published that was written two or three years prior to the publication date, and that has been superseded by further advances in a particular technology or discipline.

Correspondingly, book publishers can also be divided into several different categories, each applicable to a different type of writing. Some emphasize textbooks, while others emphasize trade books intended for book store sale. Some specialize in specific technologies or categories of products (many leading software firms have their own publishing arms or have alliances with other publishers), while others decide to emphasize either current or future computer technologies, but not both. It pays to check the publication policy of various publishers before submitting proposals (discussed next).

PROPOSALS, QUERY LETTERS, AND OUTLINES

Most books about professional writing provide detailed guidance on the process of developing a query letter (a form of business letter), a proposal, and an outline. For the sake of space, we'll summarize some of the major points with respect to this process and provide an example of a query letter and proposal that led to a published book. For further information and examples, you might want to consult a general book about writing.

Proposals for computer books and articles, regardless of how technical the subject matter is, should always be oriented to the *commercial* applicability of the subject matter. That is, will a book about your subject be a success in the marketplace? Will the title of your article on the cover of a magazine sell copies?

A proposal should contain, at a minimum:

1. The title of your article or book, along with a brief summary of the contents.
2. Why this article or book is needed in the marketplace.
3. Who your target audience is (programmers, analysts, managers, etc.).
4. (More applicable for books) why your book will be a success.
5. Your qualifications for writing the book or article, such as extensive experience with the product or technology about which you are writing. More importantly, if you can state it, why you are *the* person who should write this book.
6. Competition, such as other books, articles in other magazines, etc., and how your writing is different *and better* than any earlier writing on the subject matter.

A *general* rule of thumb, but one that should be examined case-by-case, is that book proposals should be accompanied by an outline, while article proposals may be accompanied by an outline if the article is not written yet, or by the article itself if completed. The best policy is to verify the submission policy of each publisher, which will also let you know if simultaneous submissions (with another publisher) are acceptable as well as give you other information.

In the next section is the query letter I wrote back in 1983 for the First Edition of this book. Since that time, I've written well over 200 query letters and proposals. Even with 22 books completed or under contract, that's about a 10 percent success rate. Be patient, and be persistent!

A SAMPLE QUERY LETTER

Figure 10-1 illustrates a sample query letter.

SUMMARY

Look again at Chris Date's consulting success profile at the end of Chap. 7 and his reference to teaching, writing, and consulting, all feeding off one another. Chapter 7 discussed some of the many subjects dealing with computer system

```
                              Alan R. Simon
                              8225 Cutter Terrace
                              Colorado Springs, CO 80918
                              (303) 594-9535
                              September 3, 1983


McGraw-Hill Book Company
Attn: Mr. Tyler G. Hicks
Editor in Chief
Computing and Software
1221 Avenue of the Americas
New York, NY 10020


Dear Mr. Hicks:

   Attached is an outline for a proposed book titled How to Be a
Successful Computer Consultant. I am sending you this outline for
publication consideration by McGraw-Hill Book Company.

   I am founding partner of Computer Education and Consulting, a
Colorado Springs, Colorado, computer consulting firm. Our firm is
involved in a variety of activities, including seminar training for
both beginning and advanced users, custom software development, and
general consulting services. I formed this organization as a sole
proprietorship and recently added three partners to the firm. While
organizing Computer Education and Consulting, I spent many months
researching small business management, tax considerations, marketing
strategies and seminar techniques. Because there was no one book
```

FIGURE 10-1   Sample query letter.

dealing specifically with computer-related consulting, I relied on general consulting material and small business management references, coupled with my experience in the computer field.

The explosive growth of computer use in businesses and homes is well documented. The advent of the "personal computer age" has, in addition to providing computer owners with powerful tools to manage their information and environments, afforded an outstanding opportunity to provide computer-related services to others. "Computer literacy" has become a common industry buzzword. Many personal computer owners have a unique chance to find a niche in this growing field developing custom programs, conducting educational services, and writing articles for the many computer magazines being published. How to Be a Successful Computer Consultant conveys pertinent and timely information in several areas: starting and organizing a consulting operation, managing a growing firm, and an in-depth look at computer services.

Because most personal computer owners already have full-time jobs that may not even be related to the computer field, a theme I intend to emphasize throughout the book is the part-time operation of a consulting firm. Computer Education and Consulting was started while I was a full-time U.S. Air Force officer and all four partners are still USAF computer officers. I am, therefore, extremely familiar with the problems, such as conflict-of-interest situations, that may surface when organizing a business while still employed by another company. However, the advantage of having job security while embarking on a new venture often outweighs these problems.

In addition to my experience in the consulting field and as an Air Force computer officer, I have been employed as a computer programmer, systems analyst, and consultant by the Arizona attorney general's office and the University of Arizona. I taught computer classes at the University of Arizona during graduate school and currently teach computer classes for the Chapman College (California) residence education center in Colorado Springs. I have both bachelor's and master's degrees in College of Business computer programs from Arizona State University and the University of Arizona.

I hope I have conveyed the importance of a book such as How to Be a Successful Computer Consultant to both the potential readers and McGraw-Hill Book Company. I feel that a large, untapped market exists for this book and that many people would be able to benefit from this information being provided in one concise location. A sample chapter is available upon request. Thank you for your consideration of my submission, and I look forward to hearing from you.

Sincerely,

Alan R. Simon

FIGURE 10-1   (*Continued*)

development; Chap. 8 discussed the basics of training and seminars. In this chapter, we've taken a look at the business of writing.

Writing, like seminars, serves a dual purpose. In one sense, it can be a revenue source by itself—in some cases, a major revenue source. In nearly all cases, though, regardless of the commercial success of what you write, there are definite marketing advantages to your writing activity, primarily that of establishing your professional and technical credentials.

END NOTE

1. The information in this chapter is adapted from Alan R. Simon and Jordan S. Simon, *The Computer Professional's Guide to Effective Communications*, McGraw-Hill, New York, 1993, Chap. 10.

PART THREE

CONTINUING
CONCERNS

MANAGING OPERATIONS

During the early chapters of this book, we discussed many of the managerial and business topics that are important to you as the owner of a consulting firm. We dealt with these subjects from the viewpoint of beginning your practice: what decisions should be made to establish your company, build your client base, and define your product line.

We will now return to these topics, but address them as ongoing activities of an established firm. That is, once you have succeeded in building your practice from the ground up, how do you keep it growing?

We will discuss the importance of operational planning, accounting and tax-related activities, personnel management, insurance concerns, marketing, utilizing outside resources, and, if necessary, cutting back on unprofitable operations.

OPERATIONAL PLANNING

During the early stages of your consulting activities, you developed a business plan that discussed plans for your services, marketing activities, financial needs, and other subjects. As time passes, your business plan needs reviewing to ensure that it reflects the state of your firm's operations. Additionally, an annual *operations plan,* based on your business plan, should be developed to identify special opportunities, problems, financial and personnel needs, and anything else of concern over the coming year.

For example, your business plan projected earnings and break-even points several years into the future from the time it was written. Are those estimates still accurate? Is more or less outside capital actually required than had been estimated?

Additionally, new markets and opportunities that were unforeseen several years earlier may have evolved; these should be included as an integral part of your operational plans.

Your operations plan for the coming year should include the following sections:

1. *Products and services.*   Will any new products or services be added to your repertoire this year? Will any be removed because of unprofitability, changing markets, or other reasons? Will new markets be exploited for existing products and services, such as expanding from medical and dental applications to legal ones?

2. *Marketing.*   What is your projected advertising budget, and through what media? What public relations methods will be employed?

3. *Financial.*   What are the upcoming year's anticipated revenues, expenses, and net earnings? Is any additional capital needed from operations? If so, from what sources? Will cash flow be sufficient to cover existing and projected expenses? Do you plan to invest your firm's assets in spin-off businesses or other investment opportunities?

4. *Personnel.*   Do you plan to hire any employees this year? If so, will they work full-time or part-time? Will they be operational (writing software, conducting seminars) or support (secretarial, administrative)? Do you project using any outside accountants or attorneys or subcontracting any work to others?

5. *Information.*   What new areas of both business and the computer industry do you feel a need to learn more about? For example, if you wish to seek venture financing 18 months from now, you probably need to learn more about venture capital firms, what industries they are currently investing in, and the mechanisms of selling public stock. Similarly, if you foresee a

need to better understand new computer technology because you anticipate several major product releases, you might want to review the computer literature closely to learn about those new operating systems, hardware, or other products.

Your operations plan should serve as your short-term (one year or less) guideline to ensure efficient management of your practice, just as your business plan should meet your long-range strategic planning requirements. By consciously forcing yourself to appraise all aspects of your company at least once a year, hopefully you will be able to plan for a continually growing firm that isn't surprised by foreseeable problems or missed opportunities.

BOOKKEEPING AND ACCOUNTING

Not many topics strike as much fear in business people as bookkeeping and accounting. Words like "tedious," "difficult," "confusing," and similar adjectives tend to be in the forefront of thoughts.

Why, then, bother with maintaining a set of records? Of course, there's the obvious reason; you have a legal requirement to file tax returns, and the only way to obtain the necessary information is to keep accurate records of your income and expenditures. The more organized your records are the simpler it is for you or your accountant to complete your required federal and state tax forms.

There are two other very important reasons for maintaining accurate and informative records. First, prospective investors and lenders need to gauge the solvency of your business operations. An accurate accounting of your income and expenses, assets and liabilities, and cash flow provides an insightful picture of your financial situation. Well-organized accounting procedures also demonstrate your business prowess rather than portray you as a disorganized manager.

Additionally, your financial records help you effectively manage your operations by telling you if you have too much overhead cost, aren't earning enough from a particular service or product to make it worthwhile, or by identifying exceptional growth in another operations area. Pricing decisions can be based on recorded information. In short, it will be difficult to successfully run a business and almost impossible to make it grow without informative bookkeeping and accounting.

So, whether you view accounting as a necessary evil or as an invaluable management tool, we've established that it is required. In this section we'll look briefly at business bank accounts, discuss cash versus accrual accounting, and look at the difference between single- and double-entry financial ledgers. Then we'll look at how to automate your accounting as much as possible to alleviate some of the tedium and better organize your records.

BANK ACCOUNTS

Back in Chap. 3 we saw that among the tasks to do when forming a business was to open a business bank account. Again, this is important because you must establish your business as a financial entity separate from your personal finances, even though it may not be a different legal entity.

Accountant Bernard Kamoroff, in his book *Small-Time Operator,* lists several rules to follow regarding business bank accounts.[1]

1. *Keep your business finances separate from your personal ones.*   Business expenses should be paid by check from your business account to provide accurate documentation. Inevitably, some minor expenses such as pens, file folders, or stationery may be paid by cash but they should be done so out of a petty cash fund.

I might add that you may wish to obtain a business charge card such as MasterCard, Visa, or American Express. You may be in a bookstore, for example, and see a book entitled *How to Be a Successful Computer Consultant* and have an overwhelming urge to purchase it, but not have a business check with you (most business checkbooks are of the large three-ring notebook variety and are cumbersome to take everywhere). By charging your purchase to your business account directly, you have a record of expenditures as well as several weeks or more of "free" credit by paying for your purchase upon subsequent payment of your charge card bill.

2. *Deposit all income directly into your business account.* Most likely you won't be accepting charge cards for services rendered, since few consulting firms operate in that manner. Most payments will be by check, with a few by cash. Directly depositing the payments into your account provides an audit trail of all income.

3. *Any withdrawals from the business account should be in the form of cash transactions.* This means that you will either write a check payable to cash or yourself or directly transfer the funds into your personal account. If you write a check from your business account for a personal expenditure, the accuracy of your record keeping is complicated with possible confusion of whether any given payment was for business or personal use. Even if you note a payment was for personal use your end-of-month and end-of-year calculations are unnecessarily complicated by the distinctions you must make.

4. *Balance your bank account regularly, upon receipt of each statement.* This will help prevent bounced checks, endless hours of trying to figure where in the last five months a 17-cent error occurred, and is just generally good practice.

5. *Any expenses that are partly personal and partly business should be paid from your personal account.* Your business account can then reimburse you via cash transfer (and the appropriate notation) for the business portion of the expense. This is less complicated than reimbursing the business account for your portion and having to adjust the dollar amount appropriately.

CASH ACCOUNTING VERSUS ACCRUAL ACCOUNTING

You are probably familiar with cash accounting (though maybe not the term) from your own personal tax returns.

Simply stated, any income and expenses are recorded in the period received or paid, respectively. This means that if you perform a consulting service for someone on December 15, 1997, and collect payment on January 15, 1998, the income will be shown on your 1998 tax return. Similarly, if you purchase a book on December 20, 1997, and pay the bill on January 3, 1998, the expense will also be included with those for 1998.

Accrual accounting, however, states that revenue and expenses are recognized at the time they are earned or incurred, regardless of whether any funds change hands at that time. Our first income example would be reflected on the 1997 books, as would our book purchase.

Which method should you use for your business? Most consulting firms could use either method, but consult your accountant to determine any requirements you may have to use the accrual method. Those employing the cash method could time purchases and billings to some degree to provide a favorable tax picture depending on taxable-income patterns.

For example, if next year will likely provide less income than the current one, collections for services near the end of the year can be delayed until after the new year, shifting those earnings into a lower tax year. The opposite is also true: collections could be accelerated into the current year if next year's income will be substantially higher than this one's. Similar manipulations could be done with payment of business expenses.

Users of accrual accounting can perform similar financial magic by accelerating purchases or delaying billings, and they may have even more flexibility than cash accounting users.

Cash accounting provides a slightly less accurate picture of financial operations than accrual accounting. A given year's income or expenses may not be accurately reflected because of uncollected (but earned) revenue or unpaid (but incurred) expenses. It does, however, present a more accurate cash flow picture for a reporting period than accrual accounting.

Consider the situation where Bernie Jordan finishes a major contract on December 24, 1997 (just in time for Christmas Eve) that provides $5000 in revenue (payable

January 2). Other revenue for the year was $3000, and all was collected. Total 1997 expenses were $4000, all paid.

Under an accrual basis, Bernie would show 1997 pretax earnings of $4000 ($8000 revenue less $4000 expenses). The cash basis, however, will produce a net loss of $1000 ($3000 collected revenue minus $4000 expenses). Which is correct? Bernie didn't really have a loss of $1000, but if he had to suddenly pay $2000 on December 30, 1997, he couldn't very well take the money from 1997 profit, since he hasn't collected all of his revenue yet.

There is no 100 percent correct answer, but it is recommended that you use accrual accounting because of the increased accuracy of effective earnings reporting and evaluation. In fact, for a firm with consistently increasing annual earnings the accrual basis offers a better means for accelerating revenue into the current, lower-earnings year: whether your client pays before or after January 1, by billing before the end of the year the revenue can be counted in the current year.

As should be obvious, the accrual accounting should be accompanied by accurate cash flow and working capital analysis. Potential investors (and you) aren't interested merely in reportable income; cash flow is important. As we will see shortly, the purchase of a $10,000 computer system may appear on current books not as a $10,000 expense but as a depreciation expense for a portion of the asset "used." To show the $10,000 cash outflow requires more than just an income statement and balance sheet.

LEDGERS

In what form do you then record your cash or accrual accounting? You have two options here, also. You could use the standard accounting *double-entry system* or a simplified *single-entry* method.

Double-entry systems provide much greater accuracy of records than single-entry systems but are far more complex to learn and manage. We'll take a look at both systems shortly.

A single-entry system consists of a series of ledgers for income, credit, expenditures, and equipment.[2] A double-entry system typically has a continuous journal from which entries are "posted" to a general ledger. The double-entry system, as implied by the name, requires two entries for every transaction: a debit and a credit. These entries serve to offset each other so that when a *trial balance* is computed, the totals of debits and credits should be equal, providing a measurement of accuracy of transaction entry.

Confused already? Your best bet, then, is to organize your own books under the single-entry system presented next and, for now at least, skip over the double-entry section. Those of you who are at ease with accounting concepts should review the double-entry section, especially if your last exposure to journals and ledgers was in Accounting 101 during your freshman year of college.

Let's look at Bernie Jordan's transactions for the first month of 1998. Bernie completed three consulting contracts on the following dates:

January 10—Installation of legal system	$2000
January 25—Development of property management software	2500
January 28—Installation of real estate system	1500
Total	$6000

The first two payments have been collected, while the last hasn't been received yet.

During this month Bernie made the following purchases, all paid by cash or check:

January 3—Annual post office box rent	$ 25
January 10—Office supplies	15
January 15—Postage stamps	5
January 28—Box of 10 floppy disks	25
January 29—Computer printer	400
Total	$470

If Bernie were to calculate his business profit for January he would show $5530 ($6000 − $470), assuming he used the accrual accounting method. Right? Wrong. The computer printer purchase must be treated in a special manner since it is an acquisition of an asset rather than a periodic business expense. Let's look at the above transactions and how they are treated by a single-entry system.

The first ledger Bernie must maintain is the *income ledger*, a record of all business income. Since service industries are not normally subject to state and local sales tax on their revenue, no record of taxable sales and sales tax is necessary. Bernie's income ledger is shown in Fig. 11-1.

Alternatively, a separate ledger could be maintained for credit sales but duplicate entry of each contract is required, once to the income ledger and once to the credit ledger. Since most of your payments will be received following an invoice billing to your client nearly every transaction will require two entries.

The preferred method is to combine these two ledgers as shown in Fig. 11-1, filling in the date-paid column upon receipt of funds. A periodic search through the ledger will reflect those payments still due. This search process becomes even easier when you support your ledgers with a database management system or electronic spreadsheet, as we will see.

A similar ledger will be maintained for business expenditures. Figure 11-2 illustrates Bernie Jordan's expenditure ledger.

Columns should be provided for all likely expenses of your

Income Ledger for January 1998

Contract date	Client	Date paid	Amount	Memo
1/10	Jones, Smith & Johnson	1/17	$2000.00	
1/15	ABCDEF Realty	1/26	2500.00	
1/28	GHIJKL Realty		1500.00	Billed 1/30
			$6000.00	

FIGURE 11-1   Income ledger.

Expenditure Ledger for 1998

Date	Method of payment	Payee	Office expenses and postage	Supplied	Advertising expense	Non-deductible	Total	Notes
1/3	Check 235	U.S. Post Office	$25.00				$ 25.00	Box rent
1/10	Check 236	Favored Office Supplies	25.00				15.00	Paper, folders
1/15	Cash	U.S. Post Office		5.00			5.00	Stamps
1/28	Check 237	By-Mail Computer Supplies		$25.00			25.00	10 disks
1/29	VISA	Downtown Computers				$400.00	400.00	Printer

FIGURE 11-2 Expenditure ledger.

business. If you don't have any employees, you don't need a payroll column, and if you work from your home an office-rent column is unnecessary. (*Note*: If you are taking a home office deduction on your tax return, a year-end reconciliation of home office expenses is necessary for your tax return.)

By providing a total column as well as individual ones a single payment can be recorded that contains purchases in more than one category.

The nondeductible column is for personal cash withdrawals, repayment of business loans (the interest payment is tax deductible), depreciable assets, accounts payable, and legal fines or penalties.

Wait a minute. Why is Bernie's printer purchase listed as a nondeductible expense? As we said, the purchase of an asset is not treated the same as a periodic business expense. *Depreciable assets* are considered to have a useful life longer than one year and must be used over an extended period of time. A lot of paperwork, right? Well, no one said running a business was easy!

At the end of each year (assuming your business operates on a calendar-year basis) you need to summarize your income and expenditures for your tax reporting and close the books on the year. By summing the columns on your expenditure ledger you arrive at summary amounts to be entered on your tax return in the appropriate places. The same is true for your income. Any expenses are supplemented by your calculations of depreciation, home office rent and utilities, and other adjusting entries we will discuss in the tax section. Any cash or check payments for last year's credit expenses (known as accounts payable) should not be included as a business expense for this year if you use accrual accounting, since those expenses were included on last year's return; they would be entered in the nondeductible column.

Now, on with the torture. Bernie Jordan studied accounting in college (remember, he was a business school graduate) and decides to implement a double-entry system. Using the same transactions as before, his accounting journal is shown in Fig. 11-3.

Accounting Journal, 1998

Date	Account	Debit	Credit
1/03/98	Office expenses and postage Cash (P.O. box rental)	$ 25.00	$ 25.00
1/10	Accounts receivable Revenue (Jones, Smith & Johnson)	2000.00	2000.00
1/10	Office expenses and postage Cash (Office supplies)	15.00	15.00
1/15	Office expenses and postage Cash (stamps)	5.00	5.00
1/17	Cash Accounts receivable (Payment from Jones, Smith & Johnson)	2000.00	2000.00
1/25	Accounts receivable Revenue (ABCDEF Realty)	2500.00	2500.00
1/26	Cash Accounts receivable (Payment from ABCDEF Realty)	2500.00	2500.00
1/28	Supplies Cash (Floppy disks)	25.00	25.00
1/28	Accounts receivable Revenue (GHIJKL Realty)	1500.00	1500.00
1/29	Equipment Accounts payable (Printer)	400.00	400.00

FIGURE 11-3   Accounting journal.

Wait a second! *This* is a more accurate system? It looks like the Tower of Babel compared with a single-entry system. Well, we're not finished yet. The journal is merely a transaction log from which entries are posted to the general ledger.

Each account has its own ledger entry, sometimes known as a "T-Account." All debits to an account are on the left side of the T, while all credits are on the right side. For example, assuming no beginning balance, the accounts receivable ledger account would look like this:

Accounts Receivable		
1/10	2000	2000
1/17		
1/25	2500	2500
1/26		
1/28	1500	
	6000	4500
	1500	

The end of the month shows a $1500 debit balance, indicating that this amount is still owed to Bernie Jordan. Managing a complicated journal and ledger set is very tedious when done by hand, but much simpler when done with a computer *as long as you comprehend the underlying accounting principles.* Year-end processing is more complex than with a single-entry system because you must adjust some accounts and close others to prepare the books for next year.

If you are familiar enough with double-entry accounting (translation: you got an A or B in your college accounting class) you may find that, with computer assistance, you can obtain much more useful information than from a single-entry system. Consult one or more accounting books to refresh your memory. On the other hand, if you aren't familiar with accounting and this method is just too confusing, don't despair; use the single-entry method.

AUTOMATING YOUR BOOKKEEPING

Whether you choose to use a small business financial package (e.g., Intuit's QuickBook) or to develop your own internal support systems using a spreadsheet-based system (or perhaps a database application), it is highly recommended that you automate all of this financial activity for ease of reference and ease of management.

TAXES

In all previous editions of this book, I discussed the subject of taxes, including material about forms, deductibility of various expenses, changes in rules, etc. For example, the depreciation rules in effect in the early 1980s featured an Accelerated Cost Recovery System (ACRS); this was replaced by a modified version in 1986. At one time, an investment tax credit (ITC) was also part of the depreciation models; and so on.

For this edition, I've limited the discussion about tax matters to the following straightforward statement: Each and every year, check the current tax laws, with particular emphasis on what is different from the previous year. The basics still hold:

- Depending on the form of your business (sole proprietorship, partnership, or corporation), you file the appropriate form(s), following the instructions.
- You make a distinction between expenses—purchases of notebooks and postage stamps, for example—and items such as computers and printers, for purposes of how they are treated and what are applicable forms.
- You typically need to be concerned with quarterly payments of estimated taxes if you're an independent consultant.
- You should treat tax planning as an integral part of your overall financial planning.

For more details that are up-to-date, it's recommended that you consult one of the many different tax-oriented books—but make sure the book covers *current* rules and guidelines.

TIME PLANNING AND MANAGEMENT

Let's talk for a moment about time planning and management in the course of your consulting business. Those of you who came from corporate or formal organization settings where for the most part you were a "worker bee"—that is, working on one or two highly defined tasks with few interruption-driven changes in direction—may be surprised, shocked, and disheartened by the time pressures and models in the consulting world. Not only are you—usually by yourself—the operations, marketing, support, and accounting departments, but you may find yourself operating in an interruption-driven mode, rapidly changing courses to satisfy the immediate needs of a client, chasing after a short-fuse business opportunity, or doing something else that pops up out of nowhere, all while you're trying to meet those deadlines right in front of you.

Note the theme of our highly successful consultants profiled in this book: "If you think working for yourself means fewer working hours, guess again, buddy." Most people in the consulting world find themselves pulling more all-nighters and late-nighters than they had since college because of the tremendous demands on their time.

Even though, as we mentioned, the very nature of the business is interruption-driven, there are basic time-management techniques you can employ to help keep yourself from becoming hopelessly lost in the swarm of things competing for your time. These are basic strategies such as having a prioritized formal "to do" list and working through the list in the most efficient manner, keeping good records (hopefully, online through some sort of database) so you waste less time searching for phone numbers, attempting to locate an invoice, or tracking down that requirements document from last year's ABC Company project, and so on. Pocket electronic organizers (I use one) with phone numbers, daily schedules, memos, "to do" lists, expense recording, and so on are an invaluable resource, and in my opinion well worth the investment. Many of the good ones come with interfaces to PCs, so you can upload information from your portable organizer to spreadsheet and word processing software for further organization.

Alternatively, you may choose to use a laptop PC to perform on-the-road functions and record keeping such as those mentioned above. Personal digital assistants (PDAs) have recently come to market which combine the functionality and ease-of-use of pocket organizers with cellular phones, faxes, and other communications functions. These will also become invaluable time management aids.

MARKETING

The many guidelines presented in Chap. 4 still apply as your business goes from the planning stages to full-scale operation. You should keep a close watch on your advertising budget; just because you are earning more income doesn't mean you should splurge on unnecessary and illogical advertising. You may increase your *Yellow Pages* advertising from a quarter-inch box to a quarter-page display ad, but a $100,000 television advertising budget probably is still a bit extreme.

Always keep your target markets in mind when making any advertising or marketing decisions. Your public relations and word-of-mouth referrals will remain a key factor in your marketing plan; exploit them as best you can.

INSURANCE

You should determine what type of insurance your business requires. If your office is located at your residence, you home-owner's or renter's insurance should cover fire, theft, and other casualty losses. *Be sure* to notify your insurance company that you will have business equipment (computer, printer, etc.) in your home and that they will be used for business; you may have to pay a small amount more but some companies will not cover business equipment loss or damage under a residential policy.

You may also consider liability insurance (both for you and your "products") to prevent a catastrophic multimillion-dollar suit from devastating your business and personal assets.

If you use your automobile for business, either partially or totally, your policy should include the usual liability, comprehensive, and collision coverages.

You should not have to worry about business interruption insurance, since you probably won't have a retail outlet or factory whose damage could cause temporary or permanent business stoppage. Nor will you need to concern yourself with worker's compensation insurance if you don't have any employees. Once you begin employing workers, however, investigate your state's requirement for this coverage.

Insurance issues for consultants go beyond just the "pure business insurance" area, of course. Health insurance, at the forefront in the United States at the time of this writing (1998), is *very* important. For those of you doing your consulting activities on a part-time basis while employed full-time elsewhere, chances are you have some type of medical insurance, whether a major medical policy or through a health maintenance organization (HMO).

Those of you who are independent, however, must find your own health insurance; those of you who left employment elsewhere have (under current laws) eighteen months from the time of your last employment to remain on your former employer's insurance plan, but of course you now have to pay the entire premium. Possibly, your spouse's employer provides health insurance, and you can be covered under that policy as a dependent.

These issues may change if the United States ever goes to a mandated or governmentally controlled health care system; those of you readers who are outside of the United States probably have some type of government health care coverage. Regardless of what the future holds and when it happens, the important thing is to make sure that you have some type of health care coverage for you and your dependents. True, it's pretty darn expensive. If at all possible, though, make sure you have some type of coverage, because one serious illness or accident can financially devastate a family or an individual.

Life insurance, something few of us like to think about, is also important. Term, whole life, universal life...the options are endless. Shop around among various agents and independent insurers for the various policies they offer, *read extensively about the advantages and disadvantages of various types of life insurance,* and purchase the appropriate type of policy, depending on your individual needs.

Finally, you should also consider long-term disability insurance, that which covers you if for some reason you are unable to work due to a permanent disability. Disability insurance usually kicks in after a specified time period, may last for a period of several years to a lifetime, and has other characteristics that vary from policy to policy. One of the nuances that is worth investigating if you have future income streams (such as book or software royalties) is whether or not such revenue "counts against" your disability payments. For example, your policy may pay you 60 percent of your average annual consulting earnings, which may be $60,000 a year. Suppose, though, that for the next five years you have book royalty income of $35,000 a year, on average, from books you wrote before you became disabled. In many policies, your benefits will be reduced by that book royalty amount, paying you only $25,000 a year. In effect, you may have been paying for insurance coverage you'll never receive.

There is one major rule with insurance coverage: Shop around. Prices vary widely among carriers, and there is no guarantee that an insurer with low automobile coverage will be equally reasonable for liability insurance.

YOUR EMPLOYMENT STATUS

Earlier we mentioned the ongoing discussion of whether you, as a consultant, are an independent, self-employed person or a company employee. The scenarios and models we've been discussing in this book are geared for someone who truly is an independent: working for many different clients on projects of varying durations, mixing your work between your home office and a client site, controlling your own hours, and so on. As long as this is the business model you find yourself following, you should have no problem documenting yourself as an independent consultant.

If, however, you are working on a long-duration, full-time, fixed-hours contract exclusively at one business site, chances are that the tightening guidelines and regulations may classify you as a full-time employee of that company rather than an independent consultant. This would mean, for example, that even if you aren't receiving any benefits from that company (health insurance, disability insurance, life insurance, retirement and investment packages, vacation and holiday pay, etc.) you are still their employee. The implications are that (1) they must pay social security taxes and things like unemployment insurance for you, which they really don't want to do since you are only there for a finite period of time, not an entire career, and (2) you lose a great deal of your potential deductions, such as the daily drive to and from that business site (that's now nondeductible commuting mileage, not business travel). All in all, no one is happy. Of course, as an independent you still have to pay both sides of your social security tax (discussed later in this chapter).

The guidelines in this area change regularly, but for the most part if you strive to operate as a business with multiple clients, control over your own business operations and facilities, and other independence-oriented characteristics, you can put up a good argument that you are indeed an independent business person rather than a full-time employee of a given client.

HELP!

Throughout this book I've been stressing development of your business and management abilities along with your computer skills. There may come a time, though, when you face a particularly difficult or complex situation that you cannot handle by yourself. When your business was in its infancy, most of the day-to-day business operations could be handled in-house. Now that your practice (and active client list) is growing, these support activities may consume too much of your valuable time, thus stunting your firm's growth.

There are no set rules for when to use outside expertise in these areas. If you have a very strong background in accounting, for example, you may feel comfortable conducting tax planning operations further into your firm's growth cycle than someone with minimal accounting exposure.

Let's take a look at several areas and see how (or if) outside professionals could help your business.

ACCOUNTING

Many new consultants prefer to prepare their own tax returns and do their own tax planning, as well as maintain their accounting books. Again, there are no laws etched in granite, but while your business is just starting and revenues are still small, you can manage most accounting functions.

A manual journal and ledger system would be sufficient to post revenues and expenses, and as transaction volume increases, you can use your computer to implement an automated system.

Much of your tax planning can be done using knowledge gained from research. Laws concerning depreciation, investment tax credits, home office deductions, and many other topics can be found in many tax publications and guides.

When should you consider working with an accountant? When your accounting and tax needs and problems outgrow your own expertise and time available for research. For example, during my second year in the consulting profession, I moved from an apartment to a house of which I owned 60 percent, sold one car and bought another, and formed a consulting partnership. While these may seem like simple transactions, when you consider the tax implications of two possible home offices, separate business mileage deductions, and separating sole proprietorship income and expenses from those of the partnership, I was faced with an extremely complex tax planning and return situation. Though revenues were still low, the potential for an auditable error in my tax return and the desire to fully utilize all the tax-saving methods available led me to conclude that professional help (accounting, not psychiatric!) was cost-effective.

Though I probably could have researched all the possible tax consequences and eventually (by April 14) completed my tax forms, I was involved in several consulting projects at the time as well as my writing *and* my full-time Air Force job. It was, therefore, much more cost-effective to give my accountant a summary of business expenses, explain the complicating factors such as a new house and new car, and pick up the completed tax return several weeks later.

Just as we saw with self-publication of commercial software versus contracting with a publishing house, you must consider, in addition to your own expertise, your available time and the opportunity cost of spending that time on program publishing or complicated tax planning or anything else. If you have several other revenue-producing projects that would provide far more income than the amount of money you save by doing your taxes yourself, it makes good economic sense to spend a bit of money (tax-deductible, of course) and devote your time to income-producing (and business-building) projects.

MARKETING

Assuming that you have put to work the marketing principles presented in this book and elsewhere, you should have little need for advertising agencies or other marketing assistance while nurturing your business.

You may, however, find yourself suddenly and unexplainedly losing market share and revenue. If, after a thorough analysis, you still don't understand why your business share is dropping, a marketing consultant may be able to provide the answer. Again, consider the costs and benefits of using outside help. If your business revenue from a critical portion of your operations is affected, a marketing consultant may be very cost-effective. However, if the affected area is an experimental or secondary operation that contributes little to total income (and is not expected to in the future), it may be difficult to justify the expense of marketing assistance.

Other marketing services that may be utilized include conducting marketing research. If, for example, you can obtain the mailing labels of all local real estate agents from the local board of realtors, you may be able to design a questionnaire that provides much useful information without assistance. This is especially important during the early years of operation when you are trying to control expenses. A larger firm, however, may wish to use a marketing firm's resources to investigate potential markets, analyze survey results, and recommend a course of action.

LEGAL

I have already mentioned several times before that your contracts should be reviewed (and possibly negotiated) by an attorney experienced in computer and business contracts. The potential for liability and serious problems causes legal assistance to be viewed in the same light as insurance: spend a bit now to save a lot later.

General legal questions, however, may be researched through sources such as Remer's *Legal Care for Your Software*, tax law books, or other sources. You should have an understanding of the problem in question and the alternatives before consulting an attorney.

FINANCIAL

If you are considering massive expansion of your business, such as opening offices in several cities or becoming a full-time software house, you may find yourself with the need for additional capital. Your accountant should be the first person you turn to, as he or she can point out the various tax implications of the sought-after financing. You may then be directed to a venture capitalist, Small Business Administration (SBA) lender, underwriter, or other financial source. Unless you yourself are a venture capitalist turned entrepreneur, these financing actions are best left to the professionals. One slip of a contract (which your attorney should review, of course) *could* cost you control of the business to which you have devoted so much time, effort, and money.

PERSONNEL

Unless you are embarking on a massive employment campaign, you should be able to conduct interviews and make hiring decisions without using employment agencies or executive recruiters.

A classified newspaper ad should be able to attract enough potential job seekers to allow you to find a qualified person.

Further down the road you may require agency services to attract professionals from other geographic areas or assist you with screening applicants to find that one right person. In these instances, be sure that you can justify the cost of these services by the benefits, both tangible and intangible, provided.

RECORD KEEPING

As much as most people dislike maintaining records, that is as important a function as your bookkeeping, accounting, and other managerial tasks. You should organize your filing system in such a manner that it is easy for you to file and retrieve information. The information you store should include:

Tax returns, financial records, and receipts

Contracts and other legal forms

Proposals

Client project reports

Business correspondence

Important magazine and newspaper clippings

Client information

Be sure that you periodically get rid of out-of-date records and information to prevent your files from becoming too cumbersome. Remember also that an automated record management system (discussed next) is far more efficient than a filing system that is exclusively paper-oriented. Even though items such as receipts must be retained in hard copy, conceivably you could scan such receipts into your system and file them using multimedia data management software, for electronic retrieval. Maybe the paperless society will reach us some day, after all!

USING YOUR COMPUTER

How can you utilize your own computer system to help you manage your own business? We've already discussed several uses in this and previous chapters; these uses and others are listed below.

1. *Word processing.*   You will undoubtedly be writing many letters, reports, and proposals and possibly even books and magazine articles. Word processing software will speed up the creation and revision time of these written documents. You can also mass-mail letters to your clients or vendors using a mail-merge facility with your database files (discussed next).

2. *Database management.*   You can store lists of everything using a database management system. The most common uses may include (1) client lists, (2) vendor lists, (3) magazine article cross-referencing, and (4) accounting information.

3. *Spreadsheet analysis.*   Chapter 5 dealt with cash flow analysis, income statements, and other financial uses of an electronic spreadsheet. You can also perform what-if analysis on various projects, maintain a simple single-entry set of books, and prepare your tax returns (as well as analyze the tax implications of various alternative decisions).

4. *Communications.*   You can connect your computer via modem to remote databases to retrieve bibliographic information or access several software databases. For example, a client may be searching for a solution to a particularly difficult problem, and you can access these databases to learn if any software exists that may work in this situation.

5. *Graphics generation.*   You can create charts and graphs to be used in your seminars as overhead slides or handouts.

6. *Desktop publishing.*   You can publish professional-looking client newsletters, documentation, and other material.

7. *Proof of concept testing.*   Even though this falls outside the realm of your direct business operations, you can use various software and hardware components and examine characteristics such as functionality and ease-of-use *before* you recommend them to your clients.

8. *Internet usage.*   Your computer is also your gateway to the internet for product and technology research, marketing, electronic mail, electronic commerce, and many other functions.

EMPLOYEE COMPENSATION

When you begin to hire employees for your firm, you need to know what type of compensation to provide. Without adequate and motivating reward, you will have trouble attracting and retaining good employees at all levels, professional and clerical.

You must be able to recognize what motivates people in the computer profession, both financially and in terms of work. Though we will be discussing mostly your professional computer workers, the same basic principles hold true of all employees.

Employee compensation can be broken down into four major categories.[3]

1. *Salary.*   The basis of compensation is the salary portion, either as a flat rate or on an hourly basis. The employee's salary is based on job analysis, job level, survey of comparable salaries in other firms, and periodic adjustments. Naturally, a computer programmer with a master's degree will earn more than a secretary with a high school diploma.

2. *Benefits.*   Employee benefits can consist of a combination of health care, paid vacations, life and disability insurance, employee services (discounts on company services, for example), survivor benefits, and retirement plans, among others. A recent trend is to allow employees to pick and choose among a set of benefits: a young, unmarried person may not require much (if any) life insurance, while a military retiree would have little need for health insurance.

As we discussed earlier, though, there is a strong possibility that in the United States companies will be required to provide a certain minimum level of health care coverage to all workers. While this is expected to cause some turmoil with companies of all sizes, legal requirements to do so may cause shifts in other compensation factors if business needs and budgets dictate.

3. *Perquisites.*   Slightly more than benefits, "perks" would include paid vacations at a company ski resort or use of the company car (or company aircraft, if you happen to have one in your inventory!). Perks should be distributed on a somewhat limited basis in order to maintain a reward system.

4. *Short-term and long-term incentives.* Short-term incentives, such as annual bonuses, and long-term ones, like stock options and discount stock purchase plans, are important factors in motivating and retaining your key employees.

You may also consider plans like deferred compensation, where part of an employee's salary is put off until a later time when his or her tax bracket may be less than at present. You might consider offering employees working on a key project a percentage of that task's profits as an incentive bonus.

How do you decide what type of compensation packages to offer your various employees? You should research the salaries and benefits offered by firms similar to yours, as well as general compensation from compensation consultants, your accountant, or others who could help you develop a useful package. Be aware of any geographical differences in your surveys, research, and advice; employees in San Francisco or New York City need to earn more than those in Des Moines to maintain a particular standard of living.

CONTRACTS AND FEES

Anytime you and your clients enter into an agreement, whether written, spoken, or merely implied, you become parties to a contract. We dealt with contracts briefly in previous chapters in the form of license agreements, nondisclosure agreements, and work-for-hire agreements. This section will deal with contracts in a bit more detail.

Business law, specifically contract law, is a fascinating and complex area. As a consultant, you will be party to many contracts; again, some may be spoken or implied, while others are written. It is urged that *all* contracts you enter into be written, even though oral contracts are legally enforceable. By signing written contracts, both you and your clients are somewhat protected against misunderstanding, ambiguity, and deception. Any agreement, even a written letter of agreement, can be considered a contract, so be careful what you sign.

Among the applicable elements of most contracts are:[4]

1. Responsibility of each party
2. Time agreements
3. Financial arrangements
4. Products or services to be delivered
5. Needed cooperation of client during project
6. Establishment of your independent-contractor status rather than employment
7. Establishment of your advisory capacity, as opposed to being a decision maker
8. Client responsibility for review, implementation, and results
9. Your potential work with competitors (nonexclusivity of services)
10. Client's authority to contract for your services
11. Attorney's fee clause
12. Special limitation

Expect to negotiate these terms; your client may desire, for example, to preclude you from working for his or her competitors. If you agree to this, be sure that corresponding terms, such as financial compensation and terms under which the contract may be terminated, provide you with adequate protection.

One of the most important portions is financial arrangements. You should never sign an agreement that doesn't specify *exactly* what you must do or deliver and how much you will be paid (flat fee) or on what basis (hourly or daily rate, for example).[5] Some clients may wish to place you on a retainer (see Chap. 5); be sure that you don't inadvertently lock yourself into an unprofitable situation at the expense of other, better-paying contracts from other clients.

You should also quantify how often you will be paid; you may wish to accept a 30 percent retainer at the start of the project and receive portions of your total fee at various intervals. Your proposal and/or contract should specify what constitutes the end of a contract phase, such as delivery of Report A or implementation of portions 1, 2, and 3 of a client's computer system. Additionally, you should note what payments will be due if the client cancels the project at various stages. Again, be prepared to negotiate.

I can't stress enough that the money you spend to have your attorney draft and review contracts to which you will be a party is an investment in the successful operation of your business. If you draft any contracts yourself, skip the "whyforths" and the "party of the third part"; write them in English. Be aware of the consequences of anything you don't explicitly specify (remember "implied warranties" from license agreements?) and know the default conditions.

ETHICS AND CLIENT RELATIONS

Even though you are not licensed the way an attorney, physician, or accountant is, you are still a professional. A certain code of ethics applies to your client relations. Chief among your responsibilities is confidentiality. You may be tempted to brag about your inside knowledge of XYZ Corporation's expansion plans or your assistance with UVW Company's serious problems. All you do then is invite legal action and destroy your professional and personal credibility. Not too bad, huh?

Since you are an independent consultant, it is extremely likely that at times you will be working with competitors of previous clients. In order to survive in business, you must be considered trustworthy and legal by your present client, but not at the expense of a former one. Anyone who expects you to provide inside information about another one of your clients should be informed that you don't operate your practice in that manner; if they persist, proceed to another client.

Another important subject is conflicts of interest. The previously mentioned confidentiality example is also an instance of potential conflict of interest. If you assist client A with a particular contract, such as providing technical expertise for a government project it seeks, it is unethical to aid client B with the same project even if you have finished consulting with client A—and client B offers you 10 times as much money.

Additionally, you should always check with any client with whom you are under a retainer agreement to see if they intend to pursue a particular project before assisting another client with that job. Depending on your particular retainer agreement, you may find yourself in a precarious position if your main client desires your services and you have already committed yourself to working with another customer.

Sometimes unforeseen conflicts of interest may arise. Suppose, for example, that you are sponsoring a small business computer systems seminar with a local computer retailer, perhaps one of the local "superstores." Should you be expected to automatically commit any and all future clients to purchases of hardware and software from that particular retailer? Such follow-on relationships should be clearly spelled out in all agreements, such as those for sponsoring the seminar. For example, you might agree that for a period of six months, any client who attends the seminar who retains your consulting services should be brought to that particular retailer for a bid from that company; if the components can be bought elsewhere at a lower cost, however, the client is free to do so, and you, the consultant, have no further obligation to the retailer. Forcing all attendees who contact you to purchase hardware from that particular retailer isn't desirable, but the retailer's participation should entitle it to at least have an opportunity to present a bid to the clients of a seminar it co-sponsored. It's all give and take in these types of situations; just keep the long-term good of your business at the forefront of your mind when pursuing various types of relationships.

You must also honor any contractual time and cost estimates you make, such as a ceiling of hours or guaranteed delivery date.

As a professional computer consultant, you are supposed to be enough of an expert that if you estimate a project will be completed in 50 hours and be delivered in one month, your actual development time won't be off by much.

Note, though, as we've mentioned several times before, that this is true only if the scope of the project doesn't change. If your client wants to add features to custom software or doesn't provide certain guaranteed support, your obligations to honor your estimates are terminated. To be on the safe side, make sure these conditions are *written in the contract*. A clause such as "additional features beyond those specified will be handled under separate contractual arrangements" is helpful in clarifying and solving any problems that might arise.

You may consider charging separate billing rates depending on the type and amount of services. My personal feeling is that a long-term contract such as custom software development (for example, 80 to 100 hours of work) may call for a slightly lower billing rate per hour because of the "guaranteed" number of hours billed and less idle time. Other consultants charge the same hourly rate for one-day projects as for one-year contracts. The important thing is to be honest about your fees and how they are computed. If one client wants to know why another client received your services at a lower rate than you first quoted, explain that the project was of much longer duration with a guaranteed minimum number of hours.

Any agreements at negotiated special rates should contain a clause in the contract stating either a minimum number of hours per day at the negotiated rate with a minimum total fee or number of days or a conditional clause that if the project does not meet a minimum number of hours, you will be paid your standard rate in lieu of the cheaper one.[6]

Finally, you may meet people at parties or other social gatherings who ask you many questions like "What type of computer should I buy?" or "What is the best general-ledger program for Windows-based systems?" While you may not mind providing your sister-in-law or college roommate with this free consulting advice, avoid telling casual acquaintances or total strangers too much without a formal agreement. A quick answer such as "There are several good ledger programs; last month's *Byte* featured a special report" would be as far as you should go.

SUMMARY

It's not just computer and information technology that changes rapidly and frequently. The way you might have run a consulting business in 1982 is, most likely, radically different from the way you would do so today. Not only have many different tax laws changed, causing you to reevaluate things like purchases, hiring others, and other financial decisions, but even the very management mode of running a small business has changed.

We've covered a great deal of material in this chapter. Just as Chap. 7 squeezed the contents of numerous system development texts into a highly summarized form, this chapter does the same for the business management aspects. In the next chapter, we'll discuss various ways you can keep up to date with all of the things having to do with your business. For business-related issues, there are several periodicals and books listed that are worth reviewing regularly.

END NOTES

1. Bernard Kamoroff, *Small-Time Operator,* Bell Springs Publishing, Layfonville, Calif., 1982, pp. 38–39.
2. Ibid., pp. 42–49.
3. Soundview Summary of Bruce R. Ellig, *Executive Compensation—A Total Pay Perspective,* Soundview Books, Darien, Conn., 1982, p. 1.
4. Robert E. Kelley, *Consulting: The Complete Guide to a Profitable Career,* Scribner's, New York, 1981, pp. 158–159.
5. Herman Holtz, *How to Succeed as an Independent Consultant,* Wiley, New York, 1983, p. 240.
6. Ibid., p. 245.

HOW TO STAY CURRENT— YOUR LIVELIHOOD DEPENDS ON IT

I've got one word for you: Internet. In this chapter we'll cover traditional ways of staying current with the many topics important to your consulting career, but the landscape has changed so dramatically in the past two years or so that I feel confident making the following statement:

> Any time you need the answer to a question, or want to find out what's happening that could have an impact on your consulting business, try the Internet first.

The first two chapters of this book emphasized how the changes in the computer industry, both the positive ones and the negative ones, have altered not only the industry as a whole but the careers of the individuals working in the field. This chapter will look at some ways you can stay up to date with the massive amounts of information needed *just to stay competitive*, let alone get ahead, in the world of computer consulting.

WHAT YOU NEED TO COVER

So what exactly must you cover in your quest to stay current? You might break the subjects into the following groups:

1. Computer technology in general
2. Your specific areas of computing and information systems
3. Business issues
4. Consulting-specific issues

Let's look at each of these a bit more closely.

GENERAL COMPUTER TECHNOLOGY

I strongly believe in the following premise:

> No matter what one or two areas are your specialties currently, it's important to keep up to date in as many areas of computing as possible, even if they don't have any direct bearing on your current consulting functions.

For example, suppose the emphasis of your consulting work currently is in the database area. That means that the specific functions with which you are likely to be working are things like data modeling and database design, distributed databases, object-oriented databases, and so on.

It's *not* enough to limit your studies and your efforts to keep current in the database area, though. Nearly every other area of computing, even those with which you may now have no dealings and don't anticipate doing so, has some sort of interrelationship with the other areas. For example, the discipline of open systems—standards-based interoperability and connectivity among heterogeneous components—has ties to databases through standards in the area of heterogeneous database access (SQL Access, for example). Even though your current activities might be exclusively with PC-based databases, maybe only Xbase systems (dBASE, FoxPro, etc.), chances are that at some point in the future you will be faced with the opportunity to propose a system to a client that involves something like SQL Access or other database standards under the "open systems" category.

The same is true with computer aided software engineering (CASE). You may now do all of your data modeling and database design by hand, but as CASE matures you will need to have skills not only in the database aspects of CASE but also other areas, mostly from the point of inter-tool integration and cooperability. Therefore, keeping up to date with developments in CASE is important as well.

You may be thinking to yourself, hey, folks, I already work about 50 hours a week on client projects, plus another ten or so on business overhead; how the heck am I supposed to keep up to date with all of these things I'm not even using right now? Stay tuned; at the end of this chapter we'll discuss a methodology I've found helpful in doing just that.

Your Areas of Specialization

It goes without saying that as a consultant, it is mandatory that you be as up to date as possible in the specific areas in which you're specializing. Following our previous example, your particular database expertise may be the Xbase systems. That means that when a new version of dBASE or FoxPro or some other Xbase system comes out, you should know:

1. How this version differs from the previous one
2. How this version differs from other Xbase products
3. How changes affect the applications you've developed or are currently developing for your clients
4. What, if any, bugs are present in the product, and when fixes are anticipated

Most importantly, you need to know *where to go* to get answers quickly! We'll discuss some of the sources of this type of information later in the chapter.

General Business Issues

In Chap. 11 we mentioned how the tax laws change constantly. The same is true for many aspects of business, from record keeping requirements, to employee-vs.-subcontractor status issues, to overseas opportunities. Whether your consulting business is a small one-person operation or a growing one, it's as important to stay as up to date in business issues as it is for general and specific technology issues.

Consulting-Specific Issues

Finally, there are issues specific to computer consulting that you must also follow closely. For example, things like average billing rates in your geographical area, growth or decline in the use of consultants by local businesses, and which vendors are courting independent consultants for strategic relationships all are among the many issues you must add to your trackings.

PERIODICALS

So far, we've talked about *what* you must track in your efforts to stay current. Let's turn our attention to *how* you can do so. The most prevalent way is through periodicals: magazines, newspapers and newsletters, and journals. There are literally thousands of periodicals to which you can subscribe *or receive free* (discussed a bit later); how do you choose among them? (See Fig. 12-1.)

In general, you should track one or two general computing periodicals to stay abreast of overall trends in the computing field. Examples include *Computerworld, Datamation, Software Magazine,* and *Byte.* While some of these magazines have a particular slant toward a particular area of technology (*Byte* is microcomputer-oriented, *Software Magazine* obviously is oriented toward software, and so on), they tend to have a broad spectrum of technologies covered from issue to issue.

The next category would include periodicals that deal with a specific technology. Following our example of a database consultant in this chapter, you should consider closely monitoring magazines such as *Database Programming and Design, DBMS,* or *Data Based Advisor,* all of which deal heavily with databases and related issues. There also are academic journals, such as the *ACM Transactions on Database Systems,* which can provide information to those dealing with leading-edge consulting as to the latest goings-on in database research and development.

Business Periodicals

The Wall Street Journal
Forbes
Fortune
Business Week
Inc.

General Computing Periodicals

Computerworld
Software
Datamation
Open Systems Today
Byte

Specific-Use Periodicals

Data Based Advisor
Access Advisor
Database Programming and Design
MacWorld

FIGURE 12-1   Periodical reading list.

Still another grouping would be product-specific periodicals. A database consultant who heavily emphasizes FoxPro systems would benefit from a subscription to *FoxPro User Journal*. On the hardware side, a consultant who specializes in Apple Macintosh systems should track a periodical such as *MacWorld* or *MacWeek*. There also are magazines for the open systems world (*Open Systems Today*, for example), CASE (*CASE Trends, CASE Outlook*), object-oriented programming, and nearly every other discipline in the computer field. And all of these are just in the computing area; we haven't even gotten into business and consulting periodicals yet! Before you panic, though, remember I promised to share my own personal methodology in keeping up with this information overload.

Earlier I mentioned that some of the aforementioned periodicals are available at no cost. Many periodicals are available simply by annually filling out a response card detailing information about you, your business, the hardware and software you use or plan to use, and so on. For the price of a postage stamp and about ten minutes of your time (and being on about 1000 mailing lists for the rest of the year), you can receive many of the magazines and newspapers weekly or monthly or however often they're published; no other subscription costs are necessary! In my opinion, it's well worth the time to subscribe to as many of these "freebies" as possible.

In the general business realm, you have "the big four" periodicals: the daily *The Wall Street Journal* and three business magazines, *Business Week, Fortune,* and *Forbes.* Many of the things you must track are covered in columns and stories, and you can also obtain some good ideas for future business opportunities from their stories.

There are also periodicals dedicated specifically to small business issues, such as *Inc.* magazine. Topics like financing a small business's expansion are covered in an up-to-date manner in magazines such as these.

BOOKS

"Oh, no," you're groaning, "I don't see any way to keep up with fifteen or twenty magazines and periodicals, and now this guy wants me to read books also?" Don't worry, while books can be a very important part of learning a particular subject intimately, they don't necessarily represent the "front lines" as periodicals do. Rather, here are some examples of how I use computer books in my work.

One of the projects on which I recently worked dealt extensively with multilevel protocols, such as the OSI Reference Model. Since it had been some time since I had worked in that area, and since my experience was a bit rusty, I purchased four different books on various related subjects, creating my own little reference library for quick access to volumes of disparate information about protocol-related subjects.

On another project, I was tracking a potential project using the FoxPro database system. Although I had written hundreds of thousands of lines of dBASE code during my career, my FoxPro experience was far less extensive, and I needed a quick way to build on the foundations of my dBASE knowledge with respect to FoxPro capabilities. By using a book about FoxPro, I was able to do so. In short, I use books, especially computer books, on an as-needed basis. At one time I would purchase computer books that looked interesting merely as shelf filler for my library, whether I would ever use them or not. Today, given the wide array of titles, the high prices, and the speed with which the currency of the information changes, I prefer to go with an approach of "buy 'em when I need 'em."

The same is true for business and other books. For example, suppose you are in the process of seeking investment and loan capital with which to expand your business. Many of you have heard the term "credit crunch" used to describe the reticence on the part of many financial institutions to making loans during the early 1990s. Therefore, a book on small business financing written during the heady days of the mid-1980s will likely be somewhat out of date. At the point when you are seeking funds, you might *then* seek out a recent book, such as *Free Money* by Laurie Blum[1] or *Guerrilla Financing* by Bruce Blechman and Jay Conrad Levinson.[2]

Throughout all three editions of this book I have also cited references from other books about consulting in general (not necessarily computer consulting). Two of the most widely used are *Consulting: The Complete Guide to a Profitable Career*, by Robert E. Kelley,[3] and Herman Holtz's *How to Succeed as an Independent Consultant*.[4] Mr. Holtz is also the author of other books that deal with specific consulting issues, such as *The Consultant's Guide to Proposal Writing*,[5] which goes into the subject of writing proposals in great detail.

Finally, an occasional browse through a local bookstore will yield dozens of new business book titles, some of which may catch your eye if they are pertinent to your concerns of the moment.

GOVERNMENTAL PUBLICATIONS

The Internal Revenue Service, the Small Business Administration, and various cabinet-level governmental agencies (examples: Commerce Department, Defense Department) all have lots of free publications that they will be glad to send you. For example, the IRS has publications dealing not only with general tax issues and planning, but also those specifically for small businesses. The same is true of many state and local governments, who will send you publications about small business opportunities in that region or similar up-to-date information that is important for your business.

COMPUTER VENDORS

Don't overlook the value of computer hardware and software vendors as valuable sources of current information, not only about their products but about technology in general. However, always take a somewhat critical view of what they present, and consider the information in the light of their mission of marketing and sales. Vendors have tons of product brochures, "white papers," and other documents available for you. Many large vendors also sponsor no-cost "conferences" and "seminars" (really they're just sales presentations, but usually there is valuable information presented). In addition to learning about new developments in product-specific or technical areas, you will also find them a valuable means of building strategic relationships with other consultants, or the vendors themselves.

ICCA

The Independent Computer Consultants Association (ICCA) is an organization that can be of immense assistance to experienced as well as new consultants. The national ICCA organization, coupled with local and regional chapters around the country, provides an excellent way to make contacts, learn about new developments in technology and business, and stay on top of the many issues with which consultants must deal. ICCA also provides insurance programs for members (see

Chap. 11) through which independent consultants may obtain both business and personal insurance such as medical, disability, business liability, and other coverages.

ON-LINE SERVICES

Information services such as Compuserve and Prodigy have bulletin boards or forums dedicated to consulting issues and topics. One of the largest is the CONSULT forum on Compuserve, through which ICCA also provides information. Many of the subjects discussed in this book, from technology to business issues, are addressed in a near-real-time manner through these services. Membership fees vary from service to service; usually, additional charges apply to bulletin boards and forums.

Another valuable aspect of on-line services is access to databases of journal and magazine articles, accessible through keywords. For example, to find a list of all the periodicals available on line that deal with object-oriented databases and transaction models, you can specify the appropriate keywords and receive a list. When I first began consulting, I created a personalized keyword-oriented database on my own computer, into which I would diligently enter each article I was saving in my files from the numerous periodicals to which I subscribed. As you might guess, that lasted about six months; it became far too tedious to do that, and it's often worth a couple of extra dollars to search on-line lists and download appropriate articles for further investigation.

SEMINARS AND CONFERENCES

Another way to stay current—*very* current—with technical topics is to attend seminars and conferences. For example, if your specialty is data warehousing, you may want to attend the Data Warehousing World conference sponsored by Digital Consulting, Inc. (DCI). Likewise, a database consultant might consider going to DCI's *Database World* conference or *DB Expo*. Companies such as DCI also sponsor single-topic or dual-topic seminars (example: Data Modeling or Client/Server Computing and Databases).

Better yet, you should strive to attend one of these conferences as a *presenter,* or to teach one of the seminars through one of these companies (we discussed the latter in Chap. 8 when reviewing seminar and training options for your consulting practice). Not only do you meet other consultants and practitioners in the areas in which you specialize, but you are also seen as an expert in a particular subject, which can lead to consulting business.

EDUCATION

Don't overlook continuing education as a way to stay current. You may be tired of school or, like me, have the attention span of a three-year-old these days, and the thought of pursuing another degree causes chills and flu-like symptoms in every fiber of your body. Homework, classes, term papers... NOOOOOOOOO! Keep in mind, though, that continuing education does not necessarily imply pursuing a degree, but rather may involve an occasional class or two, possibly ones you audit (take without a grade). For example, I took courses in artificial intelligence and medical information systems years after receiving a master's degree, without taking any courses toward a degree. You may even take courses at a local community or junior college, such as a two- or three-week course in small business management, just for the sake of near-term knowledge.

It's important to remember that without constant diligence in keeping up to date—the subject of this chapter—your degree loses its "true value" rather quickly, regardless of the school from which you earned it and what connections you made while there. By "true value" I mean the value of the information you learned while there (but not necessarily what you learned about *how* to pursue further information; I'll discuss that in the next section). For example, I obtained my master's degree in management information systems (MIS) in 1982 from the University of Arizona. At the time—and this is still true—Arizona was one of the top schools for MIS in the United States, according to annual surveys.[6] My areas of specialization at the time were database management and what was then called automated systems analysis and is now referred to as CASE.

I can unequivocally state that nearly every individual item I learned about CASE and databases from 1980 through 1982 is now hopelessly out of date, and if I hadn't supplemented the knowledge I acquired at school with continuing education and training, as well as book writing, consulting, and other activities, I would be in...well, deep trouble today. *Don't* expect your degree to carry you past your first job assignment or two, especially in the computer industry of the 1990s.

A METHODOLOGY FOR STAYING CURRENT

I did mention in the previous section that one of the things you can take away from an educational program is the process of *how* to learn (basically, the subject of this chapter). Given how quickly technology evolves, it's imperative that you go beyond what you have learned to date and have a methodology for determining (1) what you need to learn and (2) the most efficient and cost-effective way to do so.

Here is a methodology I've used for close to fifteen years now, and it has served me well. I don't claim that it's for everyone, but if you find yourself hopelessly inundated with information overload and continuing to fall behind, you might want to give this a try.

Earlier in this chapter I mentioned that the "front lines" of staying up to date are through periodicals, particularly the free ones. I subscribe to as many of the no-cost periodicals as possible, and two or three other strategic ones (one general business magazine and one or more computer magazines). When each issue of each periodical arrives, I scan the table of contents for any articles that are of particular interest to me at that moment, with "particular interest" being defined as (1) a project on which I'm currently working, (2) a subject matter that I anticipate turning into a project shortly, or (3) is interesting by itself for some other reason. I read those articles. I may take a total of a half hour or so to skim the others, registering in the back of my mind the subject and any major premises that stand out. And then I shelve that periodical, maybe tearing out a particularly topical article for immediate use. The process is repeated for each other periodical that arrives.

When a new project arises, I have a "mental library" at the back of my mind, and can tell myself "I think I saw an article about {whatever the subject is} in either *Software Magazine* or *Datamation,* sometime in the last six months." I can then narrow my search to a dozen or so magazines, and usually locate that article (sometimes more than one) rather quickly for ready reference.

I then utilize on-line databases for further keyword-based searches among periodical databases to find other references to the subject matter. Sometimes I find that I have some of those periodicals on hand, and can then find the appropriate reference. Other times I'll download one, two, maybe a dozen articles from the information service, building up a library of information on the project at hand.

As I get further into a project and sometimes more information is needed, I then "go to the books" as described earlier. In some cases, there aren't any books available about a particular subject (and, in my case, this leads to a proposal for yet another book project!). Other times, I'll invest $100 or more in two or three top-notch books, none of which had any particular interest for me before but which now are very timely and topical.

When possible, I try to attend conferences and seminars, as well as stay up to date through the other means mentioned in this chapter.

And that's it. I don't try, at any given time, to know everything about everything. It's impossible, and any fruitless attempt to try to do so would only become a major drag on my time. Rather, I pursue what I term a "consultant's orientation," immersing myself in one or more subjects that are at the forefront at a given point in time, and staying peripherally up to date in as many other areas as possible so that I can, when necessary, build from a level of familiarity and then proceed with the "information immersion" process.

SUMMARY

In this chapter, we've discussed many different ways to stay current on the subjects that are important to your consulting career, from periodicals and books to conferences and on-line services. It's important to understand the necessity to stay up to date, because at times it can be a major drag on your time and your sanity.

Just remember; as a computer consultant you are basically in the information business, with processes oriented around the philosophy of "he (or she) who holds the information wins." The same philosophy should be applied to your own business as well. As the pace with which advances and changes in this industry continues to accelerate, you can't afford to be stuck in yesterday's technology and business practices.

END NOTES

1. Laurie Blum, *Free Money—for Small Businesses and Entrepreneurs*, 3d ed., Wiley, New York, 1992.
2. Bruce Blechman and Jay Conrad Levinson, *Guerrilla Financing*, Houghton Mifflin, Boston, 1991
3. Robert E. Kelley, *Consulting: The Complete Guide to a Profitable Career*, Scribner's, New York, 1981.
4. Herman Holtz, *How to Succeed as an Independent Consultant*, Wiley, New York, 1983.
5. Herman Holtz, *The Consultant's Guide to Proposal Writing*, Wiley, New York, 1986.
6. The general subject of computer education, as well as school rankings, is discussed in Alan R. Simon, *The Computer Professional's Survival Guide*, McGraw-Hill, New York, 1992.

CONSULTING SUCCESS PROFILE: DONALD M. JACOBS, PRESIDENT, INTECK, INC.

CAREER AND CONSULTING HIGHLIGHTS

B.A., Astronomy Mathematics, UCLA, 1962

M.S.A., George Washington University, 1970

C.P.A., C.D.P.

Worked in the early days of the space program at Jet Propulsion Laboratories, 1962–1966

Specialist in hospital information systems

Cofounder of Inteck, Inc., a Denver-based hospital information systems consulting firm

Adjunct professor at the University of Denver, with responsibilities for the Health Information Systems certificate program

(*Note:* Donald Jacobs was profiled in *The Computer Professional's Survival Guide** along with other professionals from many areas of the computer industry. Because Don was the representative "successful consultant" among those interviewed for and profiled in that book, we'll take a closer look at Don's career in the consulting field and his advice for other consultants.)

Don's company, Inteck, focuses on helping health care organizations use computers more effectively. As Don puts it, the computers "ask the questions senior health care management *should* ask, but doesn't know how to ask."

He describes Inteck as a small company by design, which consultants join for three reasons:

---

*Alan R. Simon, *The Computer Professional's Survival Guide*, McGraw-Hill, New York, 1992, pp. 110–112.

1. They like to do consulting work, which can be made up of a variety of tasks and assignments. The disadvantages of consulting (although some consultants might see these as advantages) are that extensive travel is often involved and that consultants often don't see projects all the way through to the end—they make recommendations that are either accepted or rejected, and they move on to other projects.

2. They like the people with whom they work. Inteck has a relatively unstructured management style that is suited for self-starters. An extensive office automation system (an open communications forum) is used for internal communications. Within Inteck, Don notes, there is not a lot of competition for promotions as compared to managerial roles, which is often found in large consulting firms.

3. The compensation of Inteck's consultants is typically based on the skills they bring to the company and how they apply those skills to help clients. Thus there is no formal salary structure.

Don notes that Inteck currently focuses exclusively on information systems for hospitals (of all sizes), not for all industries. Inteck focuses on the management side, providing timely, accurate information to senior hospital management.

Unlike the other consultants profiled in this book, Don says that the business climate for Inteck has actually been better in recent years in light of the economic slowdown. Since hospitals are labor-intensive businesses, competitive pressures have forced most of them to cut costs; expanding the role of information systems within hospital environments helps management compensate for cutbacks in labor through more efficient use of resources. The systems that Don's company recommends are intended to become assets of its hospital clients, part of their infrastructures.

When Inteck was first founded, its focus was on what might be termed "traditional" consulting services: evaluation of data processing systems, selection, contract negotiations, and long-range strategic planning. Today, Inteck focuses more on actually running a hospital data processing department, sometimes performing overall management roles and on other occasions supervising the training of new staff members at a client organization. Nearly 75 percent of Inteck's services are focused on operations, rather than acquisition.

It is interesting that the reason for this shift is that Don noticed what often happened at client hospitals after Inteck left the scene—for example, a host of problems often surfaced due to inexperience on the part of the customers in dealing with the environments they now possessed. Inteck's staff members were able to go back to customer management and sell more services, including those built around operations. Because this occurred in 1990–1991, coinciding with the slowdown in the U.S. economy, the timing couldn't have been better for Don Jacobs and Inteck to weather the economic storm.

When asked to list his "secrets and tips" for prospective consultants, Don notes the following:

1. You should get as close as possible to clients, *listen carefully* to them, and stay as close as possible. You should always ask yourself, when making decisions or recommendations, "What did the client say?"

2. Understand the problems and obstacles of your target project as clearly as possible.

3. Even if you are a technical consultant, try to have a management perspective as well as some degree of operational experience and background. That is, understand the costs and operational implications of your technical recommendations.

4. Watch your budget; know what the market will bear in terms of fees and prices for your services and products, and be able to contrast that knowledge with your minimum earnings and revenue requirements.

5. For those consultants operating on a solo basis, prepare yourself for industry and economic downturns by, among other tactics and strategies, being a strong financial manager, with tight control over your budget (mentioned earlier)

and the capability to prepare accurate pro forma statements and forecasts.

6. You need to determine how to keep up with the state of the art in your areas of specialization.

7. You also need to determine the scope of your business operations (local, regional, national, or international).

8. Recognize that "people [i.e., clients] buy people, not brochures"; in other words, there is no substitute for the personal touch in closing a consulting contract.

9. With respect to sales and marketing, a tactic that Don and Inteck pursue in the hospital market is looking for chains; sales to one hospital in a chain often provide near-automatic gateways into other sites.

10. Don't underestimate the potential for security, auditing, and similar services along with your "main" services.

Finally, Don lists the following attributes of successful consultants:

1. You must like working with people.
2. You must be willing to *talk* to people.
3. You must be a good listener.
4. You must be technically strong in your areas of specialization.
5. You must have opinions and visions; you can't be someone who needs to be told what to do or who constantly needs to ask "What do you think?"

THE NEXT STEPS IN YOUR CONSULTING CAREER

What's next? Where does your consulting career or business go from the point that it is at today?

Make no mistake about it, if you could look three years into the future, you would see a *significant* difference in many aspects of your professional life. You may be an independent consultant today, and you may still be one tomorrow—but will your areas of specialization be the same? Will the size and structure of your consulting business be the same?

In this chapter, we'll look at some of the many ways in which your consulting activities can evolve in the years ahead. Note the importance of the word *evolve*, implying that there is some degree of order to the changes that will occur. This isn't to say that a particular opportunity, one which cannot be foreseen today, may not cause you to toss away your current plan and follow some new path. But it does mean that you should have some idea of where you want to go, some plan, to prevent yourself from being buffeted by forces over which you have little or no control.

FORM OF BUSINESS

If, today, you are an independent consultant operating as a sole proprietorship, you may find yourself adding

- Partners
- Contract workers
- Employees

You may even find yourself adding all three. The mid-1990s has been a time of phenomenal activity in the consulting world, following the downturns of the early 1990s. As a result, many consulting companies that started as single-person ventures have grown into formidable regional presences, with account managers, recruiters, organizational structure—basically, they have become "real companies."

Is this what you want for your consulting business? If so, then you need to start *planning* for that to occur. Map out your one-year, three-year, and five-year strategies; study your competition; study the markets; and, perhaps most important, figure out the types of individuals in whom you will be placing your faith to help you achieve your vision.

If your forte is data warehousing, for example, you need to first figure out what *you* will be doing (or what you want to do) in the future. Do you want to be the primary hands-on deliverer of data warehousing architectures and implementations to your clients? If so, you need to make sure that the people you add to your team, regardless of the structure in which you do so, can handle business operations activities, marketing and sales, and the rest of the necessary functions so you can concentrate on that at which you feel you can contribute the most.

On the other hand, if you see yourself as more of a leader, the person who will watch over three or four simultaneous engagements but will not be immersed in any one of them, then you need to make sure you align yourself with qualified people who *can* be the hands-on delivery team, achieving the level of quality that you yourself would deliver if you were intimately involved in a project.

In this context, you have choices to make. Should you take on partners, and if so, how should ownership be divided among you and one or more other individuals? And if that is the route you choose, should you structure yourself as a partnership or a corporation?

The answers are, of course, "It all depends," subject to your specific circumstances, but the important thing to note is that before you start considering expansion and new forms of business organization, you must *first* figure out the role *you* want to play and then determine the roles you need to fill. The worst thing you can do is establish an expansion model in which you are trying to grow a one-person, $150,000 per year business to, say, $5,000,000 per year in revenues, and see yourself as company president, chief architect for all company projects, and hands-on delivery team project manager for two or three engagements a year, with a key role in marketing and business development as well. You don't necessarily need to disengage yourself from the hands-on activity, if that's what you like, but be prepared to establish a role for yourself along the lines of "chief technology officer," with others filling the business administration roles that are necessary to grow a consulting company.

SIZE AND PHILOSOPHY OF BUSINESS

With respect to the discussion above, there are also decisions you will have to make regarding the *type* of "larger consulting company" you wish to become.

On the surface (looking at classified job ads placed by different consulting companies, plus different firms' respective Web sites), lots of consulting companies look nearly identical to one another. They all have a set of "core competencies," they all offer "fabulous" opportunities for growth to new consultants; and so on.

Looking a bit deeper, though, differences start to appear. It's not just that, say, one firm specializes in data warehousing while another is more oriented toward Lotus Notes development, or that one firm offers a broad range of service offerings in Chicago while another offers similar services in Detroit. Rather, these differences are *philosophical* and, as a result, which approach you take will guide a lot of the choices you will make.

At the base level, there are really two types of consulting firms: project consulting firms and staffing consulting firms. There aren't any formal definitions for these terms, nor are firms necessarily one or the other—many firms emphasize project consulting while still having a staffing function, and others operate in the opposite manner—but in general:

- Project consulting firms sell *business solutions* that are almost always implemented by *teams*.
- Staffing consulting firms sell *individual expertise* that is, more often than not, placed onsite at a client's location, integrated into a client's organizational structure (either formally or informally), and then left to operate under the direction of one or more client managers.

For experienced consultants familiar with the "project firm versus body shop" argument, the point of our discussion here isn't to say that one is better than the other, or even that one is *preferable* to the other. Rather, it is simply to guide the reader, who may not fully comprehend the distinctions, in determining what his or her preferences are going forward as expansion and growth occurs. The *worst* thing you could do is to try to position your consulting practice as something that it isn't, or shouldn't be. Your prospective and current clients will become confused; your employees, subcontractors, and associates will be puzzled; and, in general, it will be very difficult for you to succeed.

For example, say that for the past five years, you have spent the majority of your time on application development projects. You started with solo efforts on small-scale client/server applications, and you are currently involved in two different development projects with teams of five subcontractors working on each. It is, you believe, time to take the next step and grow your firm. You have the knack for successful project delivery, and you feel that you can leverage that over five, ten, perhaps twenty simultaneous engagements as you add expertise to your firm.

In such a case, it is imperative that as you start hiring consulting employees, you choose people who are not only technologically skilled (e.g., very good Visual Basic and Microsoft SQL Server developers) but also

- Are "team players" when working as part of a project.
- Have an appreciation of the importance of, and can follow, software development methodologies.
- Are dedicated to the prospect of keeping their respective skills up-to-date through constant training and self-education.

You also need to make sure that the members of the project teams you compose, and thus the employees you hire, complement one another. Front-end user interface developers, back-end database developers, quality assurance specialists— all of these skills need to be orchestrated among your employees to ensure that the projects your firm pursues are adequately staffed. Further, you will probably need to choose some specialties among the various technology areas to ensure that your staff can meet the demands of a given project. This might mean, for example, that you decide to hire database specialists skilled in Microsoft SQL Server (or those who wish to learn that product) to the exclusion of Oracle, Sybase, or Informix experience.

On the other hand, if you decide to build a staffing-oriented consulting company, the general rule is, "Anything goes." Basically, you will hire—or, more likely (at least at the beginning), subcontract with—skilled professionals with marketable skills that are needed by client companies with which you have dealings. Need a Visual Basic programmer? Here's a couple of resumes, you reply; let me know if you want to interview any of these people.

In this type of firm, you have less to worry about in terms of project skills among your own employees. True, these individuals may very well be placed on a client's project team, but more often than not they will be individual contributors who will work alone, under the direction of a manager or supervisor at the client's location.

As your firm grows, it is important that

- Your account managers (sales professionals) have a clear understanding of whether they're selling projects (business solutions) or skills (staffing supplement).
- Your employees and subcontractors have a clear understanding of whose direction they are to follow on an engagement, that of a project manager from your company or of a client to whom they are assigned.
- Your business planning (Chap. 6), marketing (Chap. 4), and other consulting management functions accurately reflect the type of firm you are trying to build.

And this is just the beginning.

INDEPENDENT OR NOT

For many years, the "typical" career path of a computer consultant went something like this:

- An individual would work for several years as a programmer or analyst in a corporate or other organizational setting.
- He or she would decide that consulting seemed interesting.
- He or she might "go independent" immediately, or he or she might go to work as a consultant in an already existing firm, get some experience, and *then* become an independent consultant.

In general, there was a feeling that once someone achieved independent consultant status, working as his or her own boss in his or her own business, there was no other acceptable career choice. Specialties might change, the structure of the consulting firm might evolve, but "once independent, always independent."

Since the early 1990s, though, there has been something of an acceleration in independent consultants becoming *former* independent consultants, joining one of the many firms that have sprung up and flourished in the 1990s business climate. In some cases, the consultant realizes that running his or her own business isn't as attractive a proposition as it once seemed; the thrill of consulting, of learning and implementing new technologies, is overshadowed by all of the drudgery.

In other cases, a consultant may see possibilities for synergy from joining a firm and building a business unit within that organizational structure—basically, he or she can do much better that way than by continuing as a solo practitioner. For example, suppose you specialize in groupware—particularly Lotus Notes—and have been fairly successful at keeping yourself and a contractor or two fully engaged. Now, you find yourself presented with the opportunity to join a firm and build, from scratch, a groupware practice. The compensation package presented to you includes not only a handsome salary but also substantial equity. In this case, giving up your independence may very well be the right path.

There is often a bit of snobbery among independent consultants with respect to independent status. However, the important thing is to do what's right, and what makes the most sense, *for you.* Don't be overcome by a sense of pride or self-importance when presented with an opportunity like the one described above; when all is said and done, the only thing that really counts is your own career satisfaction.

AREAS OF SPECIALIZATION

Another way in which your consulting career may change has to do with areas in which you specialize. Some of these changes may be evolutionary, such as moving away from an emphasis on Xbase (dBASE, FoxPro, Clipper) applications to those which are built on Microsoft Access or Oracle. Other shifts may be more radical—for example, dusting off that COBOL that you put behind you a decade ago to specialize in

Year 2000 conversions, or casting aside your embedded systems expertise to concentrate on electronic commerce over the Internet.

As discussed in Chap. 2, it is imperative that you not only continually assess the marketplace demand—and going rates—for the areas in which you specialize, but also try to sense what the up-and-coming opportunities will be.

GEOGRAPHICAL CONSIDERATIONS

Finally, you may find yourself occasionally shifting the place in which you live or do your primary business. The major area of concern is that if your client base is primarily a local or regional one, you are far more susceptible to the sort of localized economic downturns that marked most of the 1980s and 1990s. If, however, you either (1) travel most of the time to provide client services or (2) telecommute or provide remote (e.g., Internet-based) services, then you are more immune to regional economic fortunes.

SUMMARY

Just as my own consulting activities today look nothing like what they did in the early 1980s, or even the early 1990s, you can be assured that your own services will also change. Whether you spend your entire consulting career as a sole practitioner, grow a sizable firm that you eventually sell to a larger consulting company, or leave independent status to pursue "the perfect opportunity" with another firm, the important thing to remember is that you have a whole range of possibilities in front of you. It's up to you to take advantage of them in the name of consulting success.

DETERMINING YOUR ROLE AS A CONSULTANT ON *THIS* ENGAGEMENT

INTRODUCTION

It is *imperative* that prior to beginning each and every consulting engagement, you take the time to do a thorough and honest (i.e., no fooling yourself!) assessment of *precisely* what your role will be. Even if, on the surface, the upcoming engagement appears to be exactly the same as the one you're just finishing up, or maybe the one before your current assignment, there *will* be differences.

No two engagements are exactly alike, and the significance of this is that your success—or, more ominously, your potential for failure—is largely dependent on your identifying a number of critical attributes and characteristics before beginning an engagement, and noting those that could potentially be problematic.

As we will discuss, this assessment involves far more than the technology with which you'll be working, your specific tasks, and the person who has engaged you and who is paying for your services. There are a number of subtleties that need to be identified, analyzed, and addressed to give you a complete, accurate picture of exactly what you can expect as you embark on this new engagement.

YOUR ASSIGNMENT

In two or three sentences, describe your "mission"—the value you will be expected to bring to this client.

_____

_____

_____

_____

_____

_____

Discussion.   Ideally, you should be able to articulate a *clearly defined* mission that is tied to some type of business objective. For example, you may write, "Develop an application that will permit Company X's employees to change benefits enrollment information. The application will feature a Web browser front end and will be hosted on Company X's intranet infrastructure."

Note that the example description above doesn't describe specific technologies or products (e.g., will both Netscape and Microsoft browsers be supported? What kind of Web server will be used?), schedules, or even the specifics of the deliverables; these all come later. The purpose of articulating the mission statement is to ensure that in the excitement of acquiring a new consulting engagement, possibly one using technologies you've been eagerly waiting to use, you don't overlook the *most important item* of all when it comes to setting a framework to help you succeed—why are you being hired in the first place?

Perhaps your mission statement isn't as clearly defined as the example above. Say you're being engaged to "Do general software development tasks, as assigned, using Visual Basic 4.0 and SQL Server 6.5." Is this lack of precision a problem? Not necessarily, but you should be aware that there is likely to be a strong distinction between an engagement with a clearly defined mission—one tied to the delivery of an application, for example—and an open-ended assignment where you're being engaged primarily for your technical aptitude and knowledge rather than your ability to deliver a specific automated function. In the former case, the many items we'll discuss can—and should—be tied back to this clearly articulated mission statement. In the latter case, the overall consulting engagement environment is likely to be a bit more uncertain, a bit more imprecise—you'll have to watch carefully to prevent problems from occurring.

THE FORM OF THIS ENGAGEMENT

Describe whether this engagement is a staffing assignment or a project.

Discussion.   There is a major difference between staffing assignments and projects! In a staffing assignment, you (and possibly others) are, basically, a temporary employee under the direction of someone at the client. The person to whom you report could, in fact, turn out to be yet another consultant from another company. The net effect of a staffing assignment is that you will receive your direction from the person to whom you are assigned for the duration of the engagement (or until a change in reporting managers occurs).

In a project, however, you are a member of a project *team*, not a temporary employee, and you report to, and receive direction from, your project team's manager.

Though the distinctions between staffing and project engagements are sometimes subtle, it's important to know exactly the form this particular engagement takes. More to the point, you need to know *exactly which person* has the authority to direct your work or determine whether or not you have successfully completed the tasks you've been assigned. When you are in a staffing role, it's typically the client to whom you've been assigned (who may *not* be the person who engaged you, as discussed next), whereas when you are part of a project team, you are insulated from the client(s) by the project manager (unless you yourself are the project manager, of course).

WHO HAS ENGAGED YOU?

Identify the person who has engaged you, his or her title and job functions, and the role he or she will play with respect to your work on this engagement.

_____

_____

_____

_____

_____

_____

Discussion.   In many situations, particularly consulting engagements at larger companies, the person who has made the "yes, we'll hire you" decision is not the person who will be your client. In these situations, it's important for you to not only identify this but also determine exactly what support you may or may not expect from the person who hired you. As discussed at length in Chap. 15, consulting engagements are sometimes the battlefields over which corporate turf battles are fought—and you, the consultant, are a 20-mm artillery shell to one of the contestants and a "must destroy at all costs" target to another. You need to get all of this straight *as soon as possible* so that you know what to expect and how to deal with adversarial situations.

YOUR SPECIFIC TASKS

Describe, in as much detail as possible, the specific tasks you'll be expected to perform on this engagement. For each task, also (1) identify the consulting engagement on which you most recently performed that task (or a similar task) and (2) perform an *honest* self-assessment of your skill level.

TASK	MOST RECENTLY PERFORMED	MY SKILL LEVEL*

*Skill levels: 5 = expert, world-class, "ain't no one better"; 4 = very good; 3 = adequate; 2 = uncomfortable; 1 = have never done; 0 = have tried to do this before, and failed.

Discussion. You need to complete the table above for two reasons. First, you need to make absolutely certain that you are not being assigned tasks for which you do not have the appropriate skills to successfully complete the tasks according to the schedule given you by the client. If you are an expert, world-class Oracle 7.3 developer, you have a very good idea of your productivity rates in various types of environments; you can use the task assignment table above to evaluate client assignments for reasonableness.

Additionally, the table above must tie back to the mission statement you articulated. In short, you need to ensure that the tasks you are being asked to perform are directly in support of the mission you have agreed to accept. Further, you can use this table as a "sanity check" to identify potential problems. If, for example, your mission is, "Manage a project team of five developers and deliver (some type of application) no later than October 31, 1997," you *should* have a task somewhere on the list that reads, "Form project team" or "Hire consultants to fill the five team member roles." If you do not, this should cause you to say, "Hey, wait a minute. If I'm signing up to take responsibility for delivering this application, shouldn't I be the person *forming* the project team, not just managing the people assigned to me?" This would be an item that you should begin handling immediately with respect to project risk management.

You should rate your skill level according to the *whole* of the characteristics of each task. For example, suppose you have a task on your list that reads "Using SuperModeler Version 5.5,* create a logical data model for the catalog order entry application." In the optimal situation, for you to rate your skill level as a "5," you would

- Be a top-notch logical data modeler.

- Have extensive experience using the SuperModeler product.

- Have used, or be very familiar with, the specific enhancements to Version 5.5 of SuperModeler (as contrasted with, for example, your last experience with the product having been with Version 2.0 back in the late 1980s).

- Have *at least* a working knowledge of the major characteristics of a catalog order entry application or a similar business-oriented application, e.g., there will be customers, products, quantity-on-hand, back-orders, etc. (contrasted with, say, all of your prior database design and modeling experience having been for defense applications and embedded electronics subsystems within weapons).

---

*"SuperModeler" is a fictional name for a data modeling CASE tool.

WHAT ARE YOUR DELIVERABLES?

Provide a *complete* list of all deliverables you are expected to produce as a result of your work on this engagement. For each deliverable, also note (1) when it's due (the exact date, if possible; otherwise, a general time frame—e.g., "mid- or late September") and (2) the form of the deliverable (e.g., compiled, unit-tested code; Microsoft Word–based functional specification; etc.).

Deliverable	Due	Form

Discussion.   Deliverables are not tasks, and tasks are not deliverables! There *should* be a direct relationship between the tasks you previously identified and the deliverables listed above. (This relationship may not necessarily be one-to-one; a given task could have more than one deliverable associated with it.)

Even those tasks that seem preparatory in nature should, for your own protection, have one or more deliverables associated with them, and the construction time for those deliverables should be factored into your time for this engagement. Here's a good example: suppose that you, as a project manager, have the following task: "Establish procedures with the systems support organization for doing weekly database backups after the application is delivered and put into production." For your own protection—i.e., making sure that this *will* happen—there should be a deliverable associated with this task, perhaps one entitled "Application XYA Production Database

Backup Procedures." This way, if client organizations choose to subsequently use application XYA as the battleground for their own conflicts, and database backups are *not* done for whatever reason, you will have covered yourself by having already produced a plan—one that will have been signed off by all client organizations—that clearly identifies the procedures that should be taking place.

YOUR UTILIZATION

Are you engaged on this assignment on a full-time or part-time basis? If part-time, are you working on one or more other engagements at the same time? Who controls how you allocate your time? Do you see any overloading conflicts?

Discussion. Many times you are *not* working on a particular engagement on a full-time basis. If you are not, and if you are dividing your time among multiple engagements, you need to clearly identify (for your own benefit) any potential conflicts in geography (different parts of the same city or different cities), timing (staff meetings, etc.), or other engagement characteristics that you anticipate. It's better to identify them *now* rather than after problems begin.

LOCATION(S)

At what location(s) will you be working? The client's site? More than one client site? Your company's office? Your home?

Another consulting company's office (if, say, you're partnering or subcontracting)?

_____

_____

_____

_____

_____

_____

Discussion.   Make sure you know all the details up front, and if any changes should occur, assess any impacts, particularly if you're engaged only part-time.

PREVIOUS EXPERIENCE WITH THIS CLIENT

Is this the first time you've worked with this client? If not, what was/were your previous experience(s) like? How has the "cast of characters" changed since your last engagement there? Are you being engaged by a person for whom you previously did work when he or she was with a different company?

_____

_____

_____

_____

_____

_____

Discussion.   The client's organizational structure—and behind-the-scenes characteristics—are discussed more fully in the next chapter. You should articulate as early as possible, though, any thoughts you have regarding previous experiences with this client—the company, the individual(s), or both. Sometimes we suppress memories of unpleasant experiences, and writing down your thoughts about previous work with the client may alert you that your eager, "Sure, I'm interested" response when queried about the work might have been too quick an answer.

YOUR EXIT STRATEGY

What, or who, determines when you have completed this engagement? Is there a possibility of follow-up work, and if so, are you interested? Is there a definite ending date, or is this engagement more open-ended?

_____

_____

_____

_____

_____

_____

Discussion.   Though this is often the furthest thing from a consultant's mind when he or she prepares to begin a new engagement, there should be a clear understanding by all parties (the client; you; the consulting company through which or with which you work, if applicable; your family; etc.) as to the circumstances under which the engagement will definitely, or probably, end, and what could or will follow afterward. Maybe you want to stay at this client and work on a new phase of your application, or possibly there's a follow-on study to the one you're being engaged to do, and you wouldn't mind staying at this client for the next three or four years. Or perhaps you view this engagement as more of the quick in-and-out variety and want to get on to something new. Whatever the situation is, you should have a fairly good idea going in as to what your exit strategy will be, and the circumstances under which you can complete your work and have it be deemed a *success*.

WHAT'S THE WORST SCENARIO YOU CAN IMAGINE DURING THIS ENGAGEMENT?

Describe, in detail, the *worst* scenario with respect to this engagement—one in which *everything* goes wrong, you are viewed as a complete and total failure, your work product is rejected, etc.

_____

_____

_____

_____

_____

_____

Discussion.   Wow! No one likes to think of the "total melt-down" scenario, but unless you at least consider all of the worst possibilities, you really don't know what the potential downside could be. It's better to confront the nightmare and have a clear understanding of the pitfalls to be avoided than to blindly forge ahead—straight into a horrific consulting situation.

WHAT'S THE BEST SCENARIO YOU CAN IMAGINE RESULTING FROM THIS ENGAGEMENT?

In contrast to the previous question, what will occur if *everything* goes right? Are you "auditioning" for a full-time position with a consulting firm, or perhaps the client? If this 4-month proof-of-concept development engagement is successful, will your firm be awarded an 18-month, $3 million development project?

_____

_____

_____

_____

_____

_____

Discussion. Just as you need to be aware of the downside, you also need to have a clear vision of what you *expect* to happen—what *could* happen—as a result of this engagement. Consulting assignments aren't only about completing the tasks at hand in support of the mission (as covered by several of the earlier questions). In many cases they are stepping-stones toward some longer-term relationship, and if you know—and articulate—what could happen as a result of success, you are often more likely to be successful.

WHAT ARE THE FIVE BIGGEST RISK FACTORS IN THIS ENGAGEMENT?

Based on your answers to the previous questions in this chapter, identify the five factors that are potentially most troublesome during this engagement. Is it the schedule? Lack of control over your own deliverables? Lack of clearly identified tasks?

_____

_____

_____

_____

_____

_____

Discussion.   Basically, the list you prepare above should give you a fairly clear answer to, "If offered it, will I accept this engagement?" You may not have a choice (say, if you work for a consulting company and you are being assigned to this engagement), but at least you can try to identify extremely risky situations and take corrective action (discussing your concerns with your manager or your client, or perhaps even leaving your firm to take a new job, if things look too bleak).

CONCLUSION

Perhaps, after skimming through the items in this chapter and the accompanying discussion, you are thinking, "That's just too tedious; I want to get to work. I'll worry about all of that stuff if problems occur."

Fine, that's your choice, but if you've ever had an extremely unpleasant consulting assignment—and there are darn few of us who can claim to have never done so—try this little exercise. Recall, as best you can, the circumstances before you began an engagement that you *could* have turned down but didn't, and spend about an hour trying to answer the questions posed in this chapter. Looking through your answers, do you notice any warning signs of what eventually happened?

Unless you're absolutely desperate for an assignment—and that happens, as many of us found out during the tough economic times of the early 1990s—you should consider using the information you gather as a result of this chapter's exercises either to help you negotiate a better consulting environment (and some clients will be grateful for your assistance!) or, if possible, to bypass the situation in hopes of a better assignment.

THE CLIENT'S ORGANIZATION: THE *COMPLETE* PICTURE

INTRODUCTION

As anyone who has been consulting for a while will tell you, clients are funny creatures. (Of course, the clients often say that about consultants, but that's another story.) A client hires you, (usually) paying substantially more for your services than it would pay a full-time employee, all under the philosophy, "You, the consultant, are the expert, and your expertise is critically needed to help us with this serious information technology problem."

And then, as often as not, the client puts so many roadblocks in your way that you feel like you're in Army boot camp. "Private! Dig that foxhole—You done? Now fill it up again and redig it 10 feet more to the right—Faster, private, faster! Can't you hear me? No, no, private, not there—fill it up and try again!"

(The computer consulting equivalent would be: "Aren't you done with that module yet? What's taking you so long, I've been waiting for—what the heck is this? I wanted a drop-down list, not a list box—I don't *care* what the specification says, it was changed. Do it over, and hurry because you're behind on testing. What? You don't have your test scripts written yet? How much an hour are we paying you?")

In all seriousness, *every* computer consultant *must* free himself or herself of the notion that a client will do everything possible to help the consultant succeed—after all, the consultant is working *for* the client, right? Well, consider these two items, for starters.

- On engagements at large companies (say, *Fortune* 2000–sized), whether the engagement is staffing or project in nature, there is likely to be at least one person working at the client who wants you to *fail* and will do everything in his or her power to make that happen.

- The client project on which you're working and spending 70 hours per week—the project with the "X Days Until Delivery" posters all over the hallways, the project with the "War Room" set up, the project around which "everyone in IT and the user community is rallying"—is very likely to be just one of half a dozen, maybe more, equally "critical" projects across the entire corporation, and at the boardroom level it is little more than a blip in the overall enterprise IT budget.

Don't fool yourself; everyone has his or her own agenda when it comes to client activity—including *your* work—and these agendas are likely to manifest themselves as time passes on your consulting engagement. The situation isn't *all* bad, but to ignore client-created obstacles—or, worse, to think that they don't exist—is asking for trouble.

The items in this chapter will give you a very clear idea of the things you need to learn about *every* aspect of your client and help you to determine what the impact could be on *your* work, *your* success.

ARE YOU WORKING FOR A USER ORGANIZATION OR FOR CORPORATE INFORMATION TECHNOLOGY?

Is the person to whom you are responsible for producing work product a member of a user organization or an IT department?

_____

_____

_____

_____

_____

_____

Discussion.   This question relates back to one of those in Chap. 14 with respect to identifying not only who has engaged you but for whom you are *really* working. In the context of getting the complete picture of the client's organization, you need to identify whether you are being engaged directly by a user organization, typically one for which you are developing an application, doing an architectural study, or performing similar application-oriented work, or whether you are being engaged by IT *on behalf* of the user organization—in effect, being engaged by a "middleman organization."

What's the difference? It varies from organization to organization, but in many cases an ongoing battle between IT and business units that began as a result of early 1990s decentralization is still raging. Briefly, many user organizations want control over their own technology-driven fate, particularly when it comes to development of applications in support of their business units. Most of us have heard business unit managers complain about lack of responsiveness, lack of support, lack of skills, and other shortcomings on the part of the remnants of the corporate data center. At the same time, IT managers and technologists complain about the lack of specifications on the part of business users regarding their application requests, the lack of time users are willing to put into the development process, and so on. Quite simply, in most cases folks from these various organizations just don't like each other very much.

No matter who controls your work, IT or the businesses, you are likely to find yourself in an adversarial position with the other side as you try to bridge the gaps and, quite simply, get your job done as best you know how. However, you *must* have a clear idea of who is engaging you, even if you are a "just a coding consultant" with very little client relationship responsibility.

WHO IS THE BIGGEST CHAMPION OF YOUR EFFORTS, AND WHY?

Identify (1) the person who you believe to be in a position to be most influential in your success, (2) his or her organizational position, and (3) his or her relationship to your work. Additionally, what are his or her motivations?

_____

_____

_____

_____

_____

_____

Discussion.   You had better be able to identify a "champion" of your work—probably not someone with whom you have day-to-day contact, maybe someone you speak to only in a passing hallway conversation once every two weeks, but nonetheless someone who

- Is in a position to advocate your work and its significance to other senior executives at the client.
- Can help advise you on the best ways to navigate the political minefields across the client organization.
- If you find yourself or your work attacked by your detractors (see the next item), will stand by you and not let you turn into yet another sacrificial consultant.
- Has a *personal* interest in your success.

Remember this: In all but the rarest circumstances, as a consultant, you personally have *no* power base at all within your client's organizational culture, and you need allies. If you're providing consulting services about cross-organizational architectural issues, for example, it should be obvious what value a champion can provide as others start to perceive your work as threatening to their positions, their power base, even their jobs. Even if you're "only" developing code, though, there should be someone to whom you can turn for assistance in working with the corporate database administrator to help get your schemas created in a timely manner, to help you schedule adequate system testing time; to help you get access to relevant corporate coding standards, to make sure that you have an adequately configured development machine—the list goes on and on.

WHO MIGHT WANT YOU TO FAIL?

Identify *every single person* (not only those people working in the client's company but also other consultants with whom you will be in contact, people in your own consulting company—*anyone*) who would benefit from your failure on this engagement. List what each one would gain from your failure.

PERSON	COMPANY/ POSITION OR ROLE	YOUR PRIOR EXPERIENCES WITH THIS PERSON	WHAT HE/SHE WOULD GAIN FROM YOUR FAILURE	YOUR "NEUTRALIZATION" STRATEGY

Discussion. To the uninitiated, this item may seem to be the ultimate in paranoia, but any consultant who has ever been "submarined" by a client or another consultant is probably experiencing a flood of emotions (not many of them pleasant) as he or she is reading this.

To get directly to the point, there *are* people who want you to fail. Consider:

- The client who has engaged you, a mid-range vice president, is considered to be one of three candidates to move into the powerful executive V.P. role within the next year. Do you really think that his or her two rivals want you—and your client—to be successful?

- You are part of an enterprise architectural planning and strategy team, made up of not only you and the client but also other consultants from another company. Do you think that the other consultants, their eyes on the follow-on development work and the resulting expanded role for their company, want *you* to be successful? Wouldn't it be better for them if *they* were perceived as the valuable consultants and you as just a drain on the client's budget?

- You are engaged by the corporate IT department to develop an application for a particular business unit. For the past two years the business unit's management team has been trying to gain control over their own development because they perceive the IT department to be nonresponsive and nonsupportive. It isn't unheard of for those in a business unit to sabotage their own development to make the point that, "Once and for all, give *us* control over development; even when bringing in a consultant, IT *still* failed." How much support are you expecting?

The list of such scenarios goes on and on. The point is that consulting is not simply about technology and business processes; the type of nasty corporate politics that entertains us in TV shows and movies is *very real,* and the military strategy of "know your enemy" is *very* applicable to each and every consultant.

WHO ARE *ALL* THE DECISION MAKERS IN THE OVERALL PROCESS OF THE WORK ON THIS ENGAGEMENT?

Identify *all* people—those working at your client company and other consultants (including those from your own company, such as the project manager)—who will be making decisions of *any* type (discussed below) throughout your engagement.

PERSON	COMPANY/ ORGANIZATION	POSITION OR ROLE	QUALIFICATIONS RATING*	POWER RATING†

*Qualifications rating (for this engagement): 5 = very knowledgeable—every confidence that "the right" decision will be made; 4 = will probably make a good decision, but may need convincing; 3 = uncertain—sometimes makes a good decision, but not necessarily in a timely manner; 2 = more often than not will make the wrong decision; 1 = totally incompetent.
†Power rating: 5 = very powerful; 4 = influential—usually gets his or her way; 3 = well thought of, but not necessarily a forceful leader; 2 = his or her suggestions are usually disregarded; 1 = people are openly insubordinate to him or her.

Discussion. It's highly unlikely that there will be a single person who will be responsible for making every decision relevant to your work, from selection of software (development tools, database management products, etc.) to approval of application architecture and designs to deciding what functionality is or isn't in scope. The very nature of consulting usually means that you find yourself dealing with a lot of people, many of whom are empowered to make decisions that will either help you in your work or provide substantial impediments to your success. It is very important that you identify all of these people as soon as possible and gauge, as accurately as possible, how qualified they are with respect to the decisions you expect them to be making relative to your engagement. Just as with your potential adversaries (discussed before), you need to know this information so that you can identify any potential problems and deal with them.

WHAT OTHER CONSULTING COMPANIES ARE PART OF THE "BIG PICTURE"?

Identify all other consulting companies that are involved in other work at the client that either is directly related to your engagement or has peripheral relationships (e.g., another consulting company is working on another application that at some point in the future will, along with the application you're developing, provide information to a data warehouse). Identify as much as you can about their reputation, your relationship with them, and your strategy for dealing with them.

COMPANY	THEIR ROLE(S) AT THIS CLIENT	THEIR REPUTATION	"FRIEND OR FOE"	YOUR STRATEGY

Discussion.   Multicompany consulting efforts have become increasingly common in the 1990s. Additionally, the increasingly integrated nature of information technology means that even companies with which you and your company aren't *directly* working may be part of the "big picture" in the client's mind. Therefore, it's important that you identify all of the players, whether they might be considered allies (e.g., a company with which yours has an ongoing strategic relationship and with which you work on many different joint engagements) or foes (e.g., a company which aims to get an exclusive outsourcing agreement at the client and views you and your company as a barrier to be removed).

WHAT IS THE CLIENT'S GENERAL ATTITUDE TOWARD CONSULTANTS?

Describe, in as much detail as possible, what you know about the client's general attitude toward consultants—how they are generally treated, how much support they receive, etc.

_____

_____

_____

_____

_____

_____

Discussion.   Those of you who are new to the consulting world may be surprised to learn that some companies use consultants grudgingly, and generally take a very adversarial stance with *all* consultants. They will flagrantly expand the scope of a project and demand that the consultant complete the work under the terms of the existing fixed-price contract; they will give consultants second-rate equipment that is insufficient to successfully accomplish the development tasks; they will schedule testing time for consultant-led projects only in the middle of the night, saving the "good" time slots for their employees; and so on.

It's important that you understand what the organizational culture is relative to dealings with consultants. You may choose to accept an engagement in a potentially adversarial environment, but at least you will know what to expect. Talk to others who have worked there before, if possible, or use your intuition during your interviewing and/or sales development time to try to get a sense of what it will *really* be like to work there as a consultant.

WHAT IS THE "DOWNSIZING" HISTORY AND FORECAST AT THE CLIENT?

List major "downsizing" events at the client over the past five years, if possible. Also list any projected or announced staff reductions planned for the next year.

_____

_____

_____

_____

_____

_____

Discussion.   On the one hand, downsizings are good for the consulting business—work still needs to be done, and the massive corporate cutbacks of the late 1980s and early 1990s is one reason for the boom in consulting services we're seeing in the mid-1990s.

At the same time, many consultants have themselves, as consultants, been caught in the middle of staff reductions that affect not only full-time employees of the client but also contracted support. It's important that you have a sense not only of what has happened at the client in the past but of what will, or could, happen in the near future. This doesn't mean, for example, that you would avoid a client with announced downsizing plans covering the next three quarters, but if there is a possibility that cutbacks could also result in project cancellations and dismissal of consulting support, then you would probably want to have a backup engagement in place or already be dividing your time between two clients.

WHAT RECENT ORGANIZATIONAL SHIFTS HAVE OCCURRED?

List as many *relevant* organizational changes at the client in the past two years as possible (and any that are expected to occur during your engagement). "Relevant" is defined as having anything to do with the scope of your work, having affected your project champion or any of the decision makers (refer to earlier questions), etc.

_____

_____

_____

_____

_____

_____

Discussion.   Who has gained influence and responsibility in recent years, and who has seen his or her role diminish—and what do those changes mean for your upcoming work? Are there any pending organizational announcements that could cause your project (or related efforts) to be moved from one organization to another, or to be postponed or cancelled? Basically, what's going on at the client that could affect your work?

WHAT INFRASTRUCTURE GROUPS WILL YOU NEED TO WORK WITH?

Identify all infrastructure IT organizations—database administration, the help desk, network services, etc.—with which you will need to work throughout your engagement.

_____

_____

_____

_____

_____

_____

Discussion.   Even if you're being engaged to do application development by an IT organization rather than a business unit, chances are that your IT "sponsor" is an application development group, and in the "big picture" it is only one of many clients to a variety of infrastructure organizations. You need to identify all of these organizations and get as much information as possible about each of them (how cooperative they are likely to be, for example).

WHAT IS THE OVERALL CORPORATE CULTURE AT THE CLIENT?

Describe as best you can the overall organizational culture at the client, as relevant to your engagement.

_____

_____

_____

_____

_____

_____

Discussion.   Many clients, particularly smaller businesses, are fairly laid back and, in general, very pleasant places to work. Other clients may have a culture that is seeded with nastiness and sows "I win, the rest of you lose" competitiveness among its employees.

Some clients are early adopters of emerging technologies and development tools; others are steeped in antiquated systems and are generally wary of new technologies and products.

No two companies are exactly the same, and it's important to understand as much as you can about the culture that will pervade your work.

WHOM ARE YOU DEPENDENT UPON— BUT DON'T HAVE CONFIDENCE IN?

Identify all people whom you expect to be dependent upon throughout your engagement (i.e., not just those with whom you'll have contact, but rather those who will be producing things that you will need in order to move ahead in your own work), and in whose ability to deliver you do *not* have complete confidence.

PERSON	COMPANY/ POSITION OR ROLE	WHAT YOU EXPECT TO NEED	POTENTIAL PROBLEMS	YOUR STRATEGY

Discussion. Maybe it's the database administrator (DBA), who is supporting 10 different application development efforts in addition to yours and has candidly told you that sometimes requests for database builds take up to a week to accomplish. Perhaps it's the SQL Server developer assigned to your project team by the client, who, it turns out, has no database experience at all. It's critical that you identify all of these individuals as soon as possible and develop a strategy for dealing with each of them, whether it's a workaround of some type, trying to seek a replacement, or doing whatever else you can to remove impediments to your success.

WHO ARE THE TECHNOLOGISTS, AND HOW SKILLED ARE THEY?

Identify all "technologists"—architects, designers, coders, testers, etc.—involved in your project and the skill level of each.

PERSON	POSITION OR ROLE	HIS OR HER SKILL LEVEL*

*Skill levels: 5 = expert, world-class, "ain't no one better"; 4 = very good; 3 = adequate; 2 = uncomfortable; 1 = has never done this before; 0 = has tried to do this before, and failed. [See the discussion in Chap. 14 on determining skill level based on *all* attributes of an assignment (tasks, technology, specific products and versions, application familiarity, etc.).]

Discussion.   Anyone who will be expected to produce something tangible, from an application architecture or design to a coded, tested module, needs to have his or her qualifications to perform this job assessed. Note that this assessment is not limited to consulting project managers; you should do this if you're an individual contributor working on a project managed by someone else! Simply put, if you're part of a team, you want to know the qualifications of *every* other team member— your subordinates, your peers, and even your "superiors" (in the sense of the team's structure).

CONCLUSION

It's all about intelligence. In the interest of world peace I'll avoid the military intelligence analogies to wars and battles, but suffice it to say that there are few situations in the consulting world as unpleasant as going into an engagement and being totally surprised and shocked by the climate in which you're working, when in reality you could have learned a great deal *before* you began that assignment.

Make no mistake about it, some companies are *nasty* places to work as a consultant! Whether you're being used as cannon fodder in ongoing interorganizational political battles, or whether there is a pervasive corporate culture that views outside consultants as simple tools to be used to the extreme until they "break," the most interesting consulting work could be completely overshadowed by the nastiness that pervades every aspect of your time spent there.

On the other hand, there are other places where consultants are treated *better* than employees with equivalent skills and equivalent responsibilities. Which setting are you walking into? Sometimes you don't know for sure, but you can *certainly* learn a great deal about what to expect, who the players are and their respective attitudes, and many other factors that will tell you a lot about what support you can expect to receive—or not receive.

EVALUATING AND RECOMMENDING TECHNOLOGIES AND PRODUCTS

INTRODUCTION

On a consulting engagement, sometimes you're being retained to perform specific development-related services using client-provided development tools: Visual Basic or PowerBuilder or SQL Server, for example. In these situations you typically don't get involved with technology and product selection (other than, say, supplemental software such as browser plug-ins or custom controls).

In other situations, you may be focusing exclusively on managerial and high-level architectural issues and, at least for the duration of that particular engagement, not getting into the details of specific products.

In many engagements, though, your role as a consultant will require you to evaluate a number of alternative products (sometimes even different technological and architectural approaches) and make a recommendation to your client—and upon accepting your recommendation, the client will be spending tens or hundreds of thousands of dollars, perhaps even millions. Examples might be:

- A client wants to know whether to use Microsoft SQL Server or Informix as the database engine for the application that will be developed.

- You are asked whether the client/server database interface should use an Open Database Connectivity (ODBC) driver or a native interface.

- The client is evaluating data warehousing tools and needs to choose among offerings from a variety of vendors for extraction, transformation, and data quality services.

- You are asked whether the application development language should be Visual Basic (the current corporate standard at the client) or some other language.

You had better do the evaluation and recommendation process *right*—the success of this particular engagement, and others that will follow, will depend in part on how well you handle the evaluation and recommendation process.

This doesn't mean that the client will automatically accept your recommendation; most consultants have been involved in product selection efforts where a particular recommendation is given to the client, who thanks the consultant and does something completely different. It's *usually* the client's responsibility to make the final decision (in fact, a careful consultant tries never to be the decision maker in these situations, only the recommending party), and if the client chooses another path, or if your recommendation is accepted and the client mishandles areas like support issues or development standards, then it's *not* your problem.

What this does mean, though, is that you need to be exhaustively thorough in every evaluation in which you find yourself involved. Increasingly, seat-of-the-pants, off-the-cuff recommendations of products or technologies will do little other than cause you problems. No one knows better than an active, technologically astute consultant how rapidly technology and products change. Not only are new products introduced with increasing frequency and rapidity, but most of us have had experience with product releases that take a large step *backward* in terms of performance, functionality, integration capability, or other characteristics. Do *you* want to be the person a client can point to and say, "That rotten consultant told us to spend $250,000 on

Product X because he (or she) used it and it was great—and the new release is *horrible!* The trade press is blasting it, the vendor is probably going to go out of business. I can't believe that consultant didn't even check those things out!"

The material in this chapter is not a garden-variety, how-to-pick-a-product discussion. Rather, it is focused on the special challenges facing you, the consultant, as you perform this role on behalf of your client.

WHAT IS YOUR CHARTER AND WHAT ARE YOUR DELIVERABLES?

Describe, in detail, your "charter"—the specific role you have been given to perform—with respect to the evaluation and/or recommendation process. What are you expected to deliver as a result of your work?

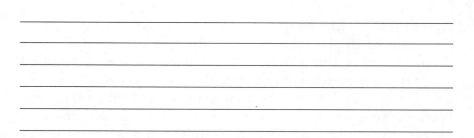

Discussion.   As with the details of your consulting engagement as a whole, you *must* have a very clear idea of *exactly* what is the task that you are being given to do. Are you simply doing preliminary research on a number of different products in a given area of technology (e.g., Web browsers) and presenting the results of your research? Or are you not only doing the research but also making a recommendation to the client as to which product should be used? Perhaps you are being handed the results of research done by some other consultant or an internal employee and given the task of making a recommendation based on that material.

Whatever the situation, you have to clearly understand exactly what it is that you are expected to do and deliver.

WHAT IS YOUR CURRENT KNOWLEDGE BASE?

Describe, in detail, your comfort level with the evaluation process at hand.

_____ _____

_____

_____

_____

_____

_____

Discussion.   Maybe you are a data warehousing consultant—one of the best there is, in your opinion—but all of the projects you've done to date have used custom-developed COBOL code to handle the "middleware" layer of extraction, transformation, data quality management, and target database loading. Now, on your current engagement, you have the task of looking at the various data warehousing product suites available and recommending whether the client should spend somewhere between $50,000 and $200,000 on one of those products, and, if so, which product should be chosen.

You need to *candidly* assess your comfort level with this role. If you've never used one of these products before, how comfortable are you with evaluating not only the user interface, with all of its drop-and-drag niceties, but the end-to-end, architectural functionality?

This isn't to say that you should be uncomfortable with this task or draw away from it. Rather, understand that you are likely to have a bit more of a learning curve with respect to your assignment than you would have if you had used one or more of these products previously and already knew what you liked and didn't like.

WHAT RESOURCES ARE AVAILABLE TO YOU?

Describe *all* resources available to you for the evaluation and/or selection task. Include results from similar evaluations done by your consulting company, previous efforts made by the client, Internet access, computer systems for hands-on testing, support from IT infrastructure groups for the hands-on testing, etc.

_____

_____

_____

_____

_____

_____

Discussion.   Make no mistake about it, it's imperative that adequate resources be available to you. No self-respecting consultant would ever recommend a product without having given it a thorough, hands-on "test drive," including as much stress testing as possible. Also, it can save a lot of time—and help you consider things you hadn't thought of already—to have access to articles; reports from Meta Group, Gartner Group, or other analysts; the vendors' Web sites; etc.

As a consultant, you are often challenged—more so than if you were doing a similar task as an employee—because of limited infrastructure and resources at your client. If, for example, you must be onsite and there is no Internet access, the client doesn't subscribe to any industry analysis service, and, in general, you have little or no support, then your task will be much more difficult than if, say, you were doing the work in your office and you had all of those resources available. *Know your environment!*

IS THE ASSIGNMENT REASONABLE?

Assess the reasonableness of your assignment in terms of time and resources available.

Discussion. Sometimes an evaluation and recommendation assignment is like a high school history exam with the following question: "Describe, in detail, the complete socioeconomic and political history of the United States from 1776 until the present, giving detailed examples. Use only this side of this page of the exam for your answer."

Laugh if you want, but many consultants have found themselves in situations where a client begins a kick-off meeting with a sentence like the following: "We have three weeks to make a recommendation for a standard data mining tool that will be used by all business units across the entire enterprise. We don't have time to get into hands-on evaluation, but let's look at the project plan…"

This really happens—a lot! Typically a client forms some type of "task force" with a relatively limited budget and unreasonable schedule, and gives the group a charter to make far-reaching, large-expenditure decisions without anywhere near the resources and time available—so the group hires consultants and passes on the mandate instead of informing their management as to the unreasonableness of the task.

This is a situation in which a consultant has a tremendous advantage over an employee: You can—no, make that *must*—give immediate feedback if you are being asked to make recommendations without adequate time and resources. It's no different from being engaged to develop an application or a portion of one and being given a totally unreasonable and unrealistic schedule. In a development situation, it will be very obvious that you can't complete your development tasks, but in an evaluation/recommendation situation, it's sometimes tempting to say, "Oh, what the heck, they [the client] weren't being reasonable anyway, so I'll just pick one of the choices."

Don't do that!

WHAT IS *REALLY* AT STAKE?

Describe in detail the implications of the evaluation/selection task for which you've been engaged.

_____

_____

_____

_____

_____

_____

Discussion. Quite simply, in some circumstances, you may be choosing among a couple of competing third-party controls, and if one doesn't work as advertised, it's really no big deal; another one can be acquired, and development will proceed.

In other circumstances, however, you may be engaged as a senior-level consultant to make a recommendation that will have architectural consequences across a large portion of the client's enterprise. For example, the client wants to move toward an enterprise system built around distributed objects, but is uncertain as to which of the competing standards it should select. The results of your work in this area will have *major* impact!

Another example: The client is a mainframe-oriented organization, and most of its transactional applications are built on top of DB2/MVS databases. You, however, have been engaged to build a data warehouse, and the client wants to know if it should stay with DB2/MVS for that environment or purchase a Unix-based DBMS such as Oracle, Sybase, or Informix. This is another situation in which your recommendation will have a major impact on the client.

Know what's *really* at stake; it will help guide your actions throughout all tasks related to the evaluation and recommendation process.

WILL YOUR SUBSEQUENT WORK BE BASED ON YOUR RECOMMENDATION?

Are you evaluating and recommending a technology or product that you will personally use in a follow-on phase of activity at the client?

_____

_____

_____

_____

_____

_____

Discussion.   If you will have to live with the results of a recommendation you make, you had better be *extra* careful throughout the entire evaluation process. This doesn't mean that you would do a sloppy job if you personally won't be using a product or technological approach, of course; rather, you should know whether such factors as usability should be geared toward your own preferences or those of others.

WHAT'S YOUR "GUT FEEL" ABOUT THE VENDORS?

What are your instincts about each vendor: Is the vendor reputable? Does it willingly provide site references? Is the sales presentation "too slick"? Has a hands-on technologist come to the product demo along with the sales person? Will the vendor willingly leave a demo copy for you to use? Is the vendor asking for money up front?

Discussion.   Sometimes a vendor's salesperson sees a consultant as a tool he or she can use to make a quick, easy sale. There could be hints of engagement work for you provided by the vendor if you recommend its product; sometimes the salesperson tries to get confidential information about the client from you (organizational structures, upcoming projects, etc.); etc.

Keep your discussions with vendors' representatives businesslike and professional, and *never* forget that you are engaged to represent your client's best interests. Try to tune into your sixth sense about the vendor as you sit through briefings and product demos; you'll be amazed what you can pick up.

WHAT ORGANIZATIONAL STANDARDS AND CONSTRAINTS ARE THERE?

Describe all organizational constraints at your client that affect your evaluation and recommendation work. Examples would be (1) no products that are in beta release or the first commercial version or (2) only products that are on the approved list of corporate standards.

_____

_____

_____

_____

_____

_____

Discussion.   There's no point wasting your time—and the client's money—if there are organizational constraints that prohibit you from even considering a particular product. As mentioned above, some clients have a "no beta" or "no V1.0" policy to which no exceptions may be made, no matter how wonderful a given product is. In other cases there may already be a "short list" of approved alternatives from which your selection must be made. (For example, "Only Oracle or Sybase DBMSs can be used for an application's database.")

Identify *all* your constraints as soon as possible; they will vary from client to client.

WHO ARE *ALL* THE PROPONENTS OF A PARTICULAR ALTERNATIVE?

Identify all people—client employees, other consultants, etc.—who are proponents of a given alternative, and why.

_____

_____

_____

_____

_____

_____

Discussion.   It's more than just technology; it's more than just corporate standards. Make no mistake about it, there's a good chance that some executive or other consultant is urging that a particular approach or product be chosen. Why? That's what *you* have to find out!

WHO ARE *ALL* THE OPPONENTS OF A PARTICULAR ALTERNATIVE?

Identify all people—client employees, other consultants, etc.—who do not want a given alternative selected, and why.

_____

_____

_____

_____

_____

_____

Discussion.   As with the proponents, you must identify anyone who will be an automatic detractor (read, enemy) of a given choice. This doesn't mean that you will automatically steer clear of that choice, but as with the consulting engagement as a whole, you had better be tuned in to the political aspects to avoid getting caught by surprise.

CONCLUSION

As with each consulting engagement as a whole, you need to do a lot of up-front homework before beginning tasks that involve the evaluation and selection of products and technologies. For the most part, there are no automatic, "safe" choices, especially when you are dealing with emerging technologies and the products built on top of them.

   Make sure your assignment is realistic, make sure you have adequate resources and time, and make sure you *clearly* understand the implications of your choice.

THE ENTERPRISE-SCALE ENGAGEMENT

INTRODUCTION

As your consulting career moves ahead and you become an experienced, "senior-level" consultant, chances are that you'll be involved in engagements that are focused on a significant portion of a large company's enterprise—perhaps even the entire enterprise. Examples of these "enterprise-scale" engagements include:

- Developing an enterprise-wide architecture based on distributed objects that will be used as the framework for all upcoming application development.

- Analyzing all existing data warehousing and business intelligence environments in the sales and marketing organizations of *each* division of a multinational corporation to see what overlap exists and what capabilities could possibly be leveraged among the units.

- Evaluating several different emerging networking technologies and making a recommendation for standardization across the client's global infrastructure.

- Cataloging all of the various electronic mail systems in use across a multinational corporation's enterprise and developing a two-year migration plan in accordance with the charter given to you by your client: "We all *will* be running the same E-mail software two years from now."

No doubt you can think of dozens more enterprise-scale consulting assignments, or have personally had experience in these situations.

Why do we place special emphasis on enterprise-scale consulting activities? For the simple reason that in addition to all of the "normal" political and organizational overtones and issues with which you must deal on any engagement (see Chap. 15), the fact that your charter crosses such a broad range of organizational entities gives you a handicap—sometimes a severe one—*before* you even begin your engagement.

Think about it. Let's say that you've been engaged by the director of the Advanced IT Architecture Group, a person who reports directly to the corporate chief information officer (CIO). He or she is probably a fairly powerful person, right? So if you've been engaged as part of a team to develop and implement a distributed object framework for all applications worldwide, you'll get everyone's cooperation and support, right?

Hah! Did you know that in most large corporations, each high-level business division is likely to have its own CIO? Did you know that in many organizations, the culture is such that the CIO has only marginal influence over certain types of IT activities of those running the business units, especially when it comes to the rapid deployment of new technologies? (The CIO is often viewed as "the person responsible for keeping all of those mission-critical mainframe legacy systems running while others work on new, interesting technologies.")

The point is that as with any consulting engagement, it takes far more than technological prowess to be successful. The chances of having real *enemies*—those who will do *anything* to prevent you from succeeding because that's not in their best interests—are significantly higher in broad, enterprise-scale engagements. As a consultant, you may have been given a charter to perform activities and produce results that are in the best interests of the corporation as a whole, but *never forget* that there will almost always be someone whose position, status, financial well-being, and possibly even job will be harmed by your success. That's the situation in the business world, and at bottom, as a consultant you really are little more than a tool of the person and organization who has engaged you, despite the significance of your formal charter.

So does that mean that you should absolutely stay away from enterprise-scale engagements? Of course not; you just need to see them as they really are: assignments where your interpersonal skills and negotiating powers are as important as your technical abilities (if not more so). Never go into one of these engagements with a feeling of self-importance or a false sense of power; that's the surest path to failure.

WHO MAKES UP THE "INNER CIRCLE"?

Describe, in detail, the "inner circle" of your engagement team, including the following

- The person who has engaged you
- All core members of the engagement team
- All auxiliary members of the engagement team
- The executive sponsor(s)

For each person, list his or her position, the role he or she will play for the engagement, the amount of time (%) he or she will participate in activities *directly* related to the engagement, and (if known) how he or she came to be a part of the engagement team.

PERSON	POSITION	ROLE	% TIME	HOW ASSIGNED

Discussion.   You want to make absolutely sure you know the opening-day lineup, the strengths of each player (and his or her weaknesses), who's on the bench, and what the game plan is. (I'm writing this just as baseball season is beginning, if you couldn't tell!)

In most situations, enterprise-scale engagements are performed by a team, rather than a single individual, for a couple of reasons: the sheer magnitude and breadth of the work that must take place, and to try and achieve as high a degree of balance as possible among positions represented. That said, it is just as likely as not that the project team will be *ill-formed*. For example:

- The core team consists of 10 members, but all of them are outside consultants or members of the core Advanced Technology Group; no business unit IT people are represented.

- Everyone assigned to the team is performing his or her role on a part-time basis, and most of them (including you) are assigned at less than 50 percent utilization.

- There are three different executive sponsors representing not only IT but the two major business areas of the corporation—but these people don't get along, and it's expected that after the kickoff meeting, the next contact the engagement team will have with them is the day the results are presented.

- You and two other consultants from your company are working on the engagement team with five internal corporate employees—each of whom was assigned to the team over his or her own strenuous objections that, "There's real work to be done; why am I wasting time on this task force that won't accomplish anything?"

Basically, the baseball lineup analogy is an appropriate one; you want to clearly and accurately determine the strengths and weaknesses of the members of the engagement team and the way it is structured. You may not have much—or any—influence over making changes to overcome these weaknesses, but at least you have a sense of what to expect and, hopefully, how to work around any shortcomings.

ARE THERE ANY DIFFERENCES BETWEEN THE FORMAL CHARTER AND THE REAL AGENDA?

Using all available information—conversations, your knowledge about the people and organizations from your own prior engagements, even your intuition—describe any differences between the formal charter of the engagement team and the real agenda.

Discussion.   If you look at enterprise-scale engagements (and their missions) purely from a technological point of view, they make a lot of sense. There is usually serious overlap of functionality and capabilities among business units within a large corporation as a result of a bottom-up approach to development of applications, systems, databases, etc. Given the advances in technology, it makes sense to take a fresh look at where capabilities could be integrated and consolidated, or a transition to new platforms and infrastructures made, to the betterment of all.

Now let's look at realities. In many situations (not all, but many), enterprise-scale engagements are tools in some type of corporate power play. Are the business units getting too large a percentage of the technology budget, to the detriment of the data center (or what remains of it)? OK, let's launch a large, all-encompassing "enterprise integration effort" with the mission of "reducing the waste in expenditures caused by overlapping functions across business units." And, by the way, that funding that's going to the business units now? It really should be brought back into corporate IT's domain, right?

This isn't to say that every enterprise-scale engagement in which you become involved will be like a plot from *Melrose Place* or a Sidney Sheldon novel, but don't for a minute fool yourself into believing that there aren't things going on behind the scenes that will have a great deal of impact on your success—or lack thereof. As with the people involved, it's essential that you know what the real story is.

WHO WILL BE THE BIGGEST WINNERS?

Assuming that the engagement team is successful in accomplishing its mission (with the definition of "successful" varying from one engagement to another), who will benefit most from your success? For each of these individuals, what is the role he or she is playing for the engagement?

Person	Current Position	What He/She Could Gain	Role for Engagement

Discussion.   It's certainly not a bad thing that people benefit from your success in your consulting role; that's what the whole consulting business is about. The point here is to add more detail to the picture you're creating of the environment in which you will be working, and to highlight a possible warning sign.

If, for example, your responses in the table above indicate that three or four individuals—mid-level to senior executives—will benefit most from, say, the establishment of a multi-business-unit data warehousing environment, and *none* of those individuals has more than a cursory role (or maybe any direct role at all) in the actual work you're doing (the last column), then you need to look more closely at the situation. Are you being engaged as a "point person" to do the "dirty work" for these people? That's possible, and if so, what are the implications of this?

WHO WILL BE THE BIGGEST LOSERS?

Again, assuming that the engagement team is successful in accomplishing its mission (with the definition of "successful" varying from one engagement to another), who will lose most from your success? For each of these individuals, what is the role he or she is playing for the engagement?

PERSON	CURRENT POSITION	WHAT HE/SHE COULD LOSE	ROLE FOR ENGAGEMENT

Discussion.   This is the flip side of the previous question. In many corporate settings, there are losers: those who are left behind when the promotions are handed out, those who find themselves losing part or all of their organization, those who have a project halted in middevelopment and control transferred to someone else—the list goes on and on.

Just as you need to identify your enemies (Chap. 15) on any engagement to make sure you have as clear a picture as possible of everyone whose interests might not exactly be aligned with your own, you need to do the same thing (that is, identify potential enemies, but on a broad scale) when you cross a large number of organizational boundaries in the course of your consulting work. Remember this: Just because someone is part of your team doesn't necessarily mean that he or she wouldn't lose position or responsibility if the team's recommendations go in one direction rather than another.

WHAT SIGNIFICANT GAPS ARE THERE IN YOUR ASSIGNMENT, AND WHAT ARE THE IMPLICATIONS?

Identify any significant gaps in your charter, and possible implications for the enterprise as a whole.

_____

_____

_____

_____

_____

_____

Discussion. Sometimes an enterprise-scale engagement has an area or two that has been declared as "out of scope." While your initial reaction might be along the lines of, "Whew, one less thing I need to look at!" you need to understand the implications of leaving those areas alone.

For example, suppose you are part of a study team looking at an enterprise-wide data warehousing strategy, the results of which will (if adopted) form an architectural basis for *all* data warehouse and data mart implementations in a multinational corporation—except for the U.S. Sales and Marketing organization.

So why is that? On the one hand, as a consultant, you can easily take the view, "Hey, it's not my company; if that group doesn't want to play nice, then it's not my problem." And you would not be entirely incorrect in taking that position.

At the same time, you need to consider the implications of excluding U.S. Sales and Marketing from the scope of your work and determine what the impacts are. If, for example, your team is proposing a particular architectural approach to produce a data mining front end to help forecast market trends in support of proactive activities by sales representatives across the world, you need to consider questions such as:

- Is there any way to integrate U.S. sales data with sales date from the rest of the global business units if the United States won't be part of the implementation-phase activities? If so, does there need to be specialized, customized data transfer that might not conform to the tools the client puts in place as part of the data warehousing initiative?

- If U.S. sales are 55 percent of global volume, will the models that will be built in support of the data mining activities still be accurate if the U.S. data isn't available? How about if U.S. data isn't available on a monthly or quarterly basis, but only semiannually?

The point is that if you're chartered to take an enterprise-wide approach to your assignment, then it's *your* responsibility as a consultant to determine if areas that have been designated as "out of scope" really should be part of the activities. You may not have the power or influence to change the scope, nor do you necessarily want to, but you *don't* want to make recommendations and produce deliverables that, when looking at the enterprise-wide picture, are inadequate because of the exclusion of certain areas.

WHAT CAN I GAIN FROM NEXT-PHASE ACTIVITIES, AND WHAT CHANNELS ARE NOW OPEN TO ME?

Describe potential consulting work for you (or your consulting company) that may result from your current activities and how you can best use the contacts you make to help make this work a reality.

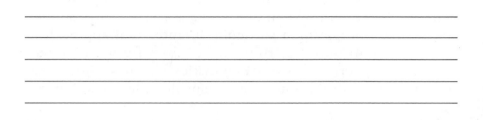

Discussion.   Though "what else is in it for me?" might appear to be a standard question that any consultant would consider throughout any engagement, the possibilities are usually broader on an enterprise-scale assignment simply because of the increased number of people—and client organizations—with whom you'll have at least some contact during your work.

Basically, always keep in mind during an engagement that when you are interviewing or meeting with someone for your work at hand, you have a wonderful opportunity to sell your abilities and those of your company for work that may have nothing at all to do with the current engagement. Do this subtly; no one likes to think that he or she is being held captive in a room with you on the pretext of conducting a work-related interview while all the time *your* agenda is to give a sales pitch for future consulting work. Use these opportunities as an introduction and manage the conversations accordingly.

CONCLUSION

Again, it's all about seeing your consulting assignment as it really is—the opportunities that await you if you are successful, the obstacles that will be in your way, the people on whom you are dependent, etc. And, as stated at the beginning of this chapter, the broader the scope of your consulting activities on an engagement in terms of the client's organization, the greater the chances that political and organizational issues could easily overshadow the technology aspects of your work.

One final word: The items discussed in this chapter apply not only to enterprise-scale consulting activities but also to activities that span multiple enterprises, such as developing an architecture that will provide supply-chain automated inventory management across many different companies. If you find yourself providing consulting services in this type of situation, then pay careful attention to this chapter's discussion and make sure that you do your homework for *all* organizations involved, across *all* companies.

THE DIFFICULT CLIENT

INTRODUCTION

And then there's the client from you-know-where.

This chapter isn't about ordinary disagreements with your client, such as each of you having different thoughts concerning which product to select or whether an interface between two systems should be synchronous or asynchronous. This isn't about having your recommendations dismissed with a curt, "Looks OK, but we're not going to take that path; thanks for your time, anyway, and send us your last invoice."

You *know* when you have a difficult client—someone who

- Returns every single version of your deliverable (for example, some type of specification) with angrily scribbled comments (usually with lots of exclamation points!!!!!), many of which contradict the comments he or she made on the previous version you submitted.

- Continually makes subtle, or sometimes not-so-subtle, threats to call your manager at the consulting company where you work and loudly complains about the quality of your work, even though your deliverables have been acceptable to every other person who needs to approve them.

- Makes it a habit to lace nearly every sentence spoken to you with a string of profanities, and you *know* it's primarily to make you as uncomfortable as possible.

The list goes on and on and on. Simply put, there are some clients who insist on being difficult, who absolutely refuse to be pleased by your work. They'll continue paying for your services, they're just as likely as not to implement your recommendations or deploy your application, but you find yourself cringing any time you see one of them turning the corner and heading toward your work area.

The material in this chapter is designed to help you get to the heart of the matter in these situations and determine the best way to deal with circumstances that make you want to leave the consulting profession (maybe even the world of information technology) because "it's just not worth it."

In many cases you can sense a situation of this type *before* you get into it and avoid it, but other times the nastiness does not manifest itself until *after* you've been engaged. If you take the time to look at the questions in this chapter—and *think* about your answers—chances are that you'll have the information you need to create an exit strategy or, if necessary, to deal with the situation for "just a little bit longer."

Remember, it's only business; you *can't* take this type of unpleasantness personally. This doesn't mean you have to put up with it, but if you find yourself in one of these situations, it's *your* responsibility to regroup and develop a plan to bring the engagement to a close without letting things degenerate further.

WHEN DID YOU FIRST NOTICE THE SYMPTOMS?

Describe the *very first* time you thought that you might very well have a difficult client on your hands. Was it before or after you began work? What was the subject about which there was discontent? What was the resolution (if any)?

_____

_____

_____

_____

_____

_____

Discussion.   Though this sounds like a question more appropriate for a doctor's office, it's important that you have an accurate picture of the roots of the difficulty, and very often the first time you realized something might be amiss is a good indicator of the problem's core. For example, suppose you are the project manager and the proposal submitted by your company called for a five-person project team, with specific names and roles designated. Just before work begins, your company pulls two of the team members to work on another project, replacing them with consultants whose skills are noticeably weaker than those of the team members originally proposed. The client, not having the time to withdraw the project and reopen it for competition, accepts these substitutions under protest, but at the kickoff meeting lets *you* know how unhappy he or she is, and is not reticent at all about letting you know that these "bait and switch tactics" (the client's words) are unprofessional.

Beware—there will be trouble ahead!

WHO ELSE IS AWARE OF THE SITUATION?

List all other people, including those within the client's domain, who have at least a cursory realization that there is client-consultant strife.

Person	Position	Role	"Friend or Foe"

Discussion.   If a battle is forthcoming, you had better identify all of your friends and your foes. As discussed in some of the earlier chapters in this section, there are almost always some who want you to fail in your work—and their leveraging a difficult client situation through innuendo and other tactics is highly likely.

It is also possible, though, that the client who is making your professional life so difficult is an outsider, someone who habitually acts in this manner (discussed next). In such a situation, there may be an exit strategy that involves rallying allies and potential allies to help insulate you from further discontent while you finish your work in as professional a manner as possible. Basically, it pays to survey the landscape and figure out who's who and what possible battle lines may be drawn, if it comes to that.

HAS THIS HAPPENED BEFORE WITH THIS CLIENT?

To the extent you can find out, has this client ever acted this way with other consultants (those at your firm, other independents—anyone!), and if so, what were the circumstances?

_____

_____

_____

_____

_____

_____

Discussion.   In trying to get to the roots of the problem, you need to try to discover whether

- It's circumstances particular to your specific engagement, merited or not, that "flipped the client's switch."
- He or she has a reputation as a "consultant eater" and possibly even acts this way with his or her own staff.

If you are witnessing behavior that is part of the client's nature, or his or her routine interpersonal style in the office, there is little you can do to counter it; on the other hand, if this is the first time that the client has been known to "turn difficult," then there is a possibility of turning the situation around.

WHAT IS THE BEST POSSIBLE EXIT STRATEGY?

Taking reality into consideration (i.e., no fantasies about the client's being fired tomorrow and being replaced by someone who doubles your hourly rate to make up for your difficulties!), what is the best possible exit strategy from this situation?

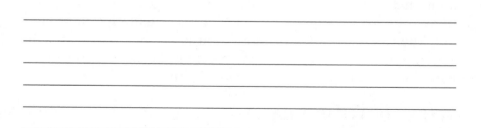

Discussion.   Perhaps you are near the end of the engagement, and the unpleasantness isn't likely to derail your deliverables, have them declared unacceptable, etc. In this case, your exit strategy may very well be to forge ahead, finish your work, have it accepted, and then leave and never look back.

On the other hand, if your difficult client is threatening to cause revolts among members of your project team—possibly to the point where they would rather quit and find another job than spend nine more months in the midst of disruptive and demoralizing conflict—then perhaps your exit strategy may be to halt work (subject to what's permissible in your contract, of course) and cut your losses on this engagement.

WHAT IS THE WORST POSSIBLE OUTCOME?

Again, taking reality into consideration, what is the *worst* possible scenario that could occur as your engagement terminates?

_____

_____

_____

_____

_____

_____

Discussion.   Before moving ahead with your plan (discussed next), you need to know not only what you would *like* to have happen (the previous question), but also the worst possible situation that *could* happen. Legal action, damaged business reputations—the list goes on and on. Though it is tempting to try and put "the worst" out of your mind, that is a dangerous approach. Your client's unpleasantness may not stop the second your work ends; be prepared for what you hope doesn't happen—but could.

WHAT IS YOUR PLAN?

Describe, step by step, your plan of action to attempt to reach an acceptable exit strategy.

STEP	ACTION	PERSON(S)	DESIRED OUTCOME	CONTIGENCY PLAN

Discussion.   Using the chart above, list, in sequential order:

- What you need to do
- The person(s) with whom you need to communicate for each action
- What your desired outcome from each action is
- If that doesn't happen, what you will *then* do

WHAT HAVE YOU LEARNED AFTER IT'S ALL OVER?

Though it is tempting to put the unpleasantness behind you, never to be thought of again, it is important that you do an "outbrief" of the situation once you have reached some type of resolution. This way, you—and those with whom you work—will hopefully be more alert to clues to help you avoid these situations in the future before you get into them, or to resolve them more quickly should they occur.

_____

_____

_____

_____

_____

_____

CONCLUSION

No matter how frustrated you get, no matter how angry, you always have to stay cool when dealing with a difficult client. Again, keep your mind focused on your exit strategy. Only in rare circumstances will you be able to turn that particular consultant-client relationship into a productive, long-running one, so focusing your efforts on this is, to be blunt, usually a waste of time.

However, you need to remember that sometimes there are high stakes involved, so you must resist the urge to rant, rave, or otherwise act as unprofessional as the client. Maintain your decorum, look forward to the end of the unpleasant situation, and bring things to a conclusion as quickly as possible.

INDEX